THE COMPLETE BOOK OF CYCLING

THE COMPLETE BOOK OF CYCLING

CHRIS BOARDMAN
with Andrew Longmore

PARTRIDGE

LONDON · NEW YORK · TORONTO · SYDNEY · AUCKLAND

TRANSWORLD PUBLISHERS
61–63 Uxbridge Road, London W5 5SA
a division of The Random House Group Ltd

RANDOM HOUSE AUSTRALIA (PTY) LTD
20 Alfred Street, Milsons Point, Sydney
New South Wales 2061, Australia

RANDOM HOUSE NEW ZEALAND
18 Poland Road, Glenfield, Auckland 10, New Zealand

RANDOM HOUSE SOUTH AFRICA (PTY) LTD
Endulini, 5a Jubilee Road, Parktown 2193, South Africa

Published 2000 by Partridge
a division of Transworld Publishers

A catalogue record for this book is available from the British Library.
ISBN 185225 2677

Line drawings by Keith Herbert/Plum Illustration

Printed in Great Britain
by Mackays of Chatham Plc, Chatham, Kent

1 3 5 7 9 10 8 6 4 2

To my long-suffering wife, Sally-Anne.
I promise I will quit soon.

Chris Boardman's Acknowledgements

Team Boardman

I would like to take a moment to introduce some of the most influential figures in my life, both sporting and personal. I want to do this partly because their names will appear in this book, partly out of a bit of self-indulgence, but mainly to illustrate that, no matter who the athlete, no-one makes it to the top without help. Yes, it is you who turns the pedals and does the training; yes, it is you who copes with the stress and pressure of competition; but without support from others it is hard to get the best out of yourself.

During my career as a rider, I have had the good fortune to come into contact with some very talented and special people. What was not good luck – and I shall pat myself on the back here – was that I recognized that they were good for me and made sure they stayed. They all have their faults and idiosyncrasies, as do we all, but, in my view, they all possess unique talents, and without any one of them my career would not have been as successful, rewarding or relatively stress free as it has been.

Keith and Carol Boardman

I want to introduce you to my parents not out of duty as a son, but as a genuine acknowledgement of what they have provided for me.

There is a fine line between encouragement and pushing. My parents instinctively knew the difference. I was never pushed to ride a bike. If anything, I was actively discouraged from racing. Yet when I made it clear that racing was the only aspect of cycling I really wanted to try, Keith and Carol made it possible for me.

I always appreciated the space they gave me, too. I saw a lot of pushy parents in my early days, parents who lived through their kids and never gave them room to grow up. Almost without exception, those riders left the sport in their teens. I remember one occasion in particular: I was a junior, taking part in a training camp about 150 miles from our home in Leicester; it was one of my first trips away from home and, for the first time, I had my own hotel room. Dad came down to pick me up after a couple of days, but I was having such a good time that I wanted to stay for another two days. So he left me there without any fuss, despite having had to do a 300-mile round trip for nothing, and came all the way back two days later. This was not at all fair on my part, and I doubt if Edward, my eldest, would be so leniently treated, but I really appreciated it.

Another time, even earlier in my sporting life, we'd seen a new frame at a cycling event which was being imported by the local bike shop. It had oval tubing – a big deal for a fourteen-year-old. There were only a couple left and they cost £70, which was a lot of money to our family. I'd been used to second-hand frames, which were not much different from new ones, but I dearly wanted one of those tubular frames. I don't think I mentioned it to Dad, but a few days later he came in from work with the new frame. He'd ridden 20 miles home from Chester with it strapped to his back. It was one of the most memorable moments of my childhood. Thanks, Dad.

Sally-Anne Edwards

I met Sally when we were both sixteen. I purchased her phone number from a rather unscrupulous former cycling friend for a pair of new cycling shorts. Fifteen years and four children later, I reckon I got the best of the deal.

Sally has given me an unreasonable amount of support over the years, coping with my moods and frustrations, looking after our family and putting her own ambitions on ice for more than a decade. An intelligent woman, her advice, often disregarded in the early days, has more often than not proved to be right. The security and companionship she still provides gave me the confidence in the early days to take the gamble on a sporting career and, subsequently, to deal with the huge amount of stress created by that career.

Sally has gone back to university to study archaeology, geography and computers. It will be her turn soon. I'll be the house husband and she can have the career.

Peter Keen

I first met Peter Keen back in the early Eighties when he was conducting some of the first physiology tests for the British Cycling Federation down in Chichester. We very quickly developed a personal coaching relationship independent of the national team. Peter, in my opinion, is unique in the world of British coaching. He has a special ability to mix the physiological and psychological needs of an athlete. Peter is the only individual who has ever been able to get inside my head and interpret my mental state better than I can myself. Our relationship has evolved over many years and we have never stopped learning together, even if it's often the hard way.

It took a long time, but finally others in British sport recognized Peter's qualities. Recently, he was hired by the UK Sports Council to head British cycling's multi-million-pound world-class performance programme to prepare our elite cyclists for the Sydney Olympics and beyond. Although I take advice from some very knowledgeable people, I could never replace Peter as my coach. This book was compiled with the knowledge that Peter gave to me and from the things we have learned together. Without his input, I have no idea what direction my career would have taken.

Peter Woodworth

I have known Peter Woodworth longer than I have known Peter
Keen, although our working relationship didn't start until the early
Nineties.

After winning the Olympic gold in the pursuit back in 1992, things
started to become very hectic. I can remember asking Pete for advice.
I have always valued his opinion and have come to consult him on
every major decision, even if, as with Sally, I don't always take the
advice. We have never managed to find an adequate title for Pete's job
description. He has kept me out of trouble for more than six years
now, looking after all my business affairs. He has managed both the
successful world hour record attempts, my book project and a multi-
tude of other business deals, projects and problems.

We have managed to maintain a rare balance between work and
friendship over the years, a combination I would never consider
attempting with anyone else. He is the proverbial rock in my very
demanding life, and I couldn't imagine coping without his guidance
and support.

Roger Legeay

Roger was my first and, to date, only boss in professional cycling. He
introduced me to the world of professional cycling and then guided
me through it. He has always been 100 per cent supportive, especially
when things have not gone well.

In an already high-pressure job, I can't imagine a better person to
work for. He has the rare attribute of not passing on the stress of his
own position to the riders, even when the results aren't coming and
the sponsors are getting restless, or when he has had to find a new
sponsor at relatively short notice to stop us all being unemployed.

Like the others here, he is unique. Roger has always believed in me,
and repaying that faith has been one of my strongest motivations as a
professional.

There are many other people who have had a huge influence on my life, some of whom are no longer with us. I hope they understand that I can't mention them all in the space available here, but I would like to say thank you to them all.

Andrew Longmore's Acknowledgements

Thanks to Alison Barrow, Simon Thorogood and Shauna Newman of Transworld for their patience. And to Chris for his time and trust.

CONTENTS

Unless otherwise stated, photographs are Chris Boardman's own.

FOREWORD by Greg LeMond

Chris and I shared a season with Roger Legeay at the old Gan team. It wasn't a year I remember particularly fondly, mainly because I was struggling so badly with my form. I abandoned the Tour de France and retired. But I had been in cycling long enough to know that this English guy who arrived in our team with the hour record, an Olympic gold and a strange Liverpool accent was a fellow traveller. We were thrown together partly as two English speakers in a French team, but also, I think, because we recognized similarities of attitude and determination in each other. Neither of us accepted what we were told to do; we both wanted to know why.

I rode in Europe for fourteen seasons and won the Tour de France three times. It should have been more, but after my shooting accident in 1987 I always felt as if I was struggling physically. At the time, Americans were a rarity in the *peloton* and attitudes to training and racing were much more parochial than they are now. You were expected to do things the French way and not to ask too many questions. It was only when I beat Laurent Fignon in the time trial using tri-bars by eight seconds on the last stage of the 1989 Tour that people began to come to terms with innovations in equipment and technique. The traditional method of getting fit for road racing was to ride your bike for hours and hours every day. I never fully understood that, and when Chris came along, though I was coming to the end of my career, it was refreshing to know that the emphasis in his training was also on quality, not quantity. So many athletes in the US believe it is essential to train for twenty-five hours a week; Chris is an example of a top-class sportsman who did half of that, but was successful because he geared his training accurately and intelligently to specific targets.

If he would have liked one of my Tour victories, I coveted one of his hour records. I did two weeks of testing for the hour in 1990, but I realized pretty quickly how hard it was and how much time and planning would be required. Eddy Merckx always claimed that doing the hour took seven years off his life, but for Chris the record was a natural focus not just for his time-trialling skills, but for his curiosity. Chris and I talked a lot about training methods. I was looking for answers about my own form and he was looking for guidance about the world of the professional road-racer. I told him I thought he could win the Tour, which was the truth. If it hasn't worked out that way, I know it wasn't from lack of commitment. Chris was a professional in his attitude and approach long before he came to Gan for his first season in the *peloton*.

We also share the same view on drugs. The early Nineties was a difficult time to enter professional road-racing because the drug culture was rampant. Riders were joining teams with a 'medical' programme. But Chris wasn't interested and, though he wasn't going to preach to anyone, he took an ethical stance on the issue, which was pretty unusual. At times, if his results were disappointing, he must have questioned what others were doing, but he just got on with it and competed to the best of his ability. There isn't much more you can ask of a rider.

I wish Chris well with the book. I wish we could have ridden longer together and I wish he could have seen me ride at the peak of my career, rather than towards the end of it. One day, we will sit down in a roadside café, watch the Tour go by and reminisce about how good we were.

INTRODUCTION by Andrew Longmore

I first took notice of Chris Boardman on a sweltering afternoon in Lille in the high summer of 1994. I had not been in Barcelona when the 'cabinetmaker from Hoylake' riding a sleak black wonder machine won the first British Olympic cycling gold medal for seventy-two years, thereby indulging our twin national passions for the glorious amateur and world-beating inventions. Journalists at the time were puzzled by Boardman's resolute refusal to acknowledge either stereotype in the aftermath of his historic victory. Here, they said, was a cold fish. But they wrote the stories anyway, creating the image of an aloof, unapproachable athlete which Chris himself has long since given up trying to dispel.

In one sense, the portrait is accurate. Chris does bring a cold, calculating logic to his sport and, by extension, to his life. In an era of revolution in training methods and the concept of professionalism, he is arguably the most committed athlete of all. A glorious amateur he is not, and never was, even when he was relying on the haphazard pocket-money economy of pre-Lottery UK sport, and, if my instinct is correct, he never will be. Retirement will not bring peace and relaxation, just a new outlet for a restless soul.

Chris's route to the streets of Lille that summer was far from conventional. In fact, most of the hard-bitten pros who make up the most exclusive sporting community in the world felt, at best, puzzled by his appearance in their midst and, at worst, resentful of his sudden rise from Olympic gold medallist to the coveted job as leader of a top French team. The 'recordman of the hour', as the French newspaper *L'Equipe* called him in honour of his world hour record in Bordeaux the previous year, was a time triallist and a track gold medallist. He had no discernible background in road racing and knew nothing of the peculiar customs of the club he was about to join – the tactics, the etiquette, the unwritten rules. Not that a man of such individuality was about to be bothered by the cautious welcome of his peers. Chris is one of the most singular athletes I have ever met. Rules are not necessarily there to be broken, but they are there to be probed, prodded, dissected and distilled for any essential truth which might make Christopher Miles Boardman go faster on a pushbike.

The *peloton*, that group of 300 or so professional bike riders who explore the frontiers of endurance every day of their working lives, were right to treat their exotic new boy with caution in more ways than they at first understood. Chris was an oddity. He was English, for a start, and English riders – nicknamed *Les Rosbifs* by the French press – had, with a few notable exceptions like Sean Yates, never commanded much respect on the continent. In addition to this, Chris's base was time-trialling, not road racing. His youth had been spent in unyielding obeisance to the clock. His physique, 70 kgs and compact, was peculiarly suited to the rigours of the 'race of truth', or *contre la montre*, as the French call the time trial, and his mind preferred the clarity of trials to the vagaries of road-race competition. No-one could mess you about in the time trial. It was you against the clock, and the clock never lied.

Hours of pounding the roads of his native Cheshire have given Chris such a fine understanding of his own physical capacity that he is able to ride instinctively on what pro athletes call 'threshold' – a sort of physical no man's land between all-out effort and total exhaustion. It is a specialized gift and, as the double world hour record holder, an honour which puts him second only to the winner of the Tour de France in the hierarchy of European cycling champions, Chris has proved himself the most effective time triallist of all time.

Chris has chosen to stay in the Wirral, preferring to commute to races and coordinate his own training programme. Riders of a previous generation, like Stephen Roche, Sean Kelly and Robert Millar, regarded moving to Europe as obligatory. It is a reflection of the meticulousness of the training regime devised by Peter Keen, Chris's long-time coach and mentor, and of the strength of his bargaining position when he turned professional at the end of 1993, that Roger Legeay, the shrewd and paternal *directeur sportif* of the then Gan-sponsored team, broke his conventions and allowed his new rider to be based in England. But it means that Chris has remained a rider apart, which has been both a strength and a weakness.

Chris was brought up on the furthest north-west tip of the Wirral, in Hoylake, a village more famous for its golf course than its cycling. Though Chris's father, Keith, was a good enough time triallist to be considered for the 1964 British Olympic team, he was content to compete for love rather than glory, an attitude his son still finds perplexing to this day. One of Chris's favourite lines is that he doesn't enjoy riding his bike, he enjoys the success that comes from riding it. In the summers of his youth, he would more likely be found at Hoylake swimming baths offering to race all comers, any time, any distance. Chris still believes that the considerable time he spent underwater helped to improve his lung capacity. It was not until he was a teenager that riding his bike began to occupy more of his thoughts. His first race was a 10-mile time trial in June 1982, when he was thirteen. His first recorded time for the distance was a thoroughly respectable 29 minutes and 43 seconds. By October he had taken more than four minutes off his personal best and, more importantly, had developed a keen enough interest in racing to follow the training schedules set down by his father. In 1983, Chris moved from the Birkenhead Victoria Club to the North Wirral Velo, improving his times with every race until he clocked 21 minutes and 4 seconds at the end of his second season.

The following year, Keith handed over coaching duties to Eddie Soens, a tough no-nonsense former soldier, who didn't always see eye to eye with the cycling establishment, but knew talent when he saw it. Despite his early death from a heart attack, Soens has remained an influential figure in Chris's career, and an analysis of the relationship says much about Chris's unconventional nature, even at that early age. While others were put off by Soens's military gruffness, Chris sensed a fellow traveller, someone equally committed, who was prepared to look at things differently, not just accept the traditional wisdom of the sport. Soens lived to see Chris, a junior, partner three senior riders to win the gold medal in the team pursuit at the National Track Championships in Leicester. Later that year, Chris was selected, aged seventeen, for the Senior World Championships at Bassano in Italy, where he experienced for the first time the true nature of world-class competition.

Chris was now in the system, but there was one more contact that was to have a profound influence on his career. Sent by the British Cycling Federation to do some tests at the Sports Institute in Chichester, Boardman met a young, fanatical, blond-haired scientist called Peter Keen, who was also a keen amateur cyclist. Keen recalls putting this scrawny kid from the Wirral through his paces without any noticeable distinction. What impressed him, though, was Chris's dedication. He not only went away clutching a training programme designed to build up his power and strength, but took the trouble to drive all the way back down to Keen's laboratory in a beaten-up old banger to monitor the improvements a few months later. Here, thought Keen, is a kid with the will to win. The success of their partnership through Olympic gold and two world hour records, among other credits, needs little embellishment, but it propelled Chris on an extraordinary journey from the obscurity of the amateur ranks and rolling roads of Cheshire to the threshold of the most illustrious event in continental cycling.

Boardman was acutely aware of all the pressures hanging over him in the stifling air above Lille that afternoon. The prologue of the Tour de France is an event apart, frowned on as a gimmick by the purists, but loved by the organizers and sponsors, who benefit from the massive publicity generated by what the French regard as the start of *les vacances*. Boardman's method of dealing with pressure is to minimize the potential for error. Nothing is left to chance, from the meticulously planned training schedule to the minute-by-minute countdown to the start, from rigorously customized and tested equipment to the neat laying out of gloves and helmet.

The crowd which had gathered outside the Musée des Beaux Arts in the main square in Lille could see not one but two riders shimmering in the heat of the final run down the Boulevard de la Liberté. They had waited patiently for the moment when the destination of the Tour's first yellow jersey would be decided, but they were perplexed by the appearance of a rider in the light blue and white of Gan alongside their own champion Luc Leblanc. Leblanc, for sure, must have had some problem. Only the digital clock across the finishing line betrayed the truth. Boardman had shattered the previous times and obliterated the record for the fastest stage ever ridden in the Tour with a speed of 55.1 kph over the 7.2-km course. The equivalent of a novice winning the Derby by 20 lengths, I wrote at the time. Miguel Indurain, the defending champion and an acknowledged master of the discipline, was beaten by fifteen seconds. Legeay and his PR officer, Michel Laurent, danced an impromptu jig on the street. '*C'est une grande surprise pour moi. Parfait,*' said Chris, unveiling his schoolboy French to the delight of the locals, who had already nicknamed him the 'TGV Anglais'.

At the time of writing, Chris's record still stands, though the Tour has not yielded its innermost secrets quite so easily. Prior to the start of the 2000 Tour, Chris had won two more prologues, but had reached the finish in Paris only twice in six attempts, a frustrating record for a man of such single-mindedness and dedication. He is driven by an extraordinary will to win. For him, success is normality, the one and only justification for living an existence that would test the will-power of a hermit. Failure is only tolerated because of what it can teach him about success. Chris has remarkable physical powers, but he will be the first to admit that he is a natural competitor, not a natural bike rider. Bikes just happen to be his most effective vehicle for winning.

Equally significant for the readers of this book is Chris's ability to analyse and articulate what he is doing. We worked on the rough principle that if I, a sports journalist working largely outside cycling, could understand the principles of his sporting philosophy, then anyone could. For a naturally impatient human being, he has been very long-suffering in the face of a thousand basic, if innocently delivered, questions. Through the hours of taping I have glimpsed a way of life which might have been lived by the Inuit for all the relevance it has to my own languid existence.

Professional cyclists are acknowledged to be the hardest of hard men, and Chris's own considerable reserves of strength have been tested to the limit by his belated graduation into a tough school. He has tackled the task with typical attention to detail. He spent the whole of one winter on a turbo trainer specially adapted for his bike so that he could simulate the Alps without moving from the Cheshire plains, has wasted his body down to 67 kgs in an effort to master the art of climbing and competed long and hard enough on behalf of his team to command the respect of the *peloton*. He is also – and I can write this without fear of contradiction from anyone inside or outside the sport – a 'clean' rider, in cycling's clinical parlance, untainted by the drug-related arrests, accusations, rumours and suspicion which currently hang over professional cycling. Boardman will not presume to preach to others, but he will practise what he preaches himself. This book is a testimony to that philosophy and an attempt to provide cyclists and athletes with a unique insight into the ways of a true champion.

1

THE BOARDMAN PRINCIPLES

Sitting on the starting line in Barcelona for the final of the Olympic pursuit, I knew the next four and a half minutes would either change my life for ever or relegate me to another statistic in the Olympic history books. My mind was all over the place. I was thinking about how many countries were watching the event live – little old Chris Boardman from Hoylake. I heard myself say, 'I'm going to win gold,' and thought how arrogant that sounded. I'd qualified fastest in every single round, yet the overwhelming sense was that gold medals don't happen to people like me. For once I was wrong.

At the time, my wife, Sally, and I were living in a small house in Prenton. I had lost my part-time job at a local furniture shop, no money was coming in, our second child was due and I had made a vow to myself, which I probably wasn't going to keep, that if I didn't win Olympic gold I would go and get a job in the real world. I wasn't even eligible for dole money because I was spending too much time out of the country. I got a grant of £1,000 from the Sports Council and, soon after, went to the Cycling Federation's annual dinner where I won a £500 award for being the Cyclist of the Year. £1,500 was like winning the jackpot, so we celebrated by having sandwiches in the room. Life was a lot less complicated then. A month later, I was being offered more than £1,000 to turn up and open a supermarket for an hour. It was almost embarrassing.

If you pursue a sport seriously, no matter what sport it is, there will be a defining moment in your career. In cycling, it might be a local club time trial, a trial for the Commonwealth Games team or a race for Olympic gold. It doesn't matter what level it is, the principle remains the same. You can be trained to fail as easily as you can to succeed. If I had lost that Olympic final to Jens Lehmann in 1992, I might have gone back to being just another cyclist trying to make ends meet.

Looking back, the strange thing about winning the gold that day was my instinctive reaction. There's a picture of me punching the air in the moment of victory, but my face is more a grimace than a smile, hardly the euphoric response you'd expect. I remember feeling rather let down by my lack of emotion. I thought, Well, is that it then? I felt rather cheated, because it wasn't how I had imagined it might be through all those hard hours of training. I had been aiming for this one thing for ten years, then, in a blink, it was all over. The next thing you know someone is sticking a medal round your neck and dragging you into a press conference. I admit that I'm not very good at instant elation; despair is a far more common emotion for me. But – and this is going to sound arrogant again – there were logical reasons for my apparent lack of surprise. I had prepared so meticulously for the event that, when it came to the moment of winning, though at least half my brain was telling me a gold medal was impossible, I expected it. I knew I had the most technologically advanced bike in the event, and I knew my training programme, formulated by Peter Keen, was imaginative and meticulous. Those factors gave me a great feeling of confidence. The only thing I couldn't control was the speed of my opponent.

I am often accused of being too clinical in my approach to the sport. People think I ride too much on numbers and not enough on feeling. But at the heart of my philosophy is a belief in being the best you can be. It sounds so simple, but it's very hard to put into practice.

We are not talking about some old-fashioned Victorian notion of glorious amateurism. Being the best you can be involves a scientific analysis of your capabilities and how they can be improved; it involves going right back to the basics, analysing every performance and seeing where you did the right thing and where you went wrong.

It involves keeping precise records of past performances so that you can monitor your progress; it involves being honest with yourself every day in every training session and it involves tenacity, self-discipline, dedication and planning. It doesn't matter whether you're an amateur or a professional, anyone can follow those principles in the search for self-improvement. For me, analysis is the key. From the start of the year, when you look back on what went right and what went wrong in the previous year and set yourself an objective, to the end of the season, when the process of self-examination begins again.

I cannot go out on a training ride without knowing why I am doing it. I can't just think, Well, it's going to make me fitter, or, That's what everyone else does. I need to know how and why a particular training programme is going to give me a better chance of winning bike races. Much of what follows in this book is an attempt to explain the basis of that philosophy.

On the morning after I was married, I got up at 6 a.m. to ride in Pendle, Lancashire, because the route of the race took in a particular hill that featured in the national hill climb a couple of weeks later. When Harriet, the second of my four children, was born, I took Sally to the hospital on Friday night, went back to bed and, the next morning, drove to Hull so that I could ride round the course of the National Championships the day before the race. I phoned up to see whether we'd had a boy or girl. That's how fanatical I was. I'm sure it wouldn't happen now, which means I'm either more balanced or less motivated, but if I'm doing something, from cooking dinner to making something in my workshop to pursuing my cycling career, I have to do it 100 per cent. It's the one piece of advice I would give my children: I don't mind what you do, but whatever it is, do it properly. And it is the almost unspoken theme that runs through the pages of this book.

Quite where my notion of doing something properly strayed into the realms of obsession is hard to pinpoint. Some of it is genetic, but it's hard to blame my parents entirely. My father, Keith, was short-listed for the cycling team at the Tokyo Olympics in 1964, though he chose to marry my mother instead. So cycling was a natural outlet for my energies because there were always cycles around the house and, when he had finished competing at national level, Dad still raced hard in time trials around Cheshire, usually on Sunday mornings. He preferred time trials to road or track racing.

I enjoyed swimming and my time spent underwater at the local open-air baths may have contributed to my lung capacity. I can remember being given a pair of flippers as a birthday present and sleeping in them. It's more likely, however, that the aerobic ability that allows me to sustain high speeds over long periods was inherited from my parents, because my mother was a pretty good cyclist, too.

More importantly, perhaps, even than a good set of lungs was the balanced encouragement my parents provided. From early on in my school career I was never going to be a team player. I couldn't quite see the point of giving the ball to someone else to mess up. I was always attracted to solo sports, swimming and running initially, then cycling, but I suppose it was inevitable that cycling would end up as the main attraction. My father knew about cycling and was able to provide the answers to my questions – and curiosity is in my nature – but he never forced me into *his* sport. He was there to support, and, later on, when I began to compete more seriously at national junior level, he would drive all over the country to meetings, but he never made me feel that I would be letting him down if I didn't carry on to the top. Perhaps because he had competed to a high level himself, he didn't feel the need to live out his own ambitions through his son.

Though Ed, my eldest son, has already ridden round the Manchester Velodrome on a purpose-built mini-track bike and thoroughly enjoyed himself, I hope I will be able to step back far enough to allow him to develop his own interests. In fact, I might even encourage him into a different sport, not because he will be saddled – no pun intended – with the 'son of' tag, but because the way I have tackled my sport is not particularly healthy. He might, of course, be very different; he might have the natural ability to develop a more relaxed attitude to training and competition than his father ever managed.

I have never had much natural cycling ability; I have what bike riders would call a good engine – I have the physical ability to shift large amounts of oxygen around my body. But my most important quality is will-power, the sheer dogged determination to stick at something until it's done. I have said many times – and it puzzles passionate cycling people like Roger Legeay, my *directeur sportif* at Gan and then Crédit Agricole – that I do not like riding a bike. It's hard work and it hurts. But I love to succeed, and if cycling is the best means to that end, then I'm willing to make the sacrifices.

People very often confuse enjoyment with satisfaction. I don't enjoy going out and training for four hours in the cold and the rain, but I get a tremendous amount of satisfaction from knowing that I have done it and done it well. Once, when I just wasn't up to doing a particular training exercise Peter Keen had set me, he told me to go away for an evening, take Sal to the pictures and get a life. I did. But I can't remember a thing about the film because all I was thinking about was why I hadn't managed to do the training and I resented my sport for stealing the rest of my life. That's what I mean about carrying my sport to unhealthy extremes. You have to be able to switch off – something I've never quite mastered. It was only a year later that I looked back at my diary that week and saw that I'd done four hours one day, then a two-hour training ride the next, ridden a seven-and-a-half-hour classic, come home, done an hour and a half the next day and then wondered why I couldn't face doing any more. I had become so focused on my immediate objective that I hadn't taken a step back and looked at the big picture.

It is my strong belief that attitude is more important in reaching the top than physiology. Every pro cyclist has particular physical attributes; what marks out the champions is will-power and the *need* to win. Talking about winning is easy. Everyone says they want to win; no-one enters a sport aiming to lose. But some athletes are prepared to sacrifice more than others to achieve success. Daley Thompson always trained on Christmas Day, so that when it came to the Olympic decathlon, he could look across at his rivals and know that none of them had done more than him in their preparation to win. My philosophy is much the same.

I've been told there are two classes of athlete: the one whose success is driven by fear of failure and the other who succeeds because he wants to win. I belong to the negative group. To be normal, I have to win. It's not even as simple as fear of failure. It's a fear of not being in control, of not having done everything in preparation to win, from getting the last ounce out of a training schedule to making sure all my equipment is properly laid out before the start of a race.

This is what appeals to me about time-trialling. Almost from my first 10-mile club time trial, I liked the simplicity and honesty of time trials. I covered that course in just over twenty-nine minutes on a frame my father had procured from a skip. The next week I did the same course in twenty-eight minutes, so I could see evidence of progress, which is important to a restless and inquisitive mind. I wasn't winning the races, but I could see improvement. In time trials you're racing against yourself, which suits my way of thinking. There are no excuses. If someone beats you, it means (a) they have prepared better than you or (b) they are better than you. As I could never accept (b), most of my sixteen-year career has been spent trying to avoid (a). For me, that also means asking questions and keeping an open mind.

The Lotus bike, which became more famous than me after the 1992 Olympics, was a case in point. I knew the critical importance of aerodynamic forces in a race as short and explosive as the pursuit from the tests I'd done in the Motor Institute wind tunnel, but it took quite a leap of faith to put my trust in a bike as untested and innovative as the Lotus. The confidence I gained from knowing I had potentially the best bike was at least as important as the technology itself.

When I finally turned professional for the 1994 season, after breaking the world hour record the previous year, one of the most difficult aspects of riding in the *peloton* was the loss of control. On a climb, or when a break erupted, twenty-five guys would suddenly ride away without me being able to do anything about it. There might still be a hundred guys with me, but I had some difficulty accepting that inevitability. Patience not being one of my prime virtues, it took me a year or two to realize that it was like playing chess on two wheels. Sometimes you had to conserve your energy, sit back and wait until the right opportunity to attack came along.

Climbing presented particular problems for me, not just physically but mentally. I had to learn to ride at my own pace and not be drawn into keeping up with others who were either better climbers than me or who had gone too fast too soon and would burn out further up the mountain. On bad days everyone seems to ride away from you; on good days they might ride away, but slowly and surely you'll reel them in half an hour later.

All these issues are addressed in detail in this book. It's not a traditional training manual, though there are elements of the standard textbook in it. It won't tell you what to do every minute of every day, or set down day-by-day training routines, because every rider has different aims and a different psychology.

Looking back on the Olympics, eight years, countless miles, a few successes and many more failures later, I realize how mixed up, and yet calm, my mind was. There were so many negative thoughts whirring around that any sports psychologist would have had a field day. But I did manage to focus my attention on the one abiding principle of my career: my preparation could not have been more thorough. With the famed Lotus, I had the lightest, fastest bike in town. I had spent hours in the wind tunnel experimenting with the most aerodynamic riding position, and, with the help of Peter Keen, I was in the best physical shape of my life. I knew I would not be beaten because I was unprepared; I would be beaten because I wasn't good enough. This is one of the recurring themes in this book, as applicable to finding the right equipment as to eating the right food, following the right training programme, planning the right schedule, riding the fastest time trials, or climbing the highest mountains. It is the first of the five Boardman principles.

1. Be the Best You Can Be

'I want to be the best' is a common phrase among athletes. Or 'I want to be a world champion'. It's a noble sentiment, motivating, inspiring even, but it is totally meaningless. In the end, being the best is out of your control. There might be someone out there better than you. Narrowing down those goals and concentrating on the ones in your control makes for much less heartache. 'Controlling the controllable' is a phrase often used by sports psychologists, particularly to keep athletes relaxed in the lead-up to a big event, or to reduce the stress of competition. Worry about aspects of your performance that you can influence, not about what anyone else is doing. Being the best you can be is subtly different from being the best. The first is entirely within your control, the second is not.

It's not as simple as it sounds, either. Other than yourself, who knows what your best is? It's easy to cheat, to think you've exhausted every possibility when, in reality, there was plenty of scope for improvement. That extra training session on Christmas Day? Steve Redgrave, like Daley Thompson, talks about the comfort of getting to a big race and knowing that no-one on the starting line has put in more effort than him. When he looks into an opponent's eyes, that is the unspoken question Redgrave asks: Do you really think you want this more than me? The answer, for the last four Olympics at least, has been a resounding 'no'.

2. Always Set Goals

It doesn't matter if you don't necessarily achieve them as long as you've tried your best to do so. At the end of every season, I sit down with Peter Keen and Peter Woodworth and review the last season, look at what we achieved and what we failed to achieve and, most important of all, look at where and why we succeeded or failed. Failure can be as instructive as success, often more so, because failure hurts more and the lessons are harsher. The 1997 season, for example, was a disaster for me. Having decided to concentrate on being fit and absolutely ready to challenge for a top ten placing in the Tour de France, I contracted a virus a few weeks before the start that severely hampered my ability to recover after long stages, crashed on the first day in the mountains and was forced to retire on the stage to Alpe d'Huez. Despite achieving one objective by winning the prologue and the yellow jersey for the second time in four years, my season was a write-off. I had put all my eggs in one basket and dropped the lot. After the Tour, we lost the plot completely, and it was a merciful relief when the season ended.

In November 1997, we sat round the table again and looked forward to the coming season, setting goals that we thought were challenging but realistic. I may not be able to win the Tour, or even finish in the top ten general classification, so what other aims should I be looking at. Maybe I could win a classic. I know I can regain my pursuit world title, win the Tour prologue, maybe win a road stage in the Tour or the World Championships. There are plenty of other options. If you are a club cyclist and your job is the biggest priority in your life, then it would be unrealistic to expect you to win the National Championships. But you could train intelligently enough to win a local club race. It's like all those New Year's resolutions you make: learning the piano, speaking French, getting up earlier, drinking less and eating more raisins. They all go out the window the next day. Set your goals too high and your plans will be useless before the season is a month old. So set targets that are challenging but realistic.

3. Recognize, Analyse, Capitalize

I have never been able to go out training unless I know why I'm doing it and how it will improve my performance. This means answering some fundamental questions and constantly revising the techniques and exercises I do. There is no point in being told 'this will make you go faster' unless you know something about the principles involved or the process underpinning it. 'This will make you go faster because . . .' or, more specifically, 'This will improve your explosive power because . . .'

Ideally, you need to find someone who knows you and your capabilities, someone you can trust to tell you the truth. In my case, this has been Eddie Soens, my first coach, and Peter Keen, who has coached me since I was eighteen. In a wider career sense, Peter Woodworth has also acted as a monitor and guide. Peter Keen, in particular, has the ability not just to tell me why I'm doing an exercise, but to translate his technical explanation into comprehensible English.

The two years that Pete was otherwise occupied with the elite performance programme of the British Cycling Federation only served to stress the importance of his input to my own performance, which suffered badly. I overtrained in the winter of 1997 and took two years to recover any semblance of consistent form. By the end of the Tour in 1999 I was a shadow of the rider I'd once been, confused by my inability to compete and frightened of suffering in the way I'd once taken for granted. I'd lost the objective judgement and motivation that Pete's programme had given me, and the ability to analyse my performance and plan accordingly. It launched me into a vicious circle – failure had eroded my self-belief, and my lack of self-belief fostered greater failure until survival became my sole ambition.

I rode the 1999 Tour like a ghost. In my experience, it is critical to have a plan, a series of sub-plans and a coherent method of executing the plan. Plans will nearly always go wrong, but if you don't start with one, there is nothing to fall back on. Plans can easily be changed. Constantly analyse what you're doing and whether your training programme seems to be fulfilling its objectives, because only careful analysis will bring benefits to the next schedule.

4. Be Prepared to Compromise

Nothing is ever black and white, even in sport. Solutions are often a matter of compromise, of sacrificing one element of your training and fitness to improve another area. In trying, for example, to maximize my ability in the mountains, I lost a critical amount of peak power. That is just one example of the need to balance one aspect of training with another. Balancing your private life with your sporting life will probably require compromise just as much as individual aspects of your training and racing.

5. Be Passionate

Anyone who has followed my career might be surprised by this principle because I have always been regarded by the press as a very dispassionate and clinical athlete, someone who talks about my pulse rate, not the glory of the moment. But, as Fig. 1.1 illustrates, passion is not something that just emerges from nowhere; it has a base and a cause. For me, the cause is self-belief, and self-belief comes from evidence that my goal is achievable. In 1999, I lost my passion for the sport because the goal I had set myself – doing well in the general classification of the Tour – had moved beyond my reach. Instead of going back to what I knew I could do – competing in the prologue, the time trials and maybe the odd long, flat stage – I lost motivation and ended up doing nothing particularly well. I also lacked control. As the Pirelli advertisement says, 'Power is nothing without control.'

Control comes from objective analysis and the independent judgement of a coach who can instinctively provide technical and emotional support.

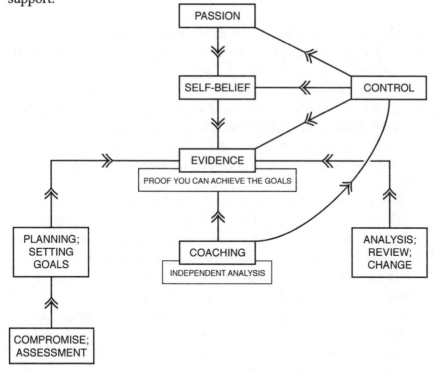

Fig 1.1 This is a diagrammatic overview of the five principles outlined above. I have made passion the most important requirement because it is the culmination of all the other ingredients in producing the evidence you need to achieve your goals. With evidence comes self-belief, and with self-belief comes passion. The critical element of control comes from an independent assessment of what you are doing right and what you are doing wrong.

2

THE STRUCTURE OF THE PRO SEASON

Just as an amateur cyclist will need to look at his calendar before starting to set out objectives for a season, so the professional cyclist has to isolate races and aims. The amateur will probably not have to worry about the added pressures of sponsors' commitments. Spanish teams have to ride the Vuelta, the Tour of Spain; and the Italians ride the Giro, the Tour of Italy. Other races are ridden because that is what the team manager wants. But, within reason, the lead riders in a team can dictate their own schedules to suit themselves, and there are plenty of races to choose from. A rider like Miguel Indurain stuck to a carefully planned schedule which worked for him. Pretty much every year he would ride the same races in preparation for his year's grand objective, the Tour. By monitoring his condition each year, and comparing it with the previous year, he could know pretty well to the day whether or not he was on schedule.

For the rest of us it's a bit more variable. Riders, though, will develop active likes and dislikes for certain races. It might be the standard of the hotels or the friendliness of the organizers; it might be the condition of the roads or the access to a particular stage route. I will always gravitate towards races with prologues and time trials, a stage race like the Paris–Nice in the spring or the Grand Prix des Nations, which was once regarded as the world time trial champion-ships, in the autumn. Magnus Backstedt has, for some weird reason, an affiliation with the mud and danger of Paris–Roubaix, so that will always be an early season objective for him, while Bobby Julich, our new recruit for the millennium season at Crédit Agricole, will gear all his preparation towards the Tour de France. Strong stage riders will eye the spring classics and the ten one-day races that make up the World Cup.

The season is divided into the main spring classics, the stage races leading up to the major three-week tours, the Giro in May, the Tour de France in June/July and the Vuelta in September, with the World Championships on road and track now moved to October. Races are graded by the UCI, the sport's governing body, and there are different qualifying criteria for the different categories of race. Here is a brief outline of some of the major races in the pro calendar year:

Spring – The Classics

Milan–San Remo: The first of ten races which make up the World Cup season, but also a hugely significant race for the Italian riders, second only in importance to their Giro. Its significance is reflected in its roll-call. Past winners have included Eddy Merckx (a mere seven times), Fausto Coppi, Francesco Moser, Raymond Poulidor, Sean Kelly and Laurent Fignon. Tommy Simpson also won it in 1964. It is the longest single-day classic, with a distance of about 300 kms decided over no more than 300 ms. The race is essentially decided at the Cipressa, about 30 kms from the finish, which is a very fast big ring climb lasting about ten minutes. Teams try to get their main men positioned for the bottom of the Cipressa, as the climb defines the group of twenty to thirty who will have a chance of winning the race. The Poggio, a false flat on the edge of a housing estate on the out-skirts of San Remo, is traditionally the place for the final attack. For the last couple of years, the field has actually stayed together and the race has been decided in the final sprint. It's more a race for someone like Erik Zabel than for me, though I found it one of the easiest of the classics to ride, because, on the whole, it's pretty flat. Not one of my favourites.

Paris–Nice: This is the first big stage race of the season. It is called the Race to the Sun, but is more often the race from the cold to the wet, with a few sunny intervals in between. It's a good race for me because the schedule includes a prologue and a time trial. I finished third overall there in 1996, clocking the fastest stage time ever recorded in a time trial. Because it's the first big rendezvous after the winter, the racing is ferocious. Everyone wants to get some credit in the bank and teams are eager to get some wins on the board, so instead of twenty riders playing to win, as would be the case in October, there are a hundred. New members of teams are anxious to impress and team-mates are jostling for position for the year. It all adds up to some fraught racing. In my first year, I rode the smaller Tour of Murcia instead of Paris–Nice because I needed a bit of a boost to my morale after the culture shock of my first few weeks as a professional. But every other year I've done the Paris–Nice, which is a useful guide to where your fitness is compared to the rest of the *peloton*.

The Tour of Flanders: This is the first of the Belgian classics and has one of the longest histories, dating back to 1913. It used to climb over an incredibly steep cobbled hill called the Koppenberg, but after an incident there when Jesper Skibby was almost run over, the route has been changed and, thankfully for most, it no longer tackles the Koppenberg. The route is about 270 kms long and includes a series of short, sharp climbs, many of them cobbled. This is a race for the Flandrian hard men like Johan Museeuw and Peter van Petegem, who won the race in 1999. The key to the race is to hit the critical points with the first thirty or so riders, but it is a race for a particular type of rider. Like a lot of the classics, it is very tactical and intense. Not one that's my idea of a good day out; the risk of injury is too high.

Paris–Roubaix: No road race that requires suspension forks can be taken seriously; it's like comparing a demolition derby to Formula One. That's my view and I'm sticking to it, but my team-mate Magnus Backstedt, who finished in the top ten in his first year as a pro, will hear none of it. He lives and breathes the Paris–Roubaix, but then, in a previous life he travelled downhill on skis at 200 kph. Enough said.

On the continent, the 273 kms of the Paris–Roubaix is second only to the Tour as a national spectacle. Television viewing figures for the Queen of the Classics touch 60 million. It's a race for the big 75–80-kilo guys, and for guys who don't mind getting wet, muddy and injured. Johan Museeuw smashed his kneecap last year, then got gangrene, which nearly killed him. He lost a whole season's racing. Personally, I think it's a circus. I can see why people enjoy watching it, but I don't want to be one of the clowns.

Liège–Bastogne–Liège: They say Paris–Roubaix is the race for the hardest men, but that LBL is the hardest classic. It's 267 kms long, with a dozen steep Ardennes climbs in quick succession, which turn the race into a war of attrition. Riders tend to just drop off at the back rather than jump off at the front. It's a race I've had my eye on for a few years because its short, sharp climbs and rolling countryside would suit my style, but, though I've managed to finish in the top twenty once, I've never managed to push on from there. It's a nasty, physical race which can do a lot of physiological damage and demands great self-belief. I don't mind that; I can cope with it. Again, it's important to be in the front group at certain critical points in the race, because once you've been dropped it's mighty hard to get back in touch. Often, the decisive break comes about 5 or 6 kms from the finish on the Saint Nicolas Climb.

Amstel Gold: This is the last in the spring round of the World Cup races, and was begun in 1966. It's a peculiar race which I've tried twice and abandoned twice. It's run over a distance of 255 kms along windy narrow roads through southern Holland, past windmills, over countless roundabouts and up a series of little climbs lined by cars and spectators. Because the narrow route and series of bends have a whiplash effect on the *peloton*, it is essential to get in the leading group. Not a race for me.

Quite a number of riders now take a break from racing for a couple of weeks to recharge their batteries for the summer tours. It's a good time to reflect on how you're feeling and what needs improving.

Spring and Summer – The Tours

This is the best time of year for me because the stage races contain time trials. The racing is much less dependent on good positioning and pure bottle; it's more about physiology, psychology and timing. The main races in my view are the Giro d'Italia, the Dauphine Libéré, the national road race championships, the Tour de France and the three World Cup events in August: the San Sebastian Classic, the Grand Prix of Hamburg and the Grand Prix of Zurich. In Britain, the arrival of the Prutour was one of the most exciting developments in cycling. Sadly, Prudential have pulled out their sponsorship after two years and, at the time of writing, the future of the race was very doubtful. It's a shame, because for our team in general, and for me in particular, it was an ideal race for restoring confidence and getting some competitive racing miles in your legs before the Tour de France. It was also good to race on familiar territory and catch up with some old friends.

The Critérium International: A strange little race run over a week-end, with a long road stage on Saturday, a 100-km stage on Sunday morning, including some short climbs, and a time trial on Sunday afternoon. It's almost an ideal itinerary for me, and I won it in 1996.

The Giro d'Italia: I've never ridden this, but I know its reputation as a tough race. It's the first of the major three-week tours and, in places, it's every bit as brutal as the Tour de France. In fact, there was a time when the organizers seemed determined to undermine the Tour de France, which starts about three weeks later, by making their route tougher. All that happened was that the major players – riders like Indurain, though he did once win both in the same year – decided that it would spoil their chances in the Tour de France and didn't ride it. Common sense seems to have prevailed, though, and Marco Pantani's double victory in 1998 proved it could be done, at least until suspicions about the legality of his victories were aroused by his high haematocrit reading in 1999. It's not a race ever likely to be on my schedule. One major tour is enough.

Dauphine Libéré: Together with the Midi Libre, this is the main preparation race for the Tour de France, and is often over many of the mountains that feature heavily in the Tour. Most of the major Tour contenders will be starting to show their form here or in the Tour of Switzerland, one of the other big Alpine tours. I found some of my best climbing form on the Dauphine Libéré, because it tended to be just one or two stages in the mountains and wasn't as intense as the Tour de France.

National Road Race Championships: Generally, the National Championships in every cycling country are held just before the Tour. To be the Italian or the French champion is quite a big deal, but to be the British champion isn't quite so prestigious. Roger Legeay, my boss, was never very happy about me competing in case I won and had to wear the jersey of the national champion rather than his sponsor's. I've stopped doing the nationals because too many people are happy to be fifty-sixth as long as you are fifty-seventh. David Millar, the highly talented young English rider with the Cofidis team, found the same problem last year. Everyone covers your breaks, and if the course is relatively easy you just end up wasting yourself for nothing. One year the race was held over a hilly course on the Isle of Man, so Robert Millar (no relation) entered and won it because he knew he could blow the others away on a tough course.

The Tour de France: The Tour will be dealt with in more detail in a separate chapter, but it is the peak of the cycling year, the Olympics, the World Championships and the World Cup all rolled into one. Tradition has made the Tour what it is – the rituals of the road and the public, who line the route in their millions each year, picnic by the roadside, wave banners and unashamedly indulge in France's most celebrated national sporting pastime.

The Tour has grown in prestige over the past two decades, though I don't fully understand why it should dominate the calendar quite so completely. Any performance in the Tour, be it a stage win, a prologue or a gallant lone breakaway, is trebly important for the sponsors of the teams on the Tour. The drugs scandal of the 1998 Tour hit the relationship between the riders and the public, but there were signs of some forgiveness the following year.

France has a culture of bike riding that is very difficult to comprehend in England. Every village, every town will have its own cycling club, so there's a ready-made set of supporters when the Tour comes to town. But that makes it 3,700 kms, and three weeks, of the most gruelling, competitive riding of the season. Some mountain stages are so taxing on the body that it is physically impossible to eat the amount of food necessary to satisfy the body's demands for compensation. It is quite normal for a rider to finish the Tour with a body fat percentage of 4–5 per cent, which would be alarmingly low on a normal person. Yet, if you do ride well, the satisfaction is that much greater because you know you have competed with, and beaten, the best.

The format of the Tour of Le Grand Boucle, as it is known – a reference to the circular belt-buckle-shaped route each year – sometimes goes clockwise around France, reaching the Alps first before going into the Pyrenees, the second of the two big mountain ranges. Sometimes the riders go down the west coast first, hitting the first of the Pyrenees mountain stages after about ten days. In my first year on the Tour, in 1994, the format included the traditional team time trial, but it was abandoned the year after on the grounds that the Tour was an individual not a team event. The discipline was included again for the Millennium Tour, which should benefit my own Crédit Agricole team.

That first year's team time trial, with the Gan team, was chaotic. We hadn't rehearsed at all and the teamwork was ragged, to say the least. I probably could have ridden faster on my own, and because I lost the yellow jersey that year, on the stage before we reached England for the first time, I was very unhappy.

The race is divided into several very distinct phases now. After the prologue, which has a surprising effect on the morale of the riders for such a short event, the early stages tend to be dominated by the sprinters and their henchmen in the chain gang, the Saeco team of Mario Cipollini, or the Mapei boys for Tom Steels. It's the team's job to keep the race together. Often, if a breakaway group has worked its way to a healthy lead on the road, the whole *peloton* doesn't come together until the last 5 kms.

With so many good sprinters, those early stages are taking on an enormously competitive edge. The long, lone break so beloved by the French is rapidly becoming an impossibility because the sprint teams close the race down, working in rotation at the front to close the gap between the *peloton* and the leading group. Most of the early stages of the 1999 Tour followed the same pattern: an early attack, a group of six to ten riders getting clear before returning to the bunch about 5–10 kms before the mayhem of the sprint finish. The late Nineties has become a golden era for the sprinters, with Cipollini, Steels, Erik Zabel, Jimmy Caspar, Jerome Blijlevens, Robbie McEwen, Stuart O'Grady, from my own team, and Jan Kirsipuu, the first Estonian ever to wear the yellow jersey. The rest of us just try to keep out of the way.

The leading riders will be keeping themselves as fresh as possible for the time trial, which usually comes after about ten days, and the first of the two mountain phases in the race. It is vital for them to conserve as much energy as possible during those early days and not to lose any time, because in the mountains they will need every ounce of their reserves. Between the stages in the Alps and the Pyrenees, the race has a transition period, often through rolling countryside with a few climbs, but nothing too steep. This is the best terrain for riders who are neither specialist climbers nor specialist sprinters, but who still have the strength to make and sustain a break over a long, hot afternoon. Max Sciandri has been an expert *rouleur*, as the French call them. Theoretically, those should be the sort of road stages that suit me, but I, and most of the others in the *peloton*, are still recovering from the mountains. Physically and psychologically the race will be decided in the mountains. By the time it heads back to Paris, often with a final time trial for added spice, the pattern is well set, and unless the leading team makes a huge mistake or has a slice of bad luck, the places are pretty well established. The atmosphere in the *peloton* changes, too, with the early competitiveness being replaced by a general camaraderie.

The Tour is the defining moment of the season for riders and teams. Physically and mentally it is easily the most draining three weeks of the year. What happens in the Tour also defines which teams and riders are competitive for the rest of the season, because those who have not performed on the Tour will need to prove themselves before the end of the season. When so many teams left the Tour in 1998, the Vuelta, the Tour of Spain, was hugely competitive and absurdly fast. There was so much spare energy in the riders' legs. But if you have a good Tour, a rider can start winding down to the end of the season.

The Tour has been the focal point of my career as a professional rider and has dealt me a number of blows since I first took part in 1994. It has been a voyage of discovery for me, sometimes uplifting, often demoralizing, but never less than interesting. These aspects – how the Tour has fitted into, shaped and changed my professional career – will be discussed in a later chapter. By the time the survivors reach Paris in late July, most are mentally and physically exhausted. No-one wants to see a bike for a few weeks. Yet the season still grinds on.

Late Summer and Autumn

Despite three World Cup races, the month of August is the lull after the storm. It is a month of transition; the big tours are over, except for the Vuelta, and the riders who have played a major part in them are getting tired mentally as well as physically, and are starting to think of packing up for the season.

The World Cup continues with the San Sebastian Classic, the Grand Prix of Hamburg and the Grand Prix of Zurich, but the fields are smaller, with only a few of the heavyweight contestants – those who have made the World Cup their priority or who need a good result to help with their ongoing contract negotiations. It is still a big deal to win a World Cup race, but they have only a fraction of the prestige of the spring classics. Those who are aiming for the World Championships will probably stay quiet before building up to the final climax of the season.

This is usually an important time for me. There are a number of individual time trials at this time of the year, the Bretling GP time trial in Germany, the Eddy Merckx time trial and, in mid-September, the Grand Prix des Nations, which was once regarded as the world time trial championship and still retains much of its prestige in the time-trialling world.

Those with the legs left go to the Tour of Spain, the Vuelta, in September, the last of the major three-week tours, but neither of my ventures there has been very profitable. The racing is no less competitive just because the Tour de France is over, and the speeds are still very high. Just about all the riders intending to be on form for the World Championships will have ridden the Tour of Spain and then Paris–Tours, the penultimate World-Cup encounter.

The World Championships themselves usually begin with the time-trial categories. For the elite men, the course is usually about 40–50 kms over varying terrain. The time trials are followed by the road races, again for different categories, culminating in the main men's event on the last day, won in 1998 by Oskar Camenzind in a wet, intense race, and in 1999 by the Spaniard Oscar Freire. I stayed safely in the commentary box.

At the other end of October come the World Track Championships, though due to the increasing demands of the professional season only a few of the *peloton* now choose to make the transition back to what, for many of them, was their starting point in bike racing.

The very last road event of the year is the Tour of Lombardy, otherwise romantically known as the Race of the Falling Leaves. It is one last chance to get something from a season, often the final refuge for the guys who were flying at the World Championships but who have a few drops left in their tanks. After ten months of pretty solid racing, most of the *peloton* have retired to the hills or the plains to reflect on the glories of their season or lick their wounds and prepare for the next one.

3

THE STRUCTURE OF A PRO TEAM

The professional cycling team is a unique sporting group. A football team share the same dressing room, training ground, hotel and coach for nine months of a season. I can go through large portions of the year without even seeing the other members of my team. Yet, on a long hot day in the Alps during the Tour de France, team spirit has to be instinctive, almost regimental. Riders have to be prepared to suffer for the team, for nothing more than a pat on the back at the end of a stage and an understanding that they will have to go through the same thing all over again the following day. In the end, no-one can ride your bike for you or lend you a fresh set of lungs. Cyclists are, by nature, individuals. But a successful cycling team has to maintain a balance between individual brilliance and collective will.

Banesto, the crack Spanish team, was entirely structured around Miguel Indurain and geared towards his victory in the Tour de France. There was only one leader and one objective. The team members' personal goals were subordinate to the overall aim of winning the yellow jersey for Indurain. They were well paid for doing so, but no other sport would countenance such a feudal division of labour. Most of the 198-strong field for a tour don't have either the intention, motivation or ability to win the race; they are hired hands, paid to protect and help their leader.

At the end of a season, or a couple of seasons, they move on to another leader and another team. It is rare for a rider to stay with one team for longer, though Indurain was an obvious exception. Integrity and professionalism are the two qualities I want to see in my colleagues. But in such an informal and temporary structure, it is hard to build a lasting trust. There are too many variables, diverse agendas and temptations for a member of the team to claim individual glory – and therefore a fat contract for next season – at the expense of the team. The difficulty for the *directeur sportif* is to harness all those different aspirations to the good of the team and the sponsors.

At one end of the spectrum is Roger Legeay, a highly respected team boss and one of the most successful and experienced managers in cycling. Roger's style is informal; he lets riders think for themselves. The team isn't particularly structured around a team leader. Roger will hire good riders, people whose attitude he likes, and then work out a race programme from there. Other teams will hire specific riders to do specific jobs.

The direct opposite to Roger would be someone like Manolo Saiz at Once, the team I nearly joined in the summer of 1997 when Gan's sponsorship was coming to an end. The Once philosophy was clear: when they go to a race, they go to win. They keep their riders happy by letting them have a chance of winning a stage if the circumstances are right, but in the big races they back the leaders – at one time Laurent Jalabert and Alex Zulle – who are paid to win.

During our negotiations, they seemed a happy team, well and firmly led by Saiz, who likes to do things his way. At Once, there would have been no question of me following my own training programme and race schedule. I had long discussions with Peter Woodworth about whether I could cope with that. Saiz wanted to control everything, yet Once are the only team to allow wives to accompany the riders on training camps. He gives the riders everything they need for their mental and physical well-being, and in return they are expected to perform 100 per cent. I would have been a work rider for Once, which would have been hard for me to take, but would have allowed me to have my moments of glory as well. The frustration would have come when my form was good, but was being used up in the service of a team leader. On the other hand, I would not have had the pressure of being the team leader. I would have had to accept the whole package.

Banesto is the ultimate team of general and foot soldiers. But it only works if the top man is successful, as Indurain was. There is a lot to be said for that approach; leadership has to come from the top, you cannot leave it to the riders to take responsibility unless you have a particularly strong team spirit. In my first year with Gan, I had the leader's jersey in the Dauphine Libéré. One of the attractions of Gan for me was that Roger would let me do my own thing. I was able to live in Cheshire and fly back and forth, and prepare and follow my own training schedule. That would not have been allowed a few years ago. Riders like Sean Kelly and Stephen Roche were expected to live on the continent and adopt a continental lifestyle, which would have killed me after six months. But Gan and Crédit Agricole have been very happy teams, in part because of the fluid structure Roger has created, which encourages everyone to work exceptionally hard for the team.

The *Directeur Sportif*

The *directeur sportif* largely sets the tone of the team. He is the financier, the fund-raiser, the hirer and firer, the tactician on the road. He organizes the team's race programme and makes the deals. An assistant will handle the logistics of a race; the *directeur sportif* will concentrate on the big picture.

I am contracted not to the sponsors, but to Roger, who owns the team and finds the sponsors. When Gan announced they were withdrawing their sponsorship in 1997, Roger's main task was to line up a replacement. The riders were contracted to him until September. After that, they were free to look elsewhere for work. For most of the 1997 summer, it looked as though the team might fold until Roger persuaded Crédit Agricole to come in. The 1998 season was sponsored half by Gan, half by Crédit Agricole, which was a little confusing. Apart, possibly, from the old-fashioned dictatorial football manager, I don't think there is another sporting role equivalent to that of a *directeur sportif* of a major cycling team. His power is almost total, and some *directeurs* – notably in the Italian teams – wield their authority to the limit.

The Team

It takes a budget of about £4 million to run a professional bike team of twenty-five riders for a season. Gan was never one of the bigger teams financially, but we made the most of what we had. The size of the budget determines the make-up of the team to a large extent, but the attitude of the *directeur sportif* is equally critical. The idea is to get the maximum exposure for the sponsors' investment, and this is a question of being realistic and understanding where the strengths of the team lie.

At Gan, we could not afford to attract a big-name rider capable of winning the Tour de France. We often didn't start a race with a team leader. But in Fred Moncassin we had one of the best sprinters, and in Cedric Vasseur, Stephane Heulot, Henk Vogels and Stuart O'Grady we had talented young riders who could win stages of major tours and smaller races, and compete at the front for the attention of the nation's television audience. The core of the old Gan team has remained with Roger under the new sponsorship of Crédit Agricole, but the purchase of Bobby Julich for the 2000 season promises to take the team into a different league. Julich is a climber who, as his third place in the 1998 Tour de France showed, has the ability to win the race.

Only occasionally has Roger's tendency to leave the riders to work it out led to unnecessary compromise and defeat. At the Paris–Camembert race, part of the Coupe de France competition, there were two guys in a breakaway – Didier Roux from Gan and Adrian Bafi, a sprinter from another team. With one last climb before the finish, Didier wanted to attack all the way up the hill to break Bafi and avoid a sprint finish that he would probably lose. But Stephane Heulot, another Gan rider who was leading the Coupe de France at the time, was paranoid about the possibility of someone else taking his jersey, even a team-mate. He started to ride across the gap to attach himself to the leading pair. Didier then couldn't attack because his team-mate was coming across. Having bridged the gap and joined the leaders, Stephane should have attacked again in order to put the pressure on Bafi, who would have had to chase. Stephane didn't; he just sat there. Didier couldn't attack because Stephane had the leader's jersey, and Bafi won the race in a sprint.

Understandably, Didier was very angry because we had two guys to one. Had Stephane come across and won the race, no problem. Had he helped Didier win the race, no problem. By being selfish and thinking only of himself, Stephane blew the race for Didier and the team. He was only interested in protecting his position and, in the unwritten rules of the road, that goes down very badly. Didier probably didn't get another chance to win a race all year and he would certainly remember that incident if it came down to helping Stephane in another race. Cyclists have long memories. You have to be damn good to be selfish.

One of Indurain's great strengths was his sense of honour. Jeremy Hunt, the promising young British sprinter, recalls one of his early races for Banesto when he was winding up for a finish and found himself on the back of his team-mate's wheel, being led out to the line. Only later did he discover that the team-mate was Indurain. That was the kind of guy Indurain was and though his popularity never won him races, it did him no harm when he needed help from another rider or team.

The *Domestiques*

A team is made up of specialists – sprinters and climbers – and overall riders, those usually capable of time-trialling well and surviving in the mountains. Richard Virenque and Marco Pantani are natural climbers by physique and temperament. Climbers, on the whole, are loners, happy with their own company, highly motivated, slightly disdainful and very single-minded. They regard themselves as the real racers, the purists. The pulse of a team, though, is regulated by the *domestiques*, the foot soldiers, the worker bees, whatever you want to call them. A good *domestique*, like the recently retired Neil Stephens of Once and Festina, is worth his weight in gold because his qualities are rare.

A *domestique* must know his limitations, either mental or physical, yet be a strong enough rider to match his team leader most of the way. Mostly, a guy who has the talent to work for someone capable of winning big stage races will have ambitions of his own. A *domestique* can have ambitions, but they must always come second to the overall objective of the team. Neil accepted quite early in his career that he had the ability to win smaller races, but that his real strength was helping others. He was a fine organizer on the road and a real team player. He wanted his team to win, and he made a very good living out of being a *domestique* because there aren't many of them around.

The duties of a *domestique* are many. He might have to ferry water bottles from the team car to his leader, give up his bike if the team leader gets a puncture, ride flat out to bring back a dangerous breakaway or to protect his man from a crosswind, pace an ailing leader up a stiff climb or work with him to close the gap on the leaders. On the whole, *domestiques* are stable characters who have rationalized their place in the *peloton* and realized how best to get their bread buttered.

The best signing we made at Gan was Eros Poli, who was a great asset to the team, both as a rider and a character, until, sadly, we let him go at the end of the 1999 season. Eros is larger than life and irrepressible. At the end of a long, hot day, we would be licking our wounds in the team bus and he would say, 'Hey, issa not so bad.' He would point out what we'd done well and go round each individual cheering them up. He is also highly ingenious. There were very limited showers available for the 150 riders at the end of a stage on the 1997 Tour, so Eros commandeered a fireman's hose, stuck it in through the bathroom window and increased capacity fiftyfold. The one thing that really gets him down is riders working for themselves more than for the team. He might be getting on a bit now, but his contribution to the team spirit in his first season at Gan was enormous. He was the first rider to be engaged for the 1998 season. Eros is too big a build to be a climber, but he won the prized Alpe d'Huez stage on the Tour de France by establishing a huge lead at the bottom of the mountain and protecting it to the top. It was an epic ride, and no-one really wanted to deprive Eros of his big moment.

Every great rider had a bodyguard, if you like, to help him through the most difficult stages. Indurain was Pedro Delgado's minder during his first years on the Tour de France, guiding Delgado to victory in 1988. When Indurain won the Tour for the first time three years later, Delgado repaid the compliment. All the great champions rely on their right-hand men to help them out: Greg LeMond, Bernard Hinault and Eddy Merckx. Once Indurain had established his domination of the Tour, Banesto had eight *domestiques* working for him, which made them a very tough team to crack.

Team Pursuit, Barcelona 1992

I did a lot of work with the sports psychologist John Syer, mainly with the British cycling team. At the Olympics in Barcelona, the development of a strong bond between the four members of the pursuit team, under John's powerful guidance, turned us from also-rans into strong contenders for a medal.

Team pursuit is a very rigid discipline. It's like rowing, and therefore an ideal subject for the sort of work John had been doing on teamwork. The key word was 'trust'. In a team pursuit, every rider must not only be aware of his own performance, but sense how his team-mates are feeling. It is no good one member riding really strongly for a lap and leaving the other members of the team behind. The changeovers, when the man on the front drops back and the next in line takes over, have to be rhythmic and smooth so momentum isn't disrupted. It is a very skilled art, relying on an instinctive understanding of teamwork.

If the first rider swings off the front and the next accelerates rather than holding the pace, everyone else has got to chase, including the guy at the back who has just finished his stint at the front. This has a damaging long-term effect on speed and stamina. In Barcelona we had one member of the team, Glenn Sword, who would sometimes do this, and when it was pointed out to him in training he would be bloody-minded and deliberately slow down instead. Once or twice, he swung up onto the banking and left the rest of us to get on with it. He was very volatile.

We had a lot of sessions with John Syer – sometimes up to four hours of pretty heavy stuff – in order to establish complete trust between the members of the team. These required total honesty from everyone. We would have to point out weaknesses in our team-mates, and be prepared to take criticism and turn it into a positive force. With Glenn, that could be difficult, but it worked, and it only worked because everyone had to bare their soul and be completely straight. I have to say, in Glenn's defence, he was the only guy not to let me down once when it came to the crunch. We finished fourth and there is still a great bond between us.

Tour de France Team Time Trial to Eurotunnel, 1994

When I came to Gan I wanted to practise some of the principles of that national team structure on a pro team. In the team time trial, now reinstated for the 2000 Tour, I was wearing the yellow jersey on my début, and we needed to hold on to it for one more day for a British rider to arrive for the historic first leg of the Tour in the UK as race leader. However, our team time trial was a shambles. It would have been perfect for a psychological preparation similar to the one in Barcelona.

The event is completely structured and the team consisted of climbers, sprinters and all-rounders who had to appreciate their differences and sacrifice some of their efforts for the benefit of the team. Climbers, for example, can destroy sprinters on the hillier sections of the time trial by pushing too hard, and on the long straight sections the sprinters can try to get their own back. Climbers will do only a short turn at the front to keep the momentum going. Everyone has to accept that they will contribute differently. Sadly, our lack of teamwork showed up badly that day. Without being arrogant, my form was so good that, at that time, I could have done the course quicker on my own. To be honest, I just wanted them to get out of the way and let me get on with it. That sort of mess could have been avoided with a more scientific approach, but it would have taken a tremendous amount of work from the team members, and I'm not sure they would have been prepared to trust each other enough. Teams change too often to establish complete trust. Good team spirit is developed more by chance. There were guys at Gan who I would really be prepared to work hard for because I knew they would do the same for me. You don't need to like team-mates particularly, but you do need to respect them.

The Team Leader

Coming, as I did, from a strange background for a road racer into the *peloton* late and unknown, I found the intensity of my new environment almost intolerable. The structure of a team depends on the nature of its leader; with Banesto, the whole team relied on Indurain's brilliance. At the end of each Tour de France, the Banesto riders knew that, if they had done their jobs and Indurain had done his, each of them would be £50,000 or so richer for the experience, because it is a tradition for the team leader to share out the overall prize in the Tour. A rigid team structure only works with the right man at the top. With Banesto, everyone knew exactly how it worked: everyone rode for Miguel, and that gave the team its strength. Everyone was happy with that because their belief in him was total.

Often, though, you find teams which have a designated leader, but his team-mates don't believe he can do the job or, as happened most famously with Greg LeMond and Bernard Hinault on the 1986 Tour, there is confusion about who is the leader. The pair finished hand in hand at the top of Alpe d'Huez, but the politics of the team was disastrous. 'It was pure war,' LeMond recalled later. 'We didn't even talk at dinner.' The pairing of Alex Zulle and Laurent Jalabert at Once didn't really work, either. It is hard for a team to have two apparent leaders.

A team leader has to have the confidence of his team, the belief that he can do better than them and that, therefore, their only option is to work for him. I have never felt I've had the confidence of my team because I haven't come up with the goods. I sense that a lot of guys in the team, though they'd never say it out loud, feel they could do better than me on certain races. In the Dauphiné Libéré in 1997, I was in trouble on some of the climbs, and they didn't think, Team leader. Even though I'm feeling better I'll stay with him, and when we get over the top of the climb, we'll try to limit our losses. They just thought, Oh, he's in trouble, I'm off. That was pretty upsetting at times. Somebody shouting, 'Come on, Chris,' while they're riding off up the road doesn't help morale, particularly if they've left you riding into a crosswind.

It was partly my own fault. I wasn't confident enough of my ability, which in turn affected my authority. It was only my fourth season as a professional, and I was already the nominal leader of a respected team. It was a strange position to be in. I felt the responsibility, but didn't want to take it on unless I was sure I could fulfil it. In some situations it was as if I was saying, No, no, I don't want you to ride for me. If you feel you can do something good, go and do it. I'll just sit and see what happens. Whereas I should have made them work for me whether I produced the goods or not, because I was the best bet.

One of the best rides I had in 1997 came on the Tour of Valencia. I had ridden in the leader's jersey for five or six days, from the prologue, before we came to the first summit finish, which was a very steep but short ten-minute climb. Escartin and all the major climbers were in the leading group, but the Gan boys worked solidly, faster and faster, to get me to the front at the bottom of the climb. They just plonked me at the bottom of the hill behind a team-mate. He peeled off when he'd had enough, and it was left to me to protect the jersey. All the specialist climbers took off up the mountain; I couldn't follow, but kept to what I knew was my limit, and, slowly but surely, I began to reel them in. I finished second or third and kept the lead. The team had done their job, I had done mine and that was very satisfying. The next day, I blew it all away in the mountains, but on that occasion it felt right. I just want the confidence to know that I can do that, and

I want them to have the confidence, too. That is what all team leaders want.

There will always be competition to be top dog within a team, unless there is a clearly defined structure and a clearly designated team leader. To an extent, it happened with me and Cedric Vasseur in 1997, but I felt it was pretty much under control. I have no problems with another rider saying, 'I really want to do well. Is it OK?' Then individual aims are open and I can respond accordingly. Often, when my form wasn't what it should have been, I was delighted that someone else was taking the pressure off me for a day. But what upset me was when people wanted to have it both ways, to keep their head down and say they were working for me only to take the opportunity when it arrived.

Tour de France, Stage to La Châtre, 1997 – Cedric Vasseur

This turned out to be one of the epic rides in the 1997 Tour, a good old-fashioned do-or-die long break that was successful against all the odds. The French, naturally, loved it, not least because Cedric's father, Alain, had won a stage on the Tour twenty-seven years before. Those sorts of lone breakaways almost never work, but when they do, they are classics. However, I was still the leader of the Gan team when Cedric disappeared up the road, and, at the end of it, someone really should have said, 'Nice ride, but what the hell were you doing?' In reality, Cedric should have said something, either on the road or in the team meeting beforehand. Then there would have been no problems, because I was in no position to make such a break myself.

The full story is that, before the stage, the team were talking about the *critériums*, the circuit races organized by towns during the summer, which provide the riders with some extra cash, and Cedric was asking if there were any for him. One of the managers said, 'No-one has asked because you're not very visible.' So that day he decided to be visible for an hour or so. I can understand that, because he has a living to earn, but he was saying one thing and doing another.

Obviously, I couldn't say anything at the end of the stage because it was a brilliant ride and the team had done well. But it was a classic example of lack of trust within a team, and it shows how easily the authority of the team leader can be undermined.

Soigneurs

Anything to do with the non-bike-riding part of the team is the job of the *soigneur*. For a major tour, we would have four *soigneurs*, each handling two members of the team. They are the contact for all the logistical details that have nothing to do with riding a bike. A *soigneur* gets up before the riders, prepares the race food, wakes the riders, takes out the suitcases and stacks them in the truck, which one of them will drive to the next hotel. The others will go to the race start to administer massage, embrocation, bandages or whatever. They will then go on to the feed zone and be ready for the riders, before whipping off to the finish to await the arrival of the *peloton*. In the meantime, the other car will have gone on to the hotel to put the suitcases in the rooms, post the room lists, put food in the rooms before dinner and sort out the menu. They will start doing the massage and, at some point in the schedule, get the dirty washing done, too.

It is an enormously critical and demanding job, and they basically do it for the love of the sport. My team is twenty years old, riders and sponsors change, but some of the *soigneurs* have been there almost since the start. Over the years, the routine and protocol have developed; the whole thing now works very efficiently, which, on a race like the Tour de France, is a real advantage. With a good back-up team, the riders don't have to think about anything other than riding their bikes, eating and sleeping. I have had the same *soigneur*, Michel, since joining the team. He has twenty years' experience and has become a good friend.

Mechanics

Mechanics change more regularly in a team. Once every couple of years a new one comes in, because riders tend to form relationships with their mechanics and sometimes take them if they leave. When I arrived at Gan I didn't know anything about road bikes, so I let the mechanics get on with sorting those out. But I have always been a perfectionist about my time trial bikes. I have built up a good relationship with all three mechanics in the team, but I suspect I get on their nerves because I've always got a new piece of kit. On the other hand, they respect that, too, because they can see that you're someone who is going to give 100 per cent to the job and, though they moan about it, they like to have new toys to play with. It varies the routine for them.

What amazed me initially about many of the riders is how traditional they are. They would be given a sponsored bike, the mechanic would look after it and they would ride it.

4

GOAL-SETTING

Step 1:
The Primary Question

Before you can go anywhere, there are two questions that you *must* have an honest answer to:

1   **What are your *real* priorities? Do you have a job? If so, how demanding is it on your time? Do you have a family? If so, how is that going to affect your sport?**
2   **How much of your time can you realistically commit to your sporting objectives and how much are you prepared to give up?**

Once you have the answers to these questions, you can move on.

Step 2:
Setting Goals – The Principle

1   **How do you choose an objective?**
2   **What is a reasonable objective?**
3   **How many objectives should I go for?**

To say 'I want to do well this year' or 'I want to do well in the premier calendar events this year' is a statement of desire; it is not, in itself, an objective. Objectives are specifically identified goals, and I would recommend between two and three objectives a year. These are what the year will be shaped around. In my case they are usually the Tour de France, the World Time Trial Championships and the World Pursuit Championships. Preferably, they should be well spaced, allowing for the different physical demands. They can be close together only if the physical demands of the goals are similar: two time trials of similar lengths, say. I have never seen true peak form held for longer than six weeks.

Once the year goals have been identified, the intermediate goals can be chosen. These should be specifically selected to coincide with the training phases for the year goals, providing motivation and, hopefully, some check points for confidence and fitness. I would suggest no more than six intermediate goals in a season. An athlete can only raise his or her game so many times in one year. For me, intermediate targets have been the Critérium International, Liège–Bastogne–Liège in the early-season phase of endurance training, the Prutour, the Midi Libre and the Dauphine Libéré, all stage races, in the build-up to the Tour de France, and the Grand Prix Eddy Merckx and the Grand Prix des Nations, both time trials, in the final phase leading up to the World Time Trial Championships.

This doesn't mean you're not allowed to take part in other races, only that preparation races are primarily about training specific aspects of your form, technique or tactics. Objective races are about results. In a preparation race, you are deliberately deflecting the pressure to perform and replacing it with a specific, positive training goal within the race. By following that structure you should be able to achieve a clearly defined direction for your training and racing programme and, equally importantly, develop confidence in the methods.

Setting Goals: The Reality

The important point to remember when you are sitting down to plan a season and set goals is to be realistic. For the amateur that means assessing your lifestyle and priorities. Saying boldly at the start of the year 'Yes, I'm going to win this, this and this' will only lead to disillusion and loss of motivation if you don't have the time to train properly to meet those objectives. The two most important elements in people's lives are their job and their family. Both have to be organized around your training because it's not just a matter of going out onto the road and riding a bike; periods of rest and the correct diet have to be structured into the rhythms of your life, too.

The first decision concerns those priorities. What comes first? The decision might not be yours alone. It is vital to talk it over with someone objectively, someone who will give you an honest and direct opinion. Peter Woodworth performs that function for me. He can look in from the outside and tell me what the options are and what the consequences of particular decisions might be. We will reflect on the way I have structured a couple of seasons later in this chapter. My wife, Sally-Anne, also has a very acute eye. She will often tell me if a schedule is unrealistic.

Once you have worked out the inhibiting factors and elicited the support of your family and friends, you can focus on realistic goals. Do you want to be top club standard? Or will you aim as high as a place on the Commonwealth Games team, for example? Having objectives means the season can be broken into bite-sized chunks, creating peaks of form, with luck, and building in periods of rest. The aim is to maintain control of your form, creating it when you want it, not at some random and totally inappropriate moment. Things will inevitably go wrong, and a look at my 1997 season illustrates the fact, but by segmenting your season, the damage can be limited to a particular phase. One objective might have to be bypassed, but others have been built into the schedule to compensate.

I believe that someone who works full time can still train hard enough to compete for a place on the British team and, if selected, perform to a good standard. You can only train for so many hours in a day before the work becomes detrimental to fitness. The sacrifices would be tremendous, the whole rhythm of family life would have to be geared to your training, but it is feasible.

This is a possible loose structure for a winter training week:

Saturday/Sundays: reserved for longer endurance-based rides. The working week would be divided into a five-day block to recover from the weekend training.

Monday/Tuesday: light training, rest and recovery.

Wednesday/Thursday/Friday: quality sessions which, by definition, should be no longer than two hours. I can get all the work I need done in two hours, provided the session is properly structured. Just riding a bike for two hours is of minimal benefit.

Wednesday evenings might be reserved for a track league or a club ten-mile time trial. In my amateur days, I would ride for an hour out to a time trial, ride the ten-mile trial and then ride home, which is an ideal combination of stamina and speed work. I won the National Championships on a similar routine, and went to the World Championships.

But it is not just finding the time to train that is critical; finding the time to rest is equally important. If training starts at eight in the evening, your body will not allow you to go to sleep until 11 p.m. at the earliest, which is compromising your rest. A possible routine incorporating work would be to ride out at 8 a.m., shower, change and be ready to start work at 10 a.m., work through until 5.30 p.m., then leave work on the bike and ride from 6–7.30 p.m. An alternative would be to take an extended lunch hour and do your main ride then. It depends on the type of work you do, the flexibility of your hours and the generosity of your employer. Either way, you should think about your diet. If you are riding at 6 p.m., you will need to eat a proper lunch, topping up your energy resources at mid-afternoon with an energy bar. Otherwise, you will be riding after six hours without food. Diet will be discussed in a later chapter; it is an integral part of a planned training programme.

Case Study:
The Best Laid Plans – Profile of a Lost Season

We have just looked at the general principles of preparing for a season: how to assess the successes and failures of the season objectively, with input from the people you know and trust, how to set targets for the coming year and then fit other sub-targets into the natural rhythms of the training schedule. For the amateur cyclist, a job move or change of lifestyle might have led to reduced time for training or prompted the need to take a decision about your future cycling career. There are many different factors at work, but the fundamental truth is that you have to be honest with yourself. Setting unrealistic goals is worse than setting none at all, because it will only erode your confidence and lead to failure.

Through the winter of 1997–8 I had to accept that I didn't have the physical ability to reach the podium in the Tour de France. I knew it was a tall order when I turned pro relatively late and from a track and time-trial background, but I had never recognized the words 'can't do' before and saw no reason why the professional ranks should be any different. But my experiences in the 1997 season were enough to persuade me that some things are out of reach. The boy from Hoylake would never wear yellow in Paris.

The 1997 season had begun very promisingly. My goal for the year was the Tour, the whole Tour and nothing but the Tour. It was a crunch year. I had done my road-racing apprenticeship, put together some promising rides in pre-tour races like the Midi Libre and the Dauphine, had completed the Tour before and now, as team leader of Gan, I had to put everything together and make a concerted challenge in the general classification of the Tour.

Together with Peter Keen, I had devised a training schedule that would take my riding weight down from 70 kgs, my standard weight, to nearer 67 kgs by the spring. The trick was to improve my power-to-weight ratio for climbing without decreasing my basic power output too much. We constructed a programme of controlled weight loss. I knew what I was trying to do and I knew why I was doing it, and through the winter I was incredibly motivated and couldn't wait to start the season.

Peter Keen had compiled some very believable figures on what would happen if I weighed less. The test case was the Tourmalet, one of the toughest climbs in the Tour schedule. He computed what difference a loss of 1.5 kgs would make over a typical hour-long climb of an average 8 per cent gradient. The answer was forty-six seconds on the climb and, overall on the Tour, about seven minutes. That information was dynamite to an info-junkie like me. I thought, If I can lose 1.5 kgs off me and 1.5 kgs off my bike it would put me in a different league. The thought was enough to send my motivation into orbit. But there was a problem. Instead of the weight loss becoming a means to an end, it became the end itself. I was losing weight in order to enhance my chances in the Tour, but – and those close to me will sigh heavily at this point – it became obsessive. I got sucked in by the prospect of losing weight and, on reflection because I didn't see it at the time, I developed a slight eating disorder.

Because I was also starting my racing schedule later than usual in order to be ready for May and June, I put all my energy into training. Training was replacing the satisfaction I usually got from racing. So when a given exercise was 300 watts for two hours, I did two and a quarter hours at 330 watts. I felt great about it because my programme was on schedule and all the training reports I sent back to Peter were buoyant and enthusiastic, so he found it hard to tell me to back off when I was absorbing the loads he set me so comfortably. On days that were set aside for rest, I would go out for a couple of hours on the bike just to burn up a few more calories. I watched my calorie intake religiously and balanced it against the calories I used up in training. I ended up losing the 3 kgs in one month instead of three.

This is a point which is relevant for any cyclist: losing weight is a very delicate business. The maximum daily deficit should be 1,000 calories. An intake of 2,400 is necessary for someone of my height and weight just to function; with the exertions of training, that intake could be increased to about 5,000 calories. During that winter, I carefully weighed and measured all my food so that I would be eating 4,000 calories a day, which is right on the limit of what the body can take before the metabolism starts to protest and slow down, which is a critical problem when you have to process large amounts of fuel during long days of racing. The body begins to shut down, and this affects your hormone and testosterone levels.

The problem didn't become acute until some time into the season. I was going well until May, finishing second to Pavel Tonkov in the Tour de Romandie, when Tonkov was considered one of the favourites for the Giro. That was a very pleasing result for me because I felt I was learning to survive in the mountains and compete with the big boys for overall classification. I was ahead of schedule at that time, but from then on my performance began to drop off. I wasn't getting dropped or anything, I was simply tiring more easily, and this got worse as the season went on. I would have a fantastic day, and the next it would be like someone had turned off the switch.

On the Tour of Catalonia, I won the prologue and was leading the tour overall when we hit the mountains. The final climb was only 3 kms long, but at a gradient of 23 per cent it was very steep. I'd had a quick look at it the day before and knew that the best way to tackle it was to ride to my own limit and not be tempted to overdo it. The team had been riding tempo in the valley and so the field was quite strung out by the time we hit the first part of the climb. I was in a perfect position. All the climbers disappeared up the road, but I rode steadily, just at my threshold, and slowly began to reel them in. I passed Tonkov and latched on to Escartin's wheel in the final climb to the line. Someone else pipped me at the line – I think I finished third – but I was only about ten seconds behind and felt really good about the way I'd ridden.

The next day, Escartin set his team to work to see if they could shift me. They did. On the previous day I'd had petrol in the tank, but that day I was running on empty. My pulse was about fifteen beats down on normal, yet I couldn't go any faster. The top end of my power range had just vanished, and the effect on my confidence was devastating. I just couldn't predict what was going to happen. Good form one day was no guarantee of good form the next and, though finding and maintaining form is not an exact science, the fluctuations should not have been so extreme. For someone who thrives on a precise understanding of what my body can do, and why, the inexplicable loss of form was doubly frustrating. Only later did we track back and isolate the problem.

From May 1997, the effects of my overtraining and drastic weight-loss programme began to take their toll. I looked great, just like a pro bike rider should, gaunt and sinewy, but I was riding terribly. Most of my best performances have been achieved at a racing weight of 70 kgs, but this time I was down to 67 kgs, even though the limit we'd set was 68 kgs. This was uncharted territory for me and my body.

By the time I arrived at the Tour de France, I knew I was tired, though mentally I was up for it. I won the prologue more on technique and experience than pure strength; I knew I was capable of doing better. The first week went almost perfectly for me. I rode well, stayed far up the field, avoided all the crashes further back and used up the minimum amount of energy.

By the time the first mountain came into view on stage nine I was actually quite confident. The first climb in any tour is usually explosive. All the climbers who have been pottering about in the field for the first few days have fresh legs and want to exert their authority, so usually there is mayhem. I was expecting to be blown away on the Col de Soulor and then to have to peg my way back steadily through the field over the Col du Tourmalet and the Col d'Aspin. That was the theory anyway.

The Tourmalet was the mountain profile I'd spent all winter dieting for. At the top of the Col de Soulor I was only a few seconds behind the leading group, but on the descent I overcooked it a bit and crashed. Nothing very dramatic, but enough to leave me with a 6-mm tear in the trapezius muscle close to my spine, an injury that was only confirmed later. I got back on my bike and set off in pursuit, but it felt like someone was continually stubbing a cigarette out on my back.

There were just two more stages until the rest day and I thought that if I could survive those two, a day of rest might cure the problem. The following day was a monster, with a mountain-top finish in Andorra. It turned out to be a devastating and historic day's racing, the day that Jan Ullrich stamped his authority on the race and over his nominal team leader and defending champion, Bjarne Riis. But those of us stuck at the back of the *gruppetto*, somehow willing our bodies through seven and a half hours of hell, didn't see or appreciate the action. It was pretty soul-destroying. I got to the rest day, and though I was unable to bend my back far enough to use my time-trial bike in the St Étienne time-trial stage, there was still a chance the pain would ease as the days wore on. On the stage to Alpe d'Huez I set off with no thoughts of stopping, but halfway up the first climb of the day, the Col du Grand Bois, the pain was certainly no better, and was arguably getting worse. Sometimes in big races, stopping and getting off the bike is a relief and release from the pressure. But here, on one of the biggest days in the year, I just didn't want to stop.

It's hard to explain why stopping the suffering should be so hard. It's just a horrible feeling having your number taken off you and climbing into the team's service car and into retirement. At least the service car is better than being given a lift in the broomwagon, the nickname for the van that sweeps up behind the race. But that day on Alpe d'Huez was even worse because we had to climb our way slowly up the mountain in the service car, and I could see all the British flags and banners waving on my behalf. Months later, you wonder what all the fuss was about, but at the time it was a very public admission of failure.

Mentally and physically I struggled to come back from that disappointment. The rest of the season was spent fighting fires and trying to salvage something from the wreckage. By the time I reached the World Time Trial Championships, I had lost all sense of direction. I hadn't a clue whether I was in good or bad form. Somehow I managed to pull out a bronze medal from somewhere, but it didn't give me any satisfaction; it just showed me I could still time trial, even when the chips were down.

The danger for me, or any racing cyclist, is that a long period of indifferent form seriously impairs your judgement. If you lose the sense of what it feels like to be in good form, you recalibrate your idea of good and bad form . . . downwards. So the bad form of two years ago becomes the mediocre form of today, and the mediocre form of two years ago becomes the good form of today. Really good form is consigned to the past. The mind plays tricks on the body. It can happen all too easily. Perhaps it did at the 1998 World Time Trial Championships, which I had targeted for a belated and much-needed flourish at the end of the season. I prepared assiduously for the event, went through all my usual routines and felt I was in reasonable, if not brilliant, form only to find that I wasn't even in the ball park. That was a considerable blow to my morale.

By the end of 1997, I had to take stock of my career and figure out which way to go next. I had reached a plateau for the first time. Roger Legeay was struggling to find a sponsor to replace Gan and the riders were therefore automatically released from their contracts from 1 September. I had been having talks with Once, the Spanish team run by Manolo Saiz, one of the most respected *directeurs sportifs* in cycling. I was approaching thirty and knew people would be looking at me and wondering whether I could keep on improving or would start going backwards. At thirty, riders are only as good as their last ride. Manolo knew what I could do and thought I would bring an extra dimension to a powerhouse team that included Laurent Jalabert and Alex Zulle. He knew my ability in the time trials and sensed that I could adapt my skills to the one-day races. But moving to Once would mean sacrificing the role of team leader for a position as a support rider, and when I thought long and hard about that idea, the disadvantages outweighed the advantages.

The advantage would be that, for once, someone else would be under all the pressure. I would be allowed to have my day, at the dictates of the team, but mostly I would be riding for someone else, and that has never been part of my character. At Gan, I have no difficulty in putting my shoulder to the wheel if someone else in the team is clearly in better form than me and can win the race, like Stuart O'Grady in the 1998 Prutour, for example. It can be very rewarding to contribute to someone else's success. But to be paid to do that day after day would destroy my motivation, as selfish as that may sound. I remember explaining to one of the new riders at Gan at one of the training camps that being a good pro sometimes involved using your own good form to help your team leader. If he goes down, you have to go down with him. That, I said, was what he was paid to do. I would feel very trapped if I had to use all my form on someone else's behalf.

Luckily, Roger came up with a new sponsor for the team in Crédit Agricole and I was able to sign a new contract with him. But the potential move to another team forced me to think very clearly about what I still wanted to achieve in the sport.

The point of this autobiographical section is to show how easily plans can be blown off course. It doesn't matter. For anyone wanting to tackle a sport, be it anything from cycling to golf, it is important to have a plan. Nine times out of ten something unforeseen will happen and the plan will have to be modified or scrapped altogether. But that, in itself, does not nullify the importance of planning and organizing your thoughts, objectives and methods. I should have known that during the winter of 1996–7 I was overtraining; I should have recognized the symptoms, understood my own obsessive nature and had the self-discipline to control my schedules. I set down targets, made schedules and, for the best possible reasons, didn't stick to them. It is the reverse problem, I should imagine, of what club cyclists experience, when they struggle to find the time to complete their training programmes, but the principle is the same.

CB's Tips:

- Don't worry about making mistakes. The trick is not to make the same mistake twice.
- Think hard about your goals and be challenging but realistic in your goal-setting. If your goals are impractical in terms of time or achievement, then you have failed before you've begun.
- Aim for a maximum of three major goals during a season, and then fit in other mini-goals which complement your training programme. Think of it as a jigsaw puzzle, the outside first and then the details inside.
- A good training schedule requires total planning of training, diet and rest. These all have to be built into the routine.
- Consult your family and friends before entering into a training programme because they have to be supportive.
- Keep a diary and race reports. They might be a pain at the time, but

they will be a useful source of measurement, and often reassurance, later on. They are also useful tools for maintaining control and good discipline.

(See Appendix B for race schedules for the 1997, 1998 and 1999 seasons.)

5

FORM AND HOW TO FIND IT

Before we get into the principles and technicalities of constructing a training programme, I want to analyse that tantalizing word that means so much to cyclists and athletes at every stage of their development. 'Form' is the most important four-letter word in the cyclist's vocabulary, but it is not one that many stop to consider. Sometimes I get the impression that riders just wait vaguely for form to come along, rather than regarding it as the product of scientific analysis. Form. The word is so simple, yet the reality is so elusive and the search for it so complex. So what is form? What does it feel like? And, most importantly, how do you find it when you want it?

Most competitive cyclists will know when they are riding well and when they are riding badly. Anyone who has done regular training, be it running, cycling or in the gym, will have a hazy understanding of form. On some days you feel as if you could run another two miles quite easily, on others it takes all your effort to put one foot in front of the other. There can even be dramatic fluctuations from one day to the next, which is very confusing if you are trying to follow a proper training programme and measure your improvement. Most athletes will experience peak form, but only a small percentage of them will be able to generate it exactly when they want it – for 100-m sprinters, for example, that means a period of ten seconds in four years. With a longer event, like the Tour de France, the calculations don't need to be quite so fine. But timing the run into form is still a great art, of which there is one acknowledged master.

Miguel Indurain, Jan Ullrich and the Art of Self-control

The true greatness of Miguel Indurain was that, year after year, he was able to find his best form for the three weeks of the year when it mattered most. If I could ask him one question it would be how did he manage to measure his preparations so precisely every year? The general answer is that he followed the same format every time. Given that his body was roughly the same as in the previous year, it stands to reason that it should respond in the same way. But there is a lot more to the question than that.

Indurain was a great athlete anyway, so his weight was usually under control. He aimed only for the Tour every year, and was much criticized, particularly in the French press, for doing so. His rhythm was similar every time. He rarely rode any of the spring classics, preferring to train on his own in the warmer climates near his home in northern Spain. He started to compete in early May, and then his results would slowly start to improve. He would win a smaller race, begin to compete in the bigger races and win the odd one, but he never overextended himself to do so. If he had been forced to dig deep, I suspect he would have let go. He had tremendous self-control and never panicked, and that was as much a part of his champion's quality as his legendary lung-power.

On single stages there would be people flying all around him, a couple of his rivals might have disappeared up the road, but still he would wait, letting his team do the work, until about forty minutes from the end of the race, when he would pull out all the stops and slowly, slowly, increase the pressure. He wouldn't even look round.

He was always aware that there was another race tomorrow, and was supremely good at calculating exactly how much to give, and when. I would be curious to know how he did it. I think it must come down to a personal philosophy and something deep in his personality, probably not a quality you could define exactly or write down. He knew intuitively. He knew himself so well that, on any given day, he could sense his capabilities.

Clearly, he had a great training programme, refined with each passing year of success, but he also had the ability to work how he felt into the schedule. Every year people would look at him and say, 'Oh, Mig's not looking so good this year; he looks a bit heavier,' and he would have the self-confidence to say, 'No, I'm carrying on with what I think is right.' He wasn't affected by outside pressures from the media, or the form of others within his team or in the *peloton*. He always had faith in himself, certain in the knowledge that when the Tour came round he would be ready. When the intensity of the Giro increased, Indurain said it was impossible to win both and stuck to the Tour. Marco Pantani has subsequently proved his theory wrong, but missing the Giro left the Spaniard fresh and ready for the start of the Tour.

In 1998, Jan Ullrich got it horribly wrong. He was actually heavier than people think. The press thought he was about 12 kgs overweight, but it was closer to 18 kgs. I'm not sure whether I am more staggered by his ability to put on so much weight in such a short time, or his ability to take it off in time for the Tour. It was incredible how he came back from such bad form in the early part of the season to finish second in the Tour, but it wasn't planned, and I suspect that he might pay the price in years to come in terms of the mental energy and the stress he went through.

Inevitably, his career will be shorter than it might have been. He must have been 2,000 calories in deficit every day for five weeks to shed such a lot of weight, and that is almost double the recommended maximum deficit. His plight highlighted how disciplined Indurain was in his preparation for the Tour. The rest of us struggle to be so precise.

What is Good Form?

Form is the difference between suffering and being in control. It means you get to the point where you are going as hard and fast as you can in your given discipline. You are breathing flat out, your legs can't go any harder, you know this is the limit, but you can control the pain and your thinking is still sharp.

There are degrees of form, but all of them are personal rather than transferable measurements. Good form, average form, poor form, peak form. It is, I suppose, another word for condition. Poor form is the mirror image of good form. You don't just go slower; you suffer. All you feel is pain. It is as if someone has taken away all the body's endorphins, all the painkillers, so you feel everything. A long bout of poor form affects the mind as much as the body. Suffering and winning is acceptable; suffering and losing is depressing. More often than not, someone else is riding better, and those in better form will dictate the pace of the race, so failure is added to suffering. The temptation is to get off and go somewhere else, but you have to go through those periods without stopping in order to have a chance of finding good form at a later date.

A case in point for me was the 1996 Tour de France. I suffered terribly, particularly in the last mountain stages, and it would have been acceptable for me to have got off and gone home. Believe me, the temptation was almost irresistible. Almost. In retrospect, fighting through it was one of my better decisions. On the last few days of the Tour I began to feel stronger and stronger. The day after the Tour finished, after twenty-two stages, I was ready to do another one. A week later I came into some of the best form of my life. Would that form have come anyway? I really don't know.

One year, in the Paris–Nice, I was riding in the top three. It was day seven, but I was feeling terrible. If anyone had attacked at that moment they would have finished me off. I had nothing left. I was very worried about the following day, which featured a short, hilly stage in the morning and a time trial in the afternoon. To my surprise and delight, I felt great, and I floated round. In fact, I recorded an average speed of over 56 kph, which was a record for a time-trial stage. Though it would be hard to go from no form to great form in twenty-four hours, form can change quite dramatically from day to day.

Exercise science has its limitations. Sometimes you just have to push through the bad patches, and only in hindsight do you know whether the decision was right or wrong. The thought of reaching

Paris for the first time kept me going through the dark days at the end of that Tour de France. I certainly wasn't thinking, If I push through this, great form is just around the corner. Unfortunately, it's not black and white, for all the advances in scientific analysis of the body. Grey is still the predominant shade.

The Search for Form

The first thing to absorb is the point made more obliquely above. We are still only in the early stages of understanding the physiology of the body. We only possess a small part of the big picture and, in my lifetime, only a few more bits of the jigsaw will be fitted together. It is dangerous – look who's talking – to get bogged down in details and an overanalysis of methods because we understand so little. Overanalysing can lead to frustration. Like a hypochondriac, every little ache or pain can take on disproportionate significance. It's often like that in the build-up to a major event. Imagine, for a moment, that you are an academic, a writer or a philosopher, and your brain keeps hurting in different places. Or that one day you master Fermat's Theorem, but the next you can't add two and two. That would drive you crazy. But that's the sort of neurosis a professional athlete has to control every day of the week. It is so easy to see one thing, draw a false conclusion and head off in completely the wrong direction. I've been guilty of that a few times; trying to be too clever and losing the plot.

So many factors govern how we feel and how we perform, but often the most basic and significant question is ignored. How do you feel? An athlete gets to know his body in minute detail, but is never going to be able to predict when form will come with 100 per cent accuracy. There is roughly a 70 per cent chance of having form when you need it. That is important to realize at the outset because it saves on the disappointment.

It is also more positive to talk about building rather than finding form. Finding form sounds like looking for a needle in a haystack, which isn't a bad analogy at times. It *is* like building in that you slowly put together the structure brick by brick, through planning properly, adopting a sensible training programme, eating a good diet and getting proper rest. Method is still critical to the process, giving you a better chance of finding the right form than if you just leap into the dark. Illness and crashes are just two factors which can upset your plans. The temptation with both is to catch up by cramming twice as much training into the same amount of time, but this risks doing more damage. I've done it myself. The plan goes out of the window for whatever reason and you get sucked into doing the wrong things. Surprisingly, the compulsory break demanded by illness or injury can also be beneficial, building a time of rest and relaxation into a season when you would never have dared contemplate having one. I have actually thought about incorporating an injury break into my training, but I bottled out because the chances are even money that when I finished my break I'd get a real injury and have to stop again. I remember crashing out of a race at the Circuit des Mines in France one time and breaking a collarbone. All I could do was use a home trainer for a week and I thought I'd blown my whole season, but when I got to my next race I was in really good form, fresh from having had the time away.

Keeping hold of form is almost as hard as finding it in the first place, particularly if it has arrived a week or two too soon. Michel Bartoli gave a classic example of mistiming his run into form in the autumn of 1998. He stormed through the autumn classics and was virtually unbeatable. But his aim was to win the World Championships, which began in October. By the time he got to the worlds, he was going well enough, but had a lot of bad luck and didn't quite have the strength left to absorb the problems. Literally a few days before and he would have won the World Championships. He'd just lost that edge.

The longest I've managed to keep peak form is six weeks. That was the period when I won the World Pursuit Championships, breaking the world record, then broke the world hour record in Manchester and was unbeaten for seven weeks.

Peter Keen instigated one of his most original training programmes to keep me in form, but the basic principle was to exercise massive self-control. When you're in form, it is tempting to absorb a greater training load because you're able to do so, but actually, this is the time to back off and resist doing too much. It's a very delicate balance. All the systems in the body are working optimally, and you must keep doing just enough training to keep them there without doing enough to damage them. Form can go at the same rate as it comes; it sort of slides away from you, like water.

CB's Tips:

- Less training is often better than more training.
- Learn to recognize form through the use of race reports, diaries and, above all, feel. When you are in form, remember the feeling so that you recognize it again.
- Exercise self-control. When you think your form is ideal, back off the training for a bit and try to keep hold of the form.
- However imprecise the timing, remember that planning is still the key to building form.

6

CONSTRUCTING A TRAINING PROGRAMME

Structured Training: The Phased Method

There are two obvious questions about phasing training schedules:
   (a) Why break training into phases at all?
   (b) How many phases should there be?
Breaking the training into manageable chunks of, say, four to six weeks tends to help concentrate the mind on what we are trying to achieve at any given point in the year. It also encourages planning and helps us to regroup when reality dawns on our fantasy world. Personally, I find that facing a four-week block of hard endurance work is more mentally tolerable. At least I know when it's going to end.

On the length of the phases, I would suggest that one phase should never exceed six weeks, otherwise you risk becoming stale and losing interest and motivation. Four weeks is a good phase length, dropping down to one week for the final taper phases before big objectives. Appendix B shows a written overview of my scheduled phases of training for the 1999 season leading into the Tour de France. It confirms that there is enough time to come down between peaks or that objectives are close enough together so that the same form can be realistically maintained from one to another. It's a kind of blueprint for the training year.

The big problem with the structure of a book like this is trying to isolate the different areas that make up a good training programme. The mental and physical states of an athlete are indivisible. Rest and diet are an integral part of an athlete's daily routine and should be incorporated into any training schedule. It's not just miles on the road or the track which will make the difference on the day of the competition; everything has to be right, from the equipment to the mind and the body. They are all part of the same whole, divided up here only for purposes of technical instruction. Just going out and pounding the pedals will not make you a better competitor, or even a better bike rider.

What is the Aerobic Threshold and Why is it Important?

First a word about the physical nature of cycling. Cycling is fundamentally an aerobic sport. You need to be aerobically efficient, i.e., you have to be able to shift large amounts of blood around the body and extract large amounts of oxygen from it as quickly as possible. Those are the main restricting factors to any performance work on a bicycle.

In his book *The Complete Manual of Sports Science*, Wilf Paish describes the aerobic energy system as 'the capacity of the body to produce energy from glycogen in the presence of an adequate supply of oxygen.' Essentially, it is the most power you can produce for an extended period of time. Physically, being over threshold will cause a burning sensation in your legs and your mind will tell you that if it carries on you will have to slow down. You will know when you're over threshold, but the only way of finding out if you are under it is to go over.

Each individual has to ascertain his or her own threshold and keep reassessing it regularly. It will vary with form, illness, fatigue and temperature. For example, sometimes, when climbing up a mountain for anything over ten minutes, cycling becomes an anaerobic exercise, which means the body has exhausted its supply of oxygen-based energy and requires a top-up. 'The body', writes Paish, 'has the capacity to store enough energy to last for about ten minutes of high-level activity.' By high-level activity he means sprinting flat out, climbing flat out, doing anything flat out. Every athlete must dig into his anaerobic reserves, whether it's a footballer suddenly sprinting 20 yards for a ball, or a middle-distance runner in the final moments of a race, or a cyclist climbing up Alpe d'Huez or sprinting for glory down Bordeaux High Street.

Peter Keen uses the analogy of baling out a boat to illustrate the aerobic threshold – the point at which oxygen supplies within the muscles are exhausted and the production of lactic acid exceeds the ability of the body to get rid of it. Without sufficient oxygen, too much lactic acid is produced in the muscles, and this has an inhibiting effect on their performance. (Try putting your hands above your head and flexing the fingers; very soon they will become stiff and unworkable as a result of the build-up of lactic acid.) When the body is still capable of baling out the lactic acid, it is working aerobically. But when the lactic acid is coming in faster than the body is able to bale it out, the body has gone over the threshold and is relying on anaerobic (non-oxygen) forms of energy. The fitter you are and the more your body and mind have been trained to cope with high levels of stress, the higher your aerobic threshold will be and the longer you will be able to sustain anaerobic effort. But this is still a largely unexplored physical area, and the mind and its ability to conquer pain and push your body plays an equally important role in developing anaerobic tolerance.

The team player – the footballer or netball player – will not spend as long in anaerobic deficit as the bike rider. Those sports call for sudden explosive effort, but also have built-in periods of recovery. That might be true on a long stage across flat country, though average speeds on the Tour de France are increasing all the time, but climbing or time-trialling requires a very careful understanding of where your aerobic threshold – your limit – is. How often have you seen climbers burst into life at the bottom of a climb, only to blow up halfway up the mountain? On the stage to Les Arcs in the 1996 Tour, Indurain suddenly hit the limits of his energy supply, partly because he had forgotten to take some liquid food with him, partly because the pressure applied to him by Bjarne Riis and the rest of the field suddenly proved too much for his resources. Perhaps his mind just said 'Enough'. Either way, the great Spaniard realized there and then that his professional cycling career had reached its peak, and his retirement was not long delayed. One moment he was riding along in typically unhurried Indurain style, the next he was struggling. Like boxers, the end of a great champion's career can be measured in minutes, even seconds.

Nowadays, the Tour is about 85 per cent aerobic and 15 per cent anaerobic, but it is the 15 per cent that will win or lose you the race or stage. For me, brought up on time-trialling, where the trick is to balance on your anaerobic threshold for the duration of the event, the 85 per cent is no problem; it's the 15 per cent that's difficult. Once the gap has opened up, if I'm in good form I can maintain it. I can sustain very high levels of work for long periods. The problem is the explosive power needed to make that gap, and that is one of the things I will be working on over the final year of my career. Laurent Jalabert has a lower aerobic threshold than me, but he wins more races because he can jump away from the *peloton* more easily. Being a successful bike rider is about balancing those forces, a balance between weight and power allied with a high aerobic threshold. You can only go over the threshold for a limited period of time. It might be two seconds, it might be three minutes. You have to decide what it's worth. You can explore your limits, but you can't make the body stay there, because in the end it will just seize up, like a car engine without oil. It's all about feel, it doesn't matter what the numbers say.

The aerobic threshold of a normally fit person would be about 4 millanol, which is a measurement of acid concentration. At the start of the year, when the body isn't used to tolerating large amounts of lactic acid, I can tolerate about 9 millanol at maximum. When I'm track trained for an explosive discipline, like pursuiting or the short prologue in the Tour, that rate rises to 15 millanol before completely cracking. Any event over fifteen minutes and the graph of output will shoot up to begin with and then drop off slowly through the remainder of the event. The trick is to keep the line steady, to go over the threshold a bit, but not by so much that you overload. In a time trial,

I'll be tweaking the rate all the time, not dramatically, just subtly. For a long time I assumed that everyone knew pretty much where their threshold was. Often they don't. From feel, I can work out how much more effort I can sustain at a given speed, whether I'm going too hard or if I need to back off slightly. What are these sensations? They are almost indescribable. It's a question of being in touch with your body and knowing where its limits are, because when you're really under pressure there is a subtle difference between pushing it to the limit and going beyond.

My own understanding probably stems from the huge number of time trials I did when I was growing up. In longer time trials of an hour or so, I can find the line and balance on it quite naturally. I can be thinking about the kids' schooling or what we might be having for dinner, anything, while sustaining almost a maximum load. What is difficult to say is whether my body was trained that way by my time-trialling background or whether I gravitated towards time-trialling because it suited my style, physique and temperament. Looking back, one or two things fit into place.

First, one of the most coveted presents I have ever been given was a pass to the local swimming pool each summer. It was heaven. All those hours messing about in and under the water at the local outdoor baths must have helped my lung capacity and oxygen efficiency.

Second, I made my racing début in a 10-mile time trial organized by the Birkenhead Victoria Cycling Club on the outskirts of Chester in 1982. The entry fee was 50 pence. The out-and-back course through the Cheshire countryside, followed by a drink at the Rake and Pikel and fish and chips for supper, became a regular part of my childhood routine.

My father, Keith, was a good enough rider to be shortlisted for selection for the Tokyo Olympics in 1964 and he competed mainly in time trials. From very early I knew the difference between a 25-mile and a 50-mile time trial; it meant I had an extra hour to play before Dad finished.

The family influences were important when I started riding, but so was the terrain. Cheshire is good time-trialling territory, not too clogged with traffic, with decent open roads and enough variety to make it interesting. But time-trialling also appealed to my logical, individual nature. I could see my improvement reflected in the clock and I didn't have to rely on anyone else for help. It was just me and the clock. If I was fast enough, I would win; simple as that. From fairly early on in my career, I came to understand that the best way to tackle a time trial, particularly the longer ones, was to sustain a steady pace throughout rather than go flat out for as long as possible and then hang on, which is a very inefficient, draining way of riding. Partly through practice, and partly because I have always been able to sustain a good pace for long periods, I developed an acute awareness of where my limits were at any given moment and how long I could keep up that pace. I'm quite proud of the fact that I've made so much use of what is a quite specific, limited ability. The hour record, for example, is the ultimate expression of aerobic threshold work.

My own threshold is a pulse rate of 180–3. I can ride within that three-beat band for over an hour and hold it there up and downhill. That is when I'm going well, and it hasn't varied much over the last six or seven years. In top form, my peak pulse is 190. At the World Championships in 1998, I averaged 170, which equates to a loss of about 50–60 watts of power.

The difficulty is that training at the intensity required to develop anaerobic efficiency is incredibly draining on both the mind and body. The only way to train effectively is to stimulate as closely as possible the stress levels experienced in competition, but you can't do that too often or the mind will start rejecting the idea, so you have to balance the physical demands with the need to keep fresh. For me nowadays creating a training programme consists of finding new ways to do the same old exercises.

Power Monitors and Pulse Meters

I use a German SRM system, a really fancy piece of kit that costs about £3,000. But pulse monitors can be picked up for £60. The pulse rate simply measures how fast the blood is being pumped round the body, and is a useful reflection of how hard your body is working. The higher the workload, the higher the demand for oxygen, the faster the pump has to work to keep up. There are three methods of measuring power: power, lactic acid and pulse. The pulse is the least accurate, but the most readily available. Taking lactate samples is rather more tricky as it involves someone driving alongside you stabbing your ear to get a sample. The only truly accurate measure of power is the SRM, but it's so expensive people haven't yet accepted its value. It measures power, averages, maximums, cadence, pedal rate (current, max and average), heart rate (current, max and average) and calories. It measures the torque through your cranks. It pretty well does everything except sing the National Anthem or ride the race for you. On the Tour de France, I wear a pulse monitor, more out of curiosity than anything else. I have always had the reputation of relying far too much on statistics, but actually I only use them as a back-up to what I feel. If I'm feeling very tired on a stage, I will check my pulse and see if it's down from the day before. If it's down ten, that equates to about 50 watts of power.

The highest pulse I've ever reached was 199 in Atlanta in 1996 in the Olympic time trial. I was on a gold medal time for three or four laps, but I couldn't cope with the high humidity. I had to throw away my helmet after a lap because I couldn't get rid of the heat fast enough. I had to slow down or I would have fainted, but I was only beaten by two Spaniards, Miguel Indurain and Abraham Olano. My pulse averaged 186 over the hour-long race. Peter Keen once got one of the girls in the British squad to do an ergometer test in the bathroom with the hot-water taps running to generate conditions of high humidity. He still believes that, although a quirky and rather unscientific method, this would be a highly effective way of training the body to cope with these conditions.

The Principles of Training

We have touched on a number of training principles in the previous chapters, but they are worth setting out again before we move on. It is critical to ask the most basic question before you start turning a pedal.

1. Why Am I Training and What Event Am I Training For?

The answer would have been set down in the planning of the race schedule set out during the winter. The wider answer is, I want to go faster on a bike. It is a simple statement, but easy to forget. Sometimes the training itself can become the end, not the means to an end. My poor 1997 season stemmed from making just that mistake. But the question demands a more specific response: a) I want to go faster on a bike on a specific day or days at a specific time, so how can I best achieve that? b) What is the event I am trying to win? Is it endurance based or do I need to develop more explosive power?

2. Variety

Training has to be as varied as possible and divided up into manageable blocks, usually of about three weeks. The mind just will not cope with doing the same thing day after day for any longer. I get the most out of myself if I can see where the work ends. If the endurance rides are really grim, it helps to be able to see the end of the phase and know that a different type of training, something more explosive and interesting, is coming next. You mustn't fall into a rut. The body can get used to a schedule, so you will need to change your angle of attack. It's like shocking your body into doing something you want it to do. Sometimes, particularly in the winter, you can go for a run or to the gym instead of going out on the bike. We will have a section later on a gym programme tailored to cycling, but I'm not yet fully convinced that working with weights makes you go faster on a bike. Personal prejudice perhaps, but valid nonetheless. What does make it worthwhile – and I have started going to the gym again over the past two years – is the variety and the simple mental benefits of a change of scene.

3. Listen to Your Body

It is the best judge. You can have all the figures in the world, but you know best how your body feels. Feeling is very important. I have a range of numbers from one to ten to describe how I've felt over a day's training. I use it in my training diary. One is near perfect, feeling great, down to ten, which is a day to stay in bed. It's easy to become obsessive about training just for the sake of it. I now know what my body should do, and when it's not capable of doing it for some reason I can find it quite depressing.

4. When in Doubt, Do Less Not More

For a highly motivated athlete it takes as much, if not more, discipline to undertrain as it does to overtrain. When I was younger and not as confident about my abilities, I would pound out a 10-mile time trial the week before the real thing, just to assure myself that I could do it. That tended to rebound on me later when I had to do it again. Make it a rule that on one day a week there is no bike. Maybe on one or two days, particularly in the winter, or else just go for a short ride to burn off some calories.

5. Rest is More Important Than Training

I have always been very bad at it. I've always regarded rest as not riding a bike. Rest, for me, is going and doing something else. I'll potter about in my workshop or do some woodwork, which was originally a possible career path and is now a hobby, when really I should be resting, watching television, reading, sleeping. I don't practise what I preach in this area and I'm going to have to start. On the Tour de France, it's different because it's an extreme environment. It is always said that riders on the Tour never run when they can walk, never walk when they can sit and never sit when they can lie down. That's about right. Every little bit counts, from standing up to do a five-minute interview to signing autographs. Energy conservation is paramount. But rest on the Tour can sometimes mean doing something else, just to give your mind a break. Greg LeMond once went and played a round of golf on his rest day, which was quite a cool thing to do. Everyone thought it was a terrible idea, and I must admit it wouldn't have been my favoured way of recuperating during a precious twenty-four hours, but it worked for him. He came back refreshed mentally, which is the key issue. In winter, a lot of riders go cross-country skiing, do weights or play volleyball, just for a change of rhythm. But, physically, rest is essential. In the middle of an important training schedule you should have a lie-in, maybe go for a walk, but be aware of the need for rest and, even if work commitments mean a morning lie-in isn't possible, build adequate periods of rest into your programme.

6. Be Honest With Yourself

It doesn't matter what it says on the training programme, however constructive and creative it is, if you feel tired, don't do it. The difficulty is that only you know what 'too tired' is.

7. Once You Have Constructed a Training Programme, Believe in It

It doesn't matter if you're feeling great and could eat up a bigger load, stick with the programme. If it says a day of rest, then rest. There are times when you will be tired, but build in rest days to absorb those. At no time should you be going into a training session with any significant fatigue. If you are, you've probably overdone it. Don't fight it; either drop down a level of intensity or go home. In the last few years, during the winter, I've been training at level one and tended to let it drift into level two, so I've ended up doing a lot of middle-quality work that didn't do me much good.

The Four Levels of Training

This is a system for measuring the intensity of training. It provides a common language that was devised by Peter Keen and is now in general use around the world. Before, a schedule might have said, 'Ride hard up that hill for ten minutes,' without giving any definition of the word 'hard'. The system is divided into four levels, each representing a different intensity of training. Because it is based on feel as much as figures, it can be adapted for riders of any level of fitness.

Level One: Steady work, pre-season work. You can keep up a conversation with a colleague quite comfortably doing level-one work because the body isn't under any strain. This level is used mainly in winter to burn fat so the body starts to increase its stores of muscle glycogen. It is low-intensity endurance work, good for recovering after a tough day's training and, for the less experienced rider, for learning basic handling skills. Heart rate: from resting rate to 45–50 beats per minute (bpm) below maximum.

Level Two: 70–80 per cent of training capacity. Heart rate: 35–50 bpm below max. My pulse rate: 140–165. You would need to pause for breath in conversation when training at this level. The top end of the level-two range is about as high as I will go in winter. It is higher-intensity endurance work, good for increasing the heart capacity, blood volume and providing a base for fitness. This is putting in the miles, the traditional way of training in the *peloton*. But it needs to be carefully regulated. I see no point in riding at level two for longer than two hours.

Level Three: Time trial work. This is about finding your threshold and trying to push it up a bit. Heart rate: 20–25 bpm below maximum. You could sustain the highest workload for about three quarters of an hour, though I would recommend a maximum of half an hour, because mentally it's so stressful. Conversation ceases at this level. This is training your body to race, and starting to work on increasing your lactic-acid tolerance.

Level Four: Over threshold. You will crack somewhere between 15 seconds and 3–4 minutes, depending on your level of fitness. This is real race-preparation training to provide explosive power either for the track or for trying to jump away from the bunch in a stage race. It brings on form, but also does the most damage to your muscles, so it has to be used sparingly and intelligently, and with large doses of rest in between. Heart rate: just below or on maximum rate.

It is possible to create literally hundreds of different training exercises, but all will be variations on those levels of intensity. These are the basic tools of the trade, around which all training programmes will be built.

Ramp Tests and Other Tortures

(See Appendix C for an example of my max profiles.)

In order to improve physically, it is really important to know what you are capable of doing in the first place. This, I'm afraid, involves tests that might hurt. But with the right attitude, testing is not only an important part of the process of establishing a training programme, but also a powerful motivational tool. If a rider can see his results improving over a period of six weeks or two months through the tests, that is a real psychological boost. An amateur cyclist might be frightened to find out their maximum because it's painful and it tests your mental strength. When you start doing tests, they generally prompt an improvement in form. If, for example, your results show a maximum power of 400 watts, which means a threshold level of roughly 300 watts, then a month or six weeks later the figures are 440 watts and a 340-watt threshold, it is very satisfying. You can see the progress. It became fashionable in the *peloton* to do some form of physiological testing in the winter. The problem is that once many of them get the results, they don't really know what to do with them. Gathering data is easy; interpreting it is harder. Not that many people can use the information beneficially. But to set meaningful ranges for training, you need to find out your maximum pulse in a controlled environment.

It is possible to do this on the road, but the best place to start would be a human performance laboratory, where the environment, temperature and conditions are better. I've seldom seen as high a pulse on the road as in the lab. There are universities and regional centres all round the country that can help, or you can contact the British Cycling Federation (see Appendix E) and ask where your nearest physiology lab is. I would recommend a test every six weeks during the season and every month during the winter.

Ergometers measure power. Make sure you are fresh and that your resting pulse is low. Do very little training for a couple of days before the test. The warm-up should be fairly brisk and take about fifteen minutes, then start the ramp test by increasing the power by around 20 watts a minute every minute (starting from 200 watts on the equipment I use) until you can't keep going any more. What is being measured is the max minute power, the average power over the last minute and the maximum pulse. From those figures, you can work backwards to set your training loads.

You can also do this on feel: you can go out and ride a time trial, carry a pulse monitor and see what your average pulse is at the end. If you averaged 175 bpm for a 10-mile time trial, you know that, for training purposes, 165–175 is the right pulse band for you to do level-three training. However, the indoor ramp test is, in my opinion, a more accurate way of judging this, and, as much of your training programme will be based on the outcome, it is worth taking a little more time and trouble to get it right.

Once you have a profile of your maximum fitness level, you can start establishing parameters for a training programme. One thing I've never been able to understand is why the body is capable of producing peak power of over 1,000 watts, yet can only produce 500 watts for any sustained length of time (say, a minute). What's the point of having the other 500-watt capacity if you can't use it properly? It's like having a car that only uses two of its four cylinders regularly. The tantalizing thought for athletes is that the spare 500 watts is in there – we know it is because we've been tested for it – but no-one has yet devised a way of consistently unlocking it. This is the sort of thing we looked into when I broke my left ankle, in order to see what the power difference between my left and right legs was. To this day, my left leg is actually stronger than my right, though the left calf is visibly smaller, and in spite of fifteen years of going through the same motion with both legs. If you plug the SRM into a computer, it will trace the power of a pedal stroke. My right leg produces a gentle curve of power which is very efficient through the whole stroke. The other leg, the one on which I broke my ankle, has a higher peak power but a choppier stroke.

Training for Different Objectives

There are essentially two ways of developing a training programme. One is to isolate the event you are training for – track, pursuit, time trial or road race – and adapt a programme accordingly, the other, more flexible way is to analyse the three ingredients that will be required for any of those events, in varying quantities, and work on those.

Peak power: This is about winning a sprint, breaking away, holding a wheel and surging up a short climb. It demands that you go into the red, over threshold, for as long as you think the effort is worthwhile.

Aerobic ability: This is about finding your anaerobic threshold, sustaining it over an increasing length of time, pushing your body to get rid of the toxins and lactic acid as fast as they are being produced. You are trying to raise that lactate tolerance level so that you can push your body over the limit for longer periods. This is time-trial work, extended breakaways and living with riders who are better than you on the climbs.

Endurance: This is the essential ingredient of a professional bike racer. Without basic endurance all other qualities are irrelevant. Endurance training heightens your body's ability to use fat as an energy source. Think of your body as containing two types of fuel: one is petrol, the high-octane fuel for high-performance motoring; the other is diesel, for longer journeys at slower speeds, where energy conservation is important. The first fuel is glycogen, the second is fat.

As a general rule, the body can store two hours' worth of glycogen – a tank of petrol, if you like. But if the race is six hours long a rider doesn't want to use up all his stores of petrol, so the body has to be trained to use the fat first – the diesel – chugging along at low speeds so the petrol can be stored for more explosive requirements, like jumping away on an attack or sprinting at the finish. A lot of riders use racing to do endurance training. It is easier on the mind than training. I used to go to Skipton via the Derbyshire Hills for my endurance work. If it's pouring with rain and there is a head wind, it's pretty grim stuff. Doing that in a race gets over the mental hurdle. The majority of endurance training is done at the beginning of the year.

Two years ago I used to do eight-hour rides to build endurance. They were just fat-burning rides, long and slow at about 32 kph with my pulse at 130. The mechanism that allows you to access the fat is glycogen, blood sugar, which is why you keep eating when you're on a bike. Always be sure there is enough blood sugar in your body to operate the fat-burning mechanism, otherwise you'll hit the wall. The downside of putting so much emphasis on endurance is that you lose the top-end power. When your body is asked to surge at 1,000 watts and it's used to producing 200, there's a natural shock. But that is the creative nature of training. Mostly, training is a balance between maintaining what you have while working on what you're lacking.

Most races for amateurs will be no more than four hours long, so if training time is limited through the week, it is more effective to work on building up your glycogen stores than burning fat. But the principle outlined earlier still applies: break the training into phases, so that when a particular type of work becomes tedious and a bit mind-bending, you know that a change of emphasis is just around the corner with the next phase. This approach helps to avoid staleness, both physical and mental, and makes the more taxing training phases more tolerable.

7

WHEELS WITHIN WHEELS

Training Programmes for Different Objectives

The Training Sheet and Race Report

I have talked about monitoring the details of your training before, but I can't stress too heavily the usefulness of logging all the information on a training day and at the end of a day's racing. The temptation after a gruelling session or a bad day at the races is to forget about it, but the effort of putting pen to paper makes you think about the day, the mistakes you made and how you felt, and it makes you think about them now, not in a day or two's time when the pain has dulled and the defeat seems less disappointing than it actually was. It is another example of the need to be honest with yourself. Writing a race report three days after the event is tantamount to cheating. You may as well not bother.

For the training sheet, we decide in advance what training exercise I will do each morning and afternoon. On the training planner sheet I will fill in how the training went, grading it from one (perfect) to ten (awful), and then write comments on the exercise in the small box next to it. I will fill that in each night, or immediately when I get back, and then I'll write an overall comment in the box at the bottom. Each day I will record figures for pulse, weight and fatigue rating (one to ten again). The sheet will then go back to Peter Keen, who will adjust the training loads accordingly. If you keep a record of all the exercises you can build up a database of performance. Another year, for example, if there is a problem or you think you're not riding as well, it sometimes helps to look back over your training routines to see that at exactly the same time last year you were feeling lousy, too.

Comparisons can be very good for morale at certain stages. Equally, looking back over a whole series of exercises and monitoring the remarks might give you a clue about your perceived state of fitness. Maybe you have been doing too much and need a day off. Sometimes it's important to take a step back from the action, and diaries can help you do that.

The simple task of filling in a race report helps you to analyse your performance. The basic information includes: race and date, type of terrain, weather conditions and feelings. How did you rate your performance that day? What mistakes did you make? What did you do well? What do you need to improve? It's quite systematic. When I come home, any problems that occurred in the race will be incorporated into the next training schedule. For example, I might have felt great throughout the race, but was unable to generate enough power to jump away from the rest of the bunch. The next training block can then address the problem and help develop more explosive speed, which would involve more high-level intensity work (levels three and four). Sometimes, as with the attached examples taken from a training and racing routine that included the Tour of Catalonia and the Route du Sud before the 1998 Tour de France, I will just write down my brief reflections on the day, including a maximum pulse rate, if necessary, and Peter Keen will print his advice for the stage or the day in the left column, because essentially these are training days in a race environment.

I have a particularly poor memory, so I make sure I fill in the forms on the same day. If you can build up all this information and try over the year to develop form models – a record of past form that can be used as a reference for the future, so that you can see what effects certain training routines had – then you can use them to go forward. My mind works like that automatically now. When I wasn't working so closely with Peter Keen, I could lie in bed at the end of a stage, run through the day, analyse the problem and devise a method of training that would put it right. At Besseges, for example, at the start of 1998,

TRAINING PLANNER – Tour of Catalonia

Week starting: 18/6/98

DAY		COACH'S WORKOUT	CHRIS BOARDMAN'S FEEDBACK AND COMMENTS
THURSDAY	AM	Catalonia stage 1: 80 km flat.	No problem. 180s in finish.
pulse			
weight	PM	Stage 1b: 8 km TT.	A good effort. 16-min warm-up. Rode well up all the way. Maxing 190, 54.8 kph.
fatigue			
FRIDAY	AM	Stage 2: 173 km, 2 minor climbs. By the time you get this you will have ridden the stage.	No problem. Boys controlled it.
pulse			
weight	PM		
fatigue			
SATURDAY	AM	Stage 3: 152 km flat. Try to ride as a recovery day. Keep cadence high and concentrate hard on keeping out of the wind.	Another controlled day. Fast finish, working mid-range to stay out of trouble. On finishing circuit got 'tested' on 3rd cat climb halfway.
pulse			
weight	PM		
fatigue			
SUNDAY	AM	Stage 4: 198 km, one 2nd cat. Looks like a stage you could keep out of trouble on, but be prepared to ride in the second group from the climb if necessary. Let it go if they go mad.	Long hot day. Nervous due to crosswinds. Rode OK. Final very nervous and technical uphill finish. Bunch just held together. Max 188.
pulse			
weight	PM		
fatigue			

TRAINING PLANNER

DAY		COACH'S WORKOUT	CHRIS BOARDMAN'S FEEDBACK AND COMMENTS
MONDAY	AM	Stage 5: 18 km TT. Full-on effort.	35 mins around circuit. 35 degrees. Humid.
pulse			
weight	PM		18 km. TT went well. A little lethargic at start. Pulse picking up to 180s. Max 188. Won by 17 secs from Olano.
fatigue			
TUESDAY	AM	Stage 6: 180 km. 1st cat. Finish. Hum! Don't allow last year's experience to dictate your thoughts now. Unless you're floating let them go on the final climb. The damage will not be absorbed without problems.	Went controlled almost all day. Let go on last climb. Don't feel great. First day. Very hot. Mid 30s.
pulse			
weight			
fatigue	PM	Alternative strategy: go with them as well as you can and don't start tomorrow, i.e. get the benefit of a full-on climb overload.	
WEDNESDAY	AM	Stage 7: 232 km. Extreme stage, 3 x1st cat with climb finish. Don't play. Either get round with damage limitation or if moderately whacked at the start climb off before you do any more damage.	7½-hour day. Pulse low, in 160s on first climb. Didn't overextend myself. Came back on descent. Next climb the same. Last climb in gruppetto. A long, hard day, but never pushed into red.
pulse			
weight			
fatigue	PM	If you didn't start, just 90 mins below 130.	

TRAINING PLANNER

DAY		COACH'S WORKOUT	CHRIS BOARDMAN'S FEEDBACK AND COMMENTS
THURSDAY	AM	Stage 8: 190 km. 2 well-spaced climbs. If you are still in the race you must be recovering reasonably well by now, so go at threshold on the climbs.	Opted to start and go to feed, didn't let myself go above 154. Let go when uncomfortable and rode on own to feed. Took 3 hours, plus or minus, mostly level 1. Sore and a little tired.
pulse			
	PM	If you didn't start, just 90 mins below 130.	(Emotionally battered.)
weight			
fatigue			
FRIDAY	AM	Recovery ride, 2 hours below 120 (yes, below 120! – if necessary behind the team car).	Up at 3.30 by choice; couldn't sleep longer. Lazy morning. Weather cool, cloudy and humid. Out late morning on own for two-hour level 1. No stress.
pulse			
	PM		Rest and planning.
weight			
fatigue			

TRAINING PLANNER – Training After 1998 Tour   Week starting: 24/7/98

DAY		COACH'S WORKOUT	CHRIS BOARDMAN'S FEEDBACK AND COMMENTS
FRIDAY	AM	45 mins upper level 2. 330–350 watts.	10 a.m. as stated. Surprisingly not too mind-bending. SRM down, but worked intermittently enough to show I was in the right range. Average 105–6 rpm, 53 mins, 160 bpm (pulse).
pulse			
	PM	Intermittent session – 2 x 10 min blocks alternating 10 secs @ 500 watts 20 secs @ 250 watts.	As stated, but without SRM, so possibly higher powers. Found it tough. Heat stress? 46 mins total. Average 160 bpm.
weight			
fatigue			

TRAINING PLANNER

DAY		COACH'S WORKOUT	CHRIS BOARDMAN'S FEEDBACK AND COMMENTS
SATURDAY pulse	AM	60 mins level 2. 290–310 watts.	Tried to do the hard session (pm) but cracked. Some carry over from yesterday. 30 mins + and with 1 x 10-min average, 422 watts, 105 rpm, 340 watts average for the whole ride.
weight fatigue	PM	Threshold session, 10-min warm-up, then 3 x 10-min blocks @ 420 watts with 10 mins recovery between each.	1 hour on the road. With 2 x 10 mins level 3. Both average 433 watts, 175 bpm+, max 179. Cadence considerably lower. Average 356 for the hour. Pulse 161.
SUNDAY pulse	AM	45 mins upper level 2. 330–350 watts.	11.30 a.m. on the road. Damp, 16 degrees C, head wind. Average 360 watts, 91 rpm, 157 bpm. 50 mins. But carried away. Long sleep. Torpid afternoon.
weight fatigue	PM	Strength-power session. Seated accelerations from 60 rpm to 120 rpm on 53 x 12. Two blocks of 10 efforts with 2 mins recovery between each effort. Maximal effort on each using minimal grip force (both to protect your arms and accentuate pedalling action). 10 mins recovery between each block.	Felt quite 'off colour'. Didn't do session.
MONDAY pulse	AM	Recovery day – 45 mins rollers – high cadence power around 200 watts.	1 hour 40 mins upper level 1. Little chain ring. Damp and warm. Average 270 watts, 94 rpm, 137 bpm. Deep sleep.
weight fatigue	PM	Repeat morning.	Just 20 mins on the ergo to top-up to 2 hours. Contemplated yesterday's afternoon session, but wasn't up to it. Early bed (9 p.m.).

TRAINING PLANNER

DAY		COACH'S WORKOUT	CHRIS BOARDMAN'S FEEDBACK AND COMMENTS
TUESDAY	AM	45 mins upper level 2. 330–350 watts.	Out late morning for just over an hour. 1 hour true upper level 2. Took 5 mins to warm up, then felt good. Average 156 bpm, 364 watts, 94 rpm and 39 kph.
pulse			
	PM	Intermittent session – 2 x 10-min blocks alternating 10 secs @ 500 watts 20 secs @ 250 watts.	Swimming with kids. 1 hour sleep. Session as stated, no problem, 45 mins.
weight			
fatigue			
WEDNESDAY	AM	60 mins level 2. 290–310 watts.	Afternoon session on treadmill – 15 mins brisk warm-up, then 15 mins average 429 watts, stable. 175 bpm, 6.5%, 24 kph, 93 rpm. 10 mins 300ish watts, 10 mins average 425 watts. 10 mins 300+ish. 5 mins 440 watts + average.
pulse			
	PM	Threshold session, 10-min warm-up, then 3 x 10-min blocks @ 420 watts with 10 mins recovery between each.	1 hour 10 minutes in total. Average 92 rpm, 350+ watts, then straight out onto the road. Windy and showers for just over an hour at level 2. Average 151, 308 watts, 91 rpm. Blew at start, recovered at 30 mins. Not a pleasant ride.
weight			
THURSDAY	AM	45 mins upper level 2. 330–350 watts.	
pulse			
	PM	Strength-power session. Seated accelerations from 60 rpm to 120 rpm on 53 x 12. Two blocks of 10 efforts with 2 mins recovery between each effort. Maximal effort on each using minimal grip force (both to protect your arms and accentuate pedalling action). 10 mins recovery between each block.	
weight			
fatigue			

I was in trouble whenever I had to sustain very high power. I came to the conclusion, after looking at my race reports, that I needed to do some more time-trial work – aerobic and just into anaerobic – sustained over about ten minutes. So I incorporated those elements into my training programme over the following ten days. Fat lot of good it did me, but that's another story.

In the Deep Midwinter

For the professionals, the first training camp of a new season – usually in early January – is a chance to get to know the new members of the team, outline goals for the year and get some miles under their belts. It is always a nervous few days to start with, because the training is intense and everyone is quietly measuring themselves against their team-mates just to see who had indulged a little too much over Christmas. For the new young rider coming into the team, the whole week can be a daunting, and often quite lonely, experience. Cycling teams are more a collection of individuals wearing the same jerseys than a team in the conventional sense. One of Roger Legeay's great skills is harnessing the individual objectives of each member of the team to the common cause. All his teams have achieved more than the sum of their parts, which is the hallmark of a good *directeur sportif*. But I would say he is the exception. Too often, young riders are left to sink or swim on their own.

At home, I usually train alone, unless there is a particularly long and gruelling piece of work to do. Then an unsuspecting companion might be drummed into action just to help pass the hours and lend some extra competitiveness and lightness to the exercise. In training camp, we usually train in groups. A typical exercise would be:

- **An hour's warm-up**
- **Divide into groups of three riders**
- **Each rider does a four-minute spell on the front, full-out (level three going into level four)**
- **He drops to the back and the next rider does the same**

- **Each rider does 6 × 4-minute spells**
- **Total time of exercise: 78 minutes**
- **An hour's warm-down**

Or you can vary the schedule depending on the fitness of the riders. In groups of three, you can do four stints of ten minutes at level three. Two hours at high speed. The trick is to give yourself the easiest ride possible by making yourself quite small, lowering your head and sitting on the drops to increase the slipstream effect when you are second or third in the group. The problem comes when one of the group is flying.

My own winter training usually starts in mid-November, after I've taken a couple of weeks off from the bike. I'll try to do anything other than ride a bike during this time because it's so important to recharge the batteries in the winter. Yes, go out and eat more than you should, drink more than usual, have a good time, anything to make sure that when you get back on the bike again you feel refreshed and ready to go. There's nothing worse than taking time off, not relaxing enough and then feeling mentally tired before you even begin the new training year. The first part of winter training, anyway, is simply about weight management and staying relatively fit. Jan Ullrich would be able to tell you a little about what happens when the calorie count escalates and the dinner dates mount up. Most of the early work is strictly level one, so actually, though you're taking exercise, you are losing fitness. Even when you come back from a break, it is important not to rush straight into a bout of high-intensity training. Variety is the spice of life at this time of year.

Other programmes will be set out in this chapter and I am, on the whole, sceptical about the idea of having a typical week. I have no typical weeks; they are all different. But this is one general set of exercises which I have followed through the winter.

Monday: One and a half hours on the mountain bike in the morning, possibly on the road, possibly off-road. Unstructured. Effort as you like. Afternoon: Gym programme – stretching, working on the legs. Monday is a good day to concentrate on your legs after a weekend ride.

Tuesday: One and a half hours on the road bike. Effort as you like. Afternoon: gym – stretching, sit-ups, pull-ups, push-ups and twenty-minute run. (Sometimes Ed, my eldest, paces me through that one.)

Wednesday: Two to three hours on the road bike, in a group, if possible. Maximum two hours on my own. This tends to be the day we go to the Two Mills Café in Cheshire. Company is very important in terms of mental stimulation. No stress, have a chat, time on the bike. Might end up at the gym for a few stretching exercises. Afternoon: off.

Thursday: Hour and a half on the mountain bike. Afternoon: off.

Friday: Hour and a half on the mountain bike. Afternoon: twenty-minute run.

Saturday: Two hours on the mountain bike, off-road, in company. Afternoon: hour in the gym – upper-body exercises.

Sunday: Stretching in the morning (about half an hour, legs and back). Afternoon: twenty-minute run. Effectively a day off.

All the bike riding through this stage should be easy. If you don't feel like doing it or the weather turns bad, just turn around and go home. At some stage self-discipline has to kick in, but the whole point of this phase is that it shouldn't be too demanding. It should be pleasant. This would be my regular routine from November through to mid-December: about sixteen hours of exercise a week – eight on a bike, four on a road bike and four on the mountain bike.

From the middle of December the amount of hours spent on the road bike increases until mid-January. The intensity of the rides would start to increase, as well as the duration.

I will discuss the different exercises you can do in the section on gym work. I am yet to be convinced that going to the gym helps you to ride a bike faster, but I think it does ease the monotony of constant road work and therefore has a part to play in the overall exercise plan. I would probably keep up the gym work until the end of January. A lot of professionals ride for twenty-four hours a week through this period, but I'm happy with fifteen to sixteen good-quality hours. For most amateurs, about twelve hours should be the maximum. If you get really tired, miss a bike session.

Twin Peaks: Training for the Pursuit and the Prologue/Improving Peak Power

In 1998 I lost the inaugural Prutour, the biggest stage race in Britain since the Tour de France passed through in 1994. It was a big event, not so much in terms of the world calendar, but for me and for British cycling, and it is a real shame that the sponsors had to pull out in 1999. I won the prologue, but lost out to Stuart O'Grady because I was unable to win the time bonus sprints consistently or jump hard enough to break away from the main *peloton*. I was happy working for Stuart, my team-mate, once he had established himself as race leader, but it was still frustrating not being able to win in my own country. The fault was repeated through much of the year until I discovered, from doing peak-power tests at the Manchester Velodrome, that my top range of power was down from roughly 1,000 to 800 watts. The test confirmed what I had felt throughout the calendar: I was nowhere as good as I used to be at making the first 100 yards in a breakaway.

In a sense, the need to find more explosive power tapped into the training programmes that had already been devised for riding the pursuit. One of the exercises, on a turbotrainer or an ergometer, involves riding at a cadence of around 60 rpm, interspersing six-second bursts of full-on power with twenty-four seconds of rest, so that you're doing two six-second bursts every minute – enough to produce very high muscle forces, but not enough to incur problems with lactic acid. The sprints can be divided into two blocks of ten minutes – twenty six-second sprints – with five minutes' rest between the two blocks. You are concentrating purely on developing muscle strength, but because the effort is short and sharp the exercise should not be too taxing mentally. The whole session, including the warm-up and warm-down, lasts about forty-five minutes.

The pursuit is a very particular discipline. Four and a half minutes of explosive all-out action is difficult to reconcile with a 4,000-km three-week stage race in terms of coherent training strategies. The temptation with the pursuit is to train for four and a half minutes flat out, but that is a destructive and mind-numbing way of preparing, and is probably guaranteed to make you exhausted and stale. The worst kind of training for a pursuit is a pursuit. It's an old adage, but essentially a correct one. Incorporating a programme of pursuit exercises into a road-race season is an exceptionally creative process, and though most club cyclists won't have to devise such a complex schedule, the principles of training for different objectives remains the same. Cycling is a combination of peak power and endurance. Riding the Pursuit World Championships a month after the Tour de France ended, as I did in 1996, is just a matter of exploring those two extremes.

The question you have to ask before every event is, What do I need to win this race. Because pursuit is such a unique event, the question is more critical. What do I need to win a four-and-a-half-minute bike race? The answer is that you need to be able to ride over threshold for almost the entire four and a half minutes. Not so far over that the line or the performance profile would noticeably drop, but enough so that, at the line, you haven't an ounce of energy left. I also need large dollops of power. I have found that I release power better at a higher cadence, around 120 rpm for an event like that. It's not desperately efficient, rather like driving a car in second gear, but it provides maximum acceleration and, for the short duration of the pursuit, it just about works.

My own ideal preparation would go roughly as follows:

Phase One (three weeks to a month): Endurance work and long road races so that you have a good level of fitness, your body is efficient and you are using all the right energy stores.

Phase Two (two weeks): Start riding shorter races, road races, *critériums* – circuit races that are usually about an hour long and are very explosive, mostly on aerobic threshold and above – and some longer time trials.

Phase Three (three weeks): 10-mile time trials using a fixed wheel and perhaps a little work on the track, just to get used to the feel of both again.

Phase Four (two weeks): Specific track work. One or two short time-trial distances and *critériums*.

Phase Five (one to two weeks): Taper phase. Halve the quantity of your training but increase the intensity to stimulate the body to repair itself faster.

That would be an ideal programme, and could be adapted for particular circumstances, either for an amateur or a professional. The skill is to follow that general outline and be able to increase your peak power without sacrificing the hours of endurance work that are still needed to ride stage races. In essence, my physiological profile would not be very different from how it was before the Tour. All the endurance work done through the winter and spring doesn't just evaporate. The edge of it is dulled a bit but, if you get the balance right, you should be able to ride a pretty fair road race at the same time as training for the pursuit. It's only if you continue the explosive training too long that the drop-off in the road-race performance will begin to kick in. The final stages of a pursuit training schedule are very destructive to the muscles. You go from doing twenty hours' training a week to eight hours because the muscle needs to recover. But it is impossible to keep doing that for too long without it having some permanent effect on the balance of your abilities.

Before the Tour de France, for example, I treat the prologue as an extended pursuit. I might do the Dauphine Libéré, for example, to get the endurance work in, then I'll concentrate on the prologue for three weeks before the Tour and hope my general endurance level is good enough to cope with the rest of the race. The preparation isn't markedly different from the pursuit. I do some track work, because it's such a good environment to concentrate on your physiological development, and I mix that with road sessions – usually about two hours' intense level-two work, riding in the low 150-pulse band – and some power work on the road to simulate the conditions of the prologue.

One exercise I do on the track is a progressive warm-up. A whistle is blown every lap at the moment I'm supposed to cross the finish line. The whistle is blown ⅒th of a second faster on each lap, until either a predetermined pulse rate is reached, say 170 beats a minute, or the warm-up is complete. It is quite a versatile exercise which can be adapted to any given speed. I also do more specific work, like a flying kilometre, which means rolling off the bank to begin rather than going from a standing start. The aim is to hold that pace for four laps, controlling pace and judging expenditure of effort. The importance of the start is to get into an efficient rhythm as soon as possible, so it's a question of breaking down each section of the pursuit, and then putting all the different bits back together again for the real thing. There is one point to note when doing high-intensity work: never do two quality sessions back to back in a day. If I do a quality session in the morning, I know the quality session in the afternoon won't be as good as it should be. I'll either be tired by the afternoon or, in the morning, I will subconsciously be holding a bit back for the afternoon, which means the morning session won't be as good as it should be. If I do two sessions in a day, the second will be lower level two, at most, or a recovery ride.

Intervals

According to Wilf Paish, interval training is the 'most abused and misunderstood term in sport'. Apparently, it is now called 'intermittent work principle', though the theory remains much the same. Interval training is designed to increase anaerobic efficiency and put pressure on the energy supply systems, initially aerobic, then anaerobic. What is often misunderstood is that the chief benefit from this form of training comes not from the maximum effort, but from the periods of recovery in between that effort. The important point to grasp is that the quality of the period of effort must be as close to maximum potential as possible, about 90 per cent.

As an illustration of interval training for a good middle-distance runner, Paish cites the following exercise: 6 × 300 ms at thirty-eight seconds with a five-minute recovery period, or 3 × 600 ms at eighty-five seconds with an eight-minute recovery period. The variables can be adapted to different stages of fitness or just for variety, but the principle remains the same – periods of intense effort interspersed with carefully prescribed periods of recovery. I tend not to go for a high number of intervals, and keep the duration of maximum effort as high as possible for, on the whole, no longer than eight to ten seconds. Short enough for lactic acid not to come into effect and impair the work, but ferocious enough to stimulate lactic acid. Allow the acid level to drop back down again and then do another one; rest and do another, until you get to the point of fatigue when the quality of the work and the amount of power you can produce begins to drop off. From experience, two blocks of ten minutes is quite enough, but the longer the period of effort, the longer the recovery period.

I can do around forty periods of intense effort in twenty minutes, or twenty if the bursts are each ten seconds long, or ten if the effort is twenty seconds long. I have a hill close to home that is part of an eight-minute circuit. It is a minute long from the bottom, and I tackle it full on from bottom to top. I've found I can take five or six of those, but for the last one the cumulative muscle damage becomes evident and can carry over for a couple of days. That sort of exercise is just as relevant to road racing – for breaking away or staying with someone – as for the track.

I have listed below a number of different training exercises that address different physical needs. There is no magic formula, but it's important to remember the philosophy behind the suggestions. A non-sprinter can't necessarily become a sprinter and a heavy sprinter is unlikely to become a great climber, but there is no reason why they cannot improve their performance in either sphere. The exercises here try to take into account your psychology as well as your physiology. They should be carefully worked into your training programme, remembering that most of them are quite intense and will need to be tempered with significant periods of rest. Do not just try to add them on to your normal training routine. The key is to allow sufficient time to absorb them so they don't damage your overall form. These are the most common deficiencies which I had to work on specifically:

1. Explosive Efforts – Jumping, Closing Gaps and Sprinting

Aim: These exercises are quite simply about producing near-maximal or maximal power for somewhere between ten and thirty seconds at a time. In my case, this would produce power in the region of 750 to 1,100 watts, way over aerobic threshold. The exercises will cause a lot of muscle damage, so only a small quantity of work can be supported in a training programme. Developing this ability can mean the difference between getting dropped or not, winning a sprint or being fifth, being able to break away or being trapped all day in a group.

This exercise is one that Peter Keen devised quite late in my career to work on pure strength. By keeping the duration of each effort down to just six seconds, you are effectively doing weights. The muscles are contracting exactly as they would when racing but without producing high levels of lactic acid. If someone suggested that you do forty near-maximal sprints in twenty-five minutes, you would regard them as mad. It's too mind-bending to contemplate. In fact, this is about the easiest session I know, because you simply don't have time to suffer. It's power training in disguise.

Exercise one: ergometer or home-trainer session.
Duration: 50 minutes.
Fifteen minutes' progressive warm-up from 100 bpm up to lower level two, followed by two minutes' easy, then two sets of ten minutes, alternating between six seconds at near-maximal power seated at about 70 rpm and twenty-four seconds with some pressure on the pedals, not freewheeling between efforts. Five minutes' recovery time between sets at quite a high cadence and a warm-down for ten minutes, followed by a stretch later in the day.

Exercise two: road, track or ergometer/home trainer.
Duration: approx. 1 hour 45 minutes.
A warm-up to suit you. If I'm on the road, I will do up to an hour at level one, then alternate between ten seconds at about 90 per cent effort in the saddle, around 90+ rpm, then twenty seconds' recovery but still pedalling. The first set can be twelve efforts, the next ten, the next eight and the last set six. Have at least five minutes' recovery between each set. Follow this with at least ten minutes' warm-down and stretching. You will be amazed how much harder this is than the six-second efforts in the last exercise. This is simulating the repeated near-maximal efforts with incomplete recovery that are the norm in the final few kilometres of a race or when there are difficult crosswinds. You are working on muscle strength and, to a large extent, on aerobic ability, due mostly to the insufficient recovery time between efforts.

2. Explosive Short Climbs – Classic Climbs

Aim: to improve climbing skills over the sort of short, sharp climbs that are generally found in British road races. Although these efforts involve quite high muscle forces and are likely to be well above aerobic threshold, they are still nowhere near as aggressive as the maximal sprints we covered in the previous category. Technique is important here, too. Think about your style as well as your intensity, and try to maintain an efficient, smooth ride. You won't be able to think about these things when racing, so it needs to be second nature by then.

Exercise three: road bike on the road.
Duration: 1 hour 30 minutes to 2 hours 30 minutes.
You will need to plan a route or circuit with hills of at least two minutes' and preferably five minutes' duration. We will assume that all your hills are three minutes long, so you must adjust the amount of effort accordingly.

As before, start with a good warm-up at a high cadence. Try to stay above 100 rpm most of the time, then, on arriving at the bottom of the first hill, sit back in the saddle with your hands on the tops of the bars in the centre. Choose a gear that gives you a cadence of about 80 rpm, ride for twenty seconds at 90 per cent effort, then back right off for ten seconds. Continue this cycle for three minutes, then rest for about five. Repeat six times, or until you feel the quality of your work is starting to drop off.

Exercise four: road bike on the road. Duration: 2 hours.
Aim: to improve your 'jump' so that you can attack a race. It is one of the hardest exercises I do and causes a considerable amount of muscle damage, so it is not one to be tried every day. This kind of exercise needs to be tackled when the rider is fresh and should come during the run-up to, but not too close to, a big objective, before the period of tapering when the volume is low but the quality is still high.

It is a simple exercise. After a good warm-up, find a one-minute climb, preferably part of a ten-minute circuit, and blast up it at maximal effort, out of the saddle on quite a big gear, say 80 rpm. Try not to sit down before the top. A maximum of six efforts, with eight to ten minutes' recovery on a fairly low gear in between.

3. Short Efforts Over Threshold – Prologues and Crosswinds

These are a subtle notch down from the previous exercises. I use them to prepare for prologues, where it is possible to ride slightly above threshold for up to fifteen minutes. In crosswinds, too, it is often necessary to ride above threshold for short periods. Only drop down to around threshold between surges to recover.

Exercise five: road or time-trial bike.
Duration: up to 2 hours 30 minutes.
Warm up for a minimum of twenty minutes and a maximum of an hour. Then ride three minutes of controlled level four in the saddle (after the first fifteen seconds to get it going). Concentrate on your style, keeping the gear low – around 100 rpm or higher – and measure

your effort so that you could not sustain it for ten minutes but remain in control for three. It isn't meant to be a totally maximal effort. Ride in a low gear for seven to ten minutes before repeating two more times. Then do another three efforts with the same rest period, but now only two minutes each.

Exercise six: race training. Duration: around 20–30 minutes.
Aim: to sharpen up your work a few weeks before a big objective. It is hard, for advanced riders and not to be done all year, only at specific times.

All around the country, from May to September, there are evening 10-mile time trials being organized by local cycling clubs. There are often only twenty or so riders, and they are usually enter-on-the-line affairs. You will need to be in a cycling club to ride in them, but that is generally the only criterion. For many, including myself, this is the first experience of race riding, but they are excellent forms of training, too, allowing you to make mistakes in race situations but without pressure. If done properly, the trial should be done in level three+, with a fixed-wheel bike, if possible, so that you are free to concentrate on effort and style rather than gear selection. Before the race, practise your warm-up on a home trainer, stopping ten minutes before the start time.

4. Threshold Efforts – Time Trials and Sustained Climbing

The last exercise crosses over into this category because to improve aerobic capacity you must push the body above its anaerobic threshold in a controlled way. Technically, this involves the body shifting oxygen in larger quantities more efficiently and dealing more effectively with lactic acid, the by-product of burning glycogen and oxygen. One way to do this is with the following exercise:

Exercise seven: TT bike, road bike or home trainer.
Duration: 1 to 2 hours.
Start with a warm-up rehearsal or at least twenty minutes on the road. Then, maybe in your time-trial position, alternate between twenty seconds at 90 per cent of your maximal effort followed by ten seconds' rest – still pedalling – and repeat a total of twelve times. Repeat after ten minutes' rolling rest, but this time with ten efforts, then eight and finally six. Finish with the usual warm-down and stretch. This exercise is mentally very tough. It pushes your body to increase its ability to tolerate lactic acid by exceeding anaerobic threshold in a controlled way, but doesn't allow enough time between efforts to completely recover. It also allows you to work on your style and technique at very high powers.

Exercise eight: more aerobic work, best on the road.
Duration: up to 2 hours total.
Aim: to improve anaerobic threshold. These exercises would be best done in the position you intend to use for time-trialling, although a standard road bike would also be suitable. If possible, arrange your route in advance to avoid interruptions from traffic lights, and try not to include descents where you can freewheel. Warm up well, then do a total of four controlled threshold efforts, with at least five minutes' rest in between each, preferably ten. Decrease the efforts each time, from fifteen minutes to twelve, ten and finally eight. This helps to keep you interested and motivated as fatigue increases and is a principle I apply in most of my training. Follow the session with the usual warm-down and stretching.

5. Endurance Work

I don't always see eye to eye with the rest of the professionals about endurance training. In the *peloton*, the tendency is to believe that endurance work is essentially a matter of doing a number of long rides to increase the body's fat-burning capability. In turn, that helps to preserve the precious stores of glycogen intact. My argument is that if you are riding long races at the weekend, this is sufficient to maintain an endurance base, and time during the week would be better spent recovering and working on more intensive, specific work.

Exercise nine: road bike. Duration: 3 to 6 hours.
These sorts of rides form a large part of my early-season or pre-season training before the racing starts. The length of the rides depends completely on your race programme. I would suggest that they need never be longer than your intended race distance, and that if your programme is made up largely of time trials then they are entirely optional. These rides are best done in company because they become very mentally demanding. Wednesday is my endurance day, when I meet up with some locals at the cycling café. Old habits die hard!

Endurance training should be done at low intensity so you avoid doing any significant muscle damage. The intensive work is best done separately, when the quality is higher and the recovery time shorter. So stick to level one.

Weight loss is also an area that can be tackled on these days. Try going without breakfast so that your body immediately starts burning up fat reserves instead of spending an hour and a half just burning off your breakfast.

NOTE: if you decide to try this, however, it is very important that you do start eating after forty-five minutes to an hour of riding. At about this time you will be metabolizing fat well, but you will be running low on blood sugar. You must eat about 60 gs of carbohydrate every hour now for the rest of the ride.

Traffic Lights

Yes, we have lots of them, don't we. Somehow they always seem to be on red at the critical moment, and it's the same for the world hour record holder as for everyone else. Like most places in the country, the traffic on the Wirral has increased dramatically over the past decade. I have devised a route through the middle of the Wirral, along lanes, which opens out after a series of roundabouts and junctions. One of the problems with being part of a group is trying to slot your way into the traffic. It's a lot easier on your own. If I want to do a long ride, I generally head off into north Wales. I might go to the Two Mills Café after an hour, pick up a group of riders, go into Wales and Cheshire, and then ride the last hour home from the Two Mills as a warm-down. You have to think hard about it, reconnoitre good open routes and get to know the terrain – the straight stretches, when you can do some sprints, and the more difficult sections which require more concentration. Sometimes, working your way through traffic can be good practice for bike-handling skills and for simulating stop-start conditions in the *peloton*.

I have often been asked why I haven't moved to the continent, where training on the road would be easier. There is no doubt that the mentality of the drivers in France is different. They often stop and wait for you. On the whole, they don't get irate and don't try to nip round you and take away all your braking space. But somehow the disadvantages of leaving Hoylake – moving all the family, mainly – have outweighed the more selfish advantages. I never felt that the compromise was so great it had to be made. I will always do the work I need; I just have to think harder than some of the continental cyclists to make sure I get it done in the right way. When I first joined Gan, Roger Legeay came over to England to check that I had the facilities I needed to train properly. He was appalled by the amount of traffic, but was satisfied that I had the discipline to do my own training and the local knowledge to make the most of the difficult on-road conditions. I still think he was a little perplexed by the mad Englishman.

To do any good-quality training, you really need a long stretch of road without lights or roundabouts. Most of my specific high-intensity work is done at the track. One of the reasons I do the majority of my training alone is the extent of the traffic. When two or more of you are trying to negotiate the same set of lights or the same roundabout at the same time, it compromises the work you're doing. I look for company nowadays on volume rides. With the right guy, you can incorporate some sprints. In the middle of some upper-level-two work, for example, one person can lead out while the other sprints for fifteen seconds.

After a two-minute rest, the roles can be reversed so the other guy sprints for fifteen seconds. It's quite a good exercise, but it needs a good long stretch of the right road.

Working in the Gym

I have written before that I am not entirely certain about the physical benefits of working with weights. For a long period in my career I never went near a gym. The only reason I've done weights is for variety. Recently, though, I've had to do some work on my muscle mass because it was extremely low and my power was suffering. Every extra ounce of muscle on a cyclist's body has to be carried around on the bike, so the advantages have to outweigh the disadvantages and it is therefore worth following a regular weight-training programme.

Mario Cipollini would doubtless have a weight-training component in his winter training sessions because the discipline of sprinting is all about strength and power. But he is a sprinter, pure and simple, and whatever he says to the contrary, the thought of actually finishing a Tour de France, as opposed to winning a couple of the early stages, doesn't enter into his calculations. Erik Zabel and, before him, Dzamolidine Abdoujaparov not only earned their money in the sprint stages in the first ten days of the Tour, but regularly featured in the race for the green jersey – for the leading point-scorer on the Tour – throughout the three weeks. Balancing the power, weight and endurance is quite a feat.

What has changed in the last couple of years is not just my need to develop a more varied set of training exercises, but also the specificity of the weight-training equipment available. There is an incredible range of gear now in most clubs, which enables the cyclist to think through the motion of pedalling a bike and devise exercises that simulate and therefore, in theory, enhance the motion. Here are a number of tips before we describe some of the exercises you can do:

■ **Don't just do an exercise for the sake of it. Think precisely about how it can help you ride a bike faster, which, after all, is the object of the** exercise. If pure muscle was the key to winning bike races, we would all look like bodybuilders. In fact, pro bike riders are incredibly sparely built and, by the end of a race like the Tour, are unhealthily gaunt. Calculate, too, how much more effort it would take to carry an extra kilo around 4,000 kms. Then go easy on the weights.

- Start light on the weights and get heavier. I do three sets of ten repetitions per exercise for most exercises.
- Don't do too much muscular work on your arms. It's not necessary. Work mainly on the legs, the lower back and the stomach, areas you will be loading on race days.
- Do weights in winter, not, on the whole, in summer, unless you need to recover from a specific injury.
- Don't get sucked into using weights as the end itself; they are only the means to an end. You will know when you have a cycling-specific exercise because you will be quite good at it and the muscle will be sore when cycling.
- If you can't complete the repetitions, don't strain. The weight is too heavy.
- Be careful with the timing of weights sessions. Never do them too close to competition. If I did a weekend endurance ride, then I would do a gym session on Monday and the emphasis would be on working on the legs. But if I had a serious long ride planned, I wouldn't do weights the day before.

Stretching Exercises and Flexibility

Often, during long road stages, you will see riders lifting themselves out of the saddle and pressing their pelvic muscles forward, straightening and trying to arch their backs to stretch their lower back muscles. Riding in a crouched position for a long time puts tremendous pressure on the stomach and back muscles, so whatever level you're riding at, it is essential to have a good stretching programme both before and after training exercises and even on rest days.

The importance of flexibility in an athlete, be it a cyclist or a footballer, is often undervalued, yet it can considerably enhance performance, decrease the chance of injury and prolong a career. Flexibility is defined as the possible range of movement in a joint or a series of joints. Hurdlers, for example, require considerable hip flexibility; footballers require flexibility in the knee, leg and ankle joints; swimmers, particularly freestyle swimmers, need flexibility in the ankle joints. Without blinding you with science, joints are strengthened and protected by ligaments, tendons and muscles. A tendon is considerably more elastic than a ligament, which makes it more prone to injury but also more adaptable for training.

There are two types of stretching: dynamic – using momentum – and static. Dynamic involves taking a muscle to its stretched position and then bouncing at the limit of the stretch. This is no longer considered the most effective method of stretching because the sudden act of muscle contraction caused by the bouncing can lead to damage in the muscle fibres. The more popular method now is static stretching, which means extending to the stretched position and then stretching a little further against the resistance. You should feel a slight pull on the muscle, not real pain. Muscles should be stretched before and after exercise and stretching incorporated into the training schedule two or three times a week to increase overall flexibility. Odd exercises, like calf or hamstring stretches, can be practised anywhere – waiting for the bus or around the office. Here are some examples:

Stretching Exercises

1) Gluteus maximus stretch (muscles in your backside). Put your back up close to the wall, raise your left knee, clasp your hands around the knee and stretch it across your body. Do the same with the right knee. Three × fifteen seconds on each side.

2) Calf stretches. Press yourself against a wall with one foot in front of the other and then press back on the backs of your feet until you feel the calf muscles stretch. Three × twenty seconds on each foot.

3) Hamstring stretch. Raise one leg up against a table and lower your trunk from the waist until it starts to hurt the hamstrings. Hold for fifteen seconds three times. Don't bounce. Hamstrings tend to tighten with constant pedalling motion, so it is important to keep them stretched – tight hamstrings can lead to pain in the lower back. Hamstrings can also be stretched by putting your foot on the back of a chair or a table and bending forward towards the toes until the muscles start to tighten.

4) Back stretch. This is critical for cyclists. Put your right arm across your chest and keep the left arm straight out, horizontal to the ground. Turn the trunk to its maximum and hold for fifteen seconds, three times on each side.

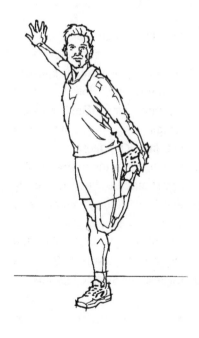

5) Quad stretch (the muscle group at the front of your thighs). This is also critical for cyclists. Stand on one leg and pull the other up behind you, holding the foot with your hand, i.e., hold your right leg with your right hand. Press up and hold for fifteen to twenty seconds, three times on each leg. It should start to hurt at the front of your thigh. Keep your back straight.

6) Shoulder stretch. Put one hand behind your back, reaching upwards, and the other over the top of your shoulder. Try to lock the fingers, hold and stretch for fifteen seconds. Repeat using the other hands.

7) Spinal mobility. The cat stretch. Kneel on all fours, with your head up. Hold for a count of ten. Arch your back, lowering the head and pushing up with the abdominal muscles, so that your body forms the shape of an arch, like a cat stretching. Hold for ten seconds and repeat ten times.

These are exercises that I use. You can adapt your own stretching exercises, but it is essential to have a good stretching programme. There is evidence to suggest that stretching aids recovery because it increases the blood flow through the muscles. It is recommended before *and* after training.

Weight-Training Exercises

Most of these exercises are aimed at strengthening the chassis, as opposed to the motor, of the body. You aren't trying to increase engine size, but rather the control of the engine. The exercises need to be stressful, but you should be able to complete them. Mix up arm and leg exercises so that no part of the body gets too tired. Generally, use fifteen to twenty repetitions, and do three sets of each exercise in rotation.

1) Triceps. Put your right knee on a bench so that you are leaning forward with your face down towards the bench and your left arm hanging loose almost down to the floor. With the weight in your left hand, pull the arm up towards the body. Do three sets of fifteen repetitions on either side, using light weights (about 15 kgs). The main rule is to start light and go heavier.

2) Arm curls. A standard exercise. Stand firm with your legs slightly apart and the weight in your right hand, palm up. Curl the weight up towards your chest. Repeat with your left arm.

3) Adapted bench press. This is designed to simulate your own bodyweight when pulling or pushing on the bars. The whole set of exercises is aimed at controlling the muscles in your arms when climbing or sprinting out of the saddle.

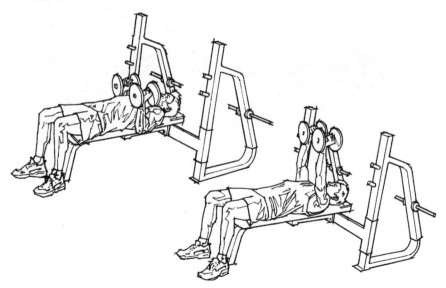

4) Tricep adapted bench press.

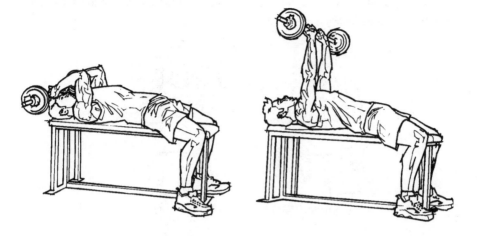

5) Base back exercise. This can be done on a machine, but also on the floor by lying face down and lifting the head, shoulders and trunk off the floor as far as possible.

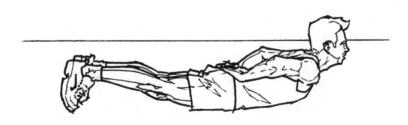

6) Sit-ups. These are for the stomach muscles.

7) Standing gluteus. This resembles the motion of pedalling, strengthening the muscles at the back of the legs and in the buttocks. I use 100-kg weights.

8) Leg extensions. For the thigh muscles. Use 40-kg weights.

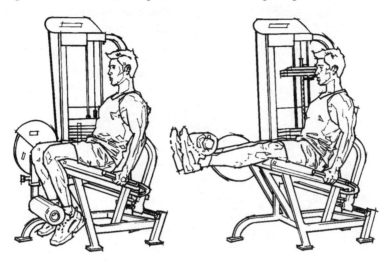

9) Standing calf raises. For the calf muscles. Put a light weight on your shoulders and push up with your calf muscles, lifting your heels off the ground. I lift 80-kg weights. Three × ten repetitions.

10) Leg press. On a machine, bring your legs up towards your chest and press out to full extension against the weights. I would use 200-kg weights.

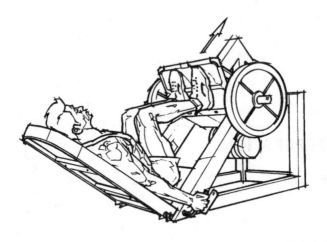

11) Dips. Start with arms extended on parallel bars. Bend your arms and push up like a vertical press-up.

8

RACE PREPARATION

The Final Week

Tapering Training

In the crudest terms, training is the process of breaking down the body's systems through exercise and allowing them sufficient time to rebuild themselves in a stronger form. Without sufficient rest, training is next to pointless.

Tapering is the final phase in a training schedule before the competition itself. As the word suggests, the volume of work is slowly reduced as the objective approaches, although there is still a significant amount of quality work involved in the final phase. The aim is to ensure that you arrive at the startline with all your body systems ready to work at their maximum. One week is typically a good length of time for a main-year-goal taper.

In professional cycling, as the calendar in chapter 2 indicates, the rhythm of racing is so intense that there's rarely time for a full week-long taper, so it's something that should be attempted only a few times a year because it involves a significantly reduced training volume. Part tapers of just two to three days should be used more regularly.

I firmly believe that you lose form at roughly the same rate you generate it: slowly. With one week to go, training should be finished, and it is highly unlikely that you will generate more form in this period through training. It is very easy to compromise your condition in this last week by trying to do too much, particularly if your training schedule has been set back by injury. You should start to feel really fresh and alert, and doing more hard training would be no problem, mentally or physically, but you should resist the temptation to do more than has been planned for the taper period. In this phase, less is definitely more.

The Final Details

The week before a major objective like the prologue of the Tour de France is the most stressful part of the year for me. Large amounts of pressure tend to lead to mistakes. My formula for dealing with that is to make as many decisions as I can in advance, mapping out how I want the week to go, in particular the last two days of it. You should factor in rest periods and think carefully about your diet to give your body all the building blocks necessary to repair damage and store sufficient fuel for the race itself. Also remember that you are using only about 40 per cent of the calories you would normally expend in training.

These are some of the questions I try to solve well before the start of the prologue:

- **Weeks or even months before the day I will view the prologue circuit for myself to make basic equipment selections, such as sizes of chain rings and sprockets. This recce will also give me a mental image of the challenge and influence the type of exercise and road type I will use in training.**
- **The day before the event, I will go round the circuit again and see how the barrier placement has affected the corners, work out the best racing line and consider how rain might alter the surface – which parts of the road might turn slippery, for example. This will be done alone, so there are no distractions.**
- **I will check the location for signing-on and the distance between the start and the team parking area to avoid any sudden surprises.**

- **When I get back to the hotel I will give the mechanics my final in-structions on my choice of tyres and gears. If in doubt, after crashing in the wet in St Brieuc, I will always play safe.**
- **That afternoon, about twenty-four hours before my start time, I will have a meeting with my *soigneur*, my mechanic and Roger Legeay, the team director, to make sure everyone knows the routine and the timetable for the following day.**

On the day itself, given that my start time is usually round about 4 p.m., my timetable would look like this:

8 a.m. Breakfast – cereal, baguette, 10 gs of butter, honey and two coffees with sugar. High carbohydrate and minimal protein at this stage of the day. In the middle of a stage race you need to increase your protein intake to compensate for the increasing breakdown of muscle.

10 a.m. One hour on the bike, typically on the prologue circuit again, with one × forty-five seconds at level three to four (over anaerobic threshold for forty-five seconds).

11.30 a.m. Sleep or read, put numbers on, pack race bag.

1 p.m. Light lunch of pasta, omelette and yogurt.

2 p.m. Leave hotel.

2.30 p.m. Arrive at start area, sign on and get official starting time. Check how long it will take to get from the warm-up area to the ramp. Return to team bus, lay out my kit and try to read.

3.20 p.m. Get ready for the warm-up.

3.30 p.m. Get on rollers for twenty minutes' progressive warm-up (see below).

3.50 p.m. End warm-up, towel down, put on helmet, glasses and gloves.

3.54 p.m. Roll to start.

4 p.m. Race.

Warm-ups

A warm-up is exactly what it says. It is not an exercise to calm the nerves. I have seen François Moreau of France and Jens Lehmann of Germany lose World Championships because they expended so much nervous energy and left a significant portion of their race on either the track or the rollers. Both of them did about three or four hours of warm-up for three four-and-a-half-minute races. In a stressful environment, the hardest thing in the world is to do nothing. So take a book or a magazine with you to help fill the time.

For warm-ups, I invariably use a static trainer, because it allows me to do two things:

■　**I can visualize the race route and how I am going to tackle it physically, mentally and technically, without interruption or distraction.**

■　**The conditions are the same each time, regardless of the weather or the terrain. There is no significant wind-chill factor on an ergometer, allowing warm-ups to be short and effective but saving the energy reserves for the race.**

I find that a progressive approach to warming up works well at quite a high cadence – 100+ rpm – starting with five minutes going from stop to lower level one, five minutes progressing to upper level one, and five minutes going up to level two. I hold that for two minutes before doing two ten-second sprints at a high cadence, with about a minute between, before winding down for the last minute. The sprints prepare you for the shock of the effort off the start. Your pulse will vary, too. It will probably be much higher than usual, which is good.

CB's Tips:

■　**This is your sporting career, so take charge of it. You do not have to do everything yourself, but be responsible for planning, organizing and delegating. Never assume that someone else will have done it.**

■　**If you have the chance, memorize the race route – or key parts of it –**

and be as familiar as possible with the place where you will be working.

- Give yourself time to plan. Get used to making notes and timetables so everyone knows their responsibilities.
- Lack of communication is the most common cause of disaster.
- Practise your warm-ups so you are comfortable with the routine of the day.
- Plan in time to fix problems.
- If possible, in terms of equipment, have two of everything.

9

THE ART OF SURVIVAL

The Psychology of Cycling

The Principles

Psychology is not something we can isolate and treat differently from any other aspect of our preparation. By doing some of the things I have outlined in previous chapters you have already started to tackle psychological problems. Structuring your approach to training helps to control all the controllable forces that affect your performance, implementing a communication strategy with the key people who will be close to you throughout training, racing and researching your objectives, both long and short term, so that you can visualize how a season might shape up and how a race might unfold, technically and physically. This is part of the mental as well as physical preparation.

I have two particular philosophies, the second of which has already been outlined in the opening chapter, but is worth restating.

- **It is OK to make mistakes, sometimes it's even good, because you can learn from them. The danger comes when you make the same mistake twice.**
- **Strive not to be the best, only to be as good as *you* can be. If you achieve that, no-one can ask for more.**

But there is another side to the mentality of cycling, and anyone who has ever ridden in a bike race will know about it. Cycling is one of the most mentally demanding sports, and it doesn't matter whether it's a stage of the Tour de France or a local club time trial, somewhere along the way your body is going to tell you to stop or slow down. What's important then, what marks out the champions from the rest, is the mind's response.

The Road to Pamplona, 1996

Even on paper the seventeenth stage of the 1996 Tour looked brutal. Eight hours and 162 miles over five mountains in 40-degree heat, with just four more stages to go till the finish. It was the furthest I had ever got in the Tour and I was determined to reach Paris, but on that day I knew I was going to suffer. All the way up the first climb, the Col d'Aubisque, I thought, I can't get up here. Dropped by the main group of the *peloton*, every muscle in my body was telling me to stop. It would have been no disgrace to stop there, but every time I thought about it another thought came into my head: Seventeen days gone. You can see Paris, you can't stop now. So for the whole day two ideas bounced off the walls of my brain in a sort of mental tennis: stop now, you can't; stop now, you can't. It was a constant battle between my emotional and physical sides.

Had I stopped, I would have gained nothing from the Tour. I had invested so much in terms of mental and physical effort, and had completed 85 per cent of the race – I just couldn't bear to stop and waste the lot. And for some reason, in that situation, you always think it's only you who is suffering.

I was dropped on every climb, but managed to claw my way back up to the main group on the descent, only to be dropped again on the next climb. I still cannot fully explain what got me through that day. There was never a good enough reason to stop, so I kept going. Partly, it was the ignominy of it. As the leader of the Gan team, I should have been half an hour up the road. Instead I was in a *gruppetto* and completely out of the race.

The one person who helped me out that day was Eros Poli, who wasn't then a member of the team. He has a very relaxing way of talking – 'Hey, don't worry about it' – and because he's so experienced, he knew exactly how fast we had to go to beat the time limit. At the back of my mind was the thought that I could get to the end of the stage and still be timed out of the race. Eros had it all under control. He had worked out where we could gain some time, how much we would lose and what percentage of the *peloton* was with us. If there are enough riders outside the time limit set by the organizers for each stage the riders aren't disqualified; if they were the Tour would be decimated. Eros thought there might be enough of us this time. Even if he was wrong, it made me feel better.

In those situations, when the race is effectively over and everyone is struggling, there is a tremendous camaraderie among the riders. Everyone wants to reach Paris and, having survived so far, everyone deserves to. So riders slow down for those who have been dropped. I made it that time, and the feeling of relief and achievement was immense. The three weeks of the Tour triggered an extraordinary run of form that lasted about six weeks through August and September, during which I broke the world hour record and won six races.

Preparing the Mind

The mental side of cycling is over 50 per cent of the sport, maybe more than that for the very top riders, when the dividing line between success and failure is so thin. Having the aerobic capacity – the engine, in other words – is one thing, having the ability to apply it is quite another. At the very top of the sport, everyone has a good engine. The difference between a top *domestique* and a Miguel Indurain or Tony Rominger is all in the mind. It is about commitment, determination and organization much more than pure physique. The problem is that, in my opinion, the ability to deal with pressure is inherent. It can be controlled, to an extent, by good discipline, planning and organization, but only so far. You either react well to pressure or you don't. This philosophy is probably not one most people want to hear, and many might disagree with it, but from experience I know that no matter how bad I feel, or how much I detest pressure, it does not affect my performance. Or if it does, it's only in exceptional circumstances.

St Brieuc, 1995

Because of the commercial demands of television, the prologue in St Brieuc was the first to be ridden in the dark, during prime-time viewing. The first riders started in the afternoon in dry conditions, but the top riders set off last and had to contend not only with virtual darkness but driving rain, which made the fast course perilously slippery. My nerves won; I am not frightened to admit it. The pressure got to me, but it was only later that I worked out why. I made an error; not a big error, but I was closer to my limit than I should have been.

There were other pressures on me that night. The team had suffered some poor results during the season and, having won the prologue the previous year and taken the yellow jersey on my first day of the Tour, I wanted to do it again. Also, my team and the sponsors expected me to do it again. I knew it was a great opportunity, provided I could hold myself together. We had gone through the build-up and I had ridden round the course to refresh my memory. I can forget the birthdays of my children, but still remember the exact configuration of a time-trial course. I felt fantastic and I knew by my gear selection for the climb – 53 × 13 – that I was flying. It was the sort of gear you might use for a descent not a climb. I grappled with my nerves during the afternoon, looking out of the hotel window and watching the rain clouds blow in, really struggling to keep myself under control. But once it started to rain it was almost a relief, because that was it, there was nothing I could do. I had a ready-made excuse for failing. I couldn't compete, I just had to get round.

I went to the start car quite happy. But Didier Roux, who had just finished the course, pointed out that he was only thirty seconds down on Jacky Durand, the leader. 'If I'm only thirty seconds down, you can win this,' he said. The people around me were going, 'Yeah, yeah,' and I started to get back into competitive mode, thinking that maybe I could do it. There was a touch of greed there, too – this was my best chance of wearing the yellow jersey in the Tour de France. I began to get more and more wound up until Roger Legeay told me victory was still possible.

I went round the first couple of bends after the start thinking, I can't believe I just got round those. There was a very technical section of the course – several sharp bends and a slight hill – but I got through it right on the edge and started the descent to the riverside. I had done the hard part of the course, and the last thing I heard Roger Legeay say was, 'You're only two seconds down. It's finished now, you can go flat out.' At the bottom of the descent was a straight section along the river, a hairpin bend and a big climb back to the top. I thought I'd done it. But I hit the bend halfway down the descent and suddenly realized how fast I was going. It was the first time I'd used an 11-sprocket and I must have been doing 80 kph through the sweeping bends. Because it was dark and the road was lit by street lamps, it was hard to see the surface of the road. I hit a slick patch of tarmac, the back wheel slipped out and that was that: a shattered ankle and a broken wrist. It could have been a lot worse had Roger not slammed on the brakes of the team car just in time. Neil Stephens, then riding for Once, told me that he was watching the race on television and had said, 'He's going to win this or he's going down.' There was no in-between that night.

To this day, I think Roger feels responsible, though nothing has ever been said. But I take responsibility; I was the guy riding the bike. Having said that, if Roger had shouted, 'Take it easy here, it's nearly finished,' I might have slowed down a bit. But the combination of being urged on and my own pumped-up state was enough to push me over the limit. Everyone was under a lot of pressure that night: Roger, me, the sponsors. It probably wasn't worth taking the risks – there were still another twenty days and 4,000 kms to go – but at that time we were all too close to the action to see it.

Mentally, the positive side of the accident was that I had a whole summer sitting in the garden with my feet up, away from the pressure of competition. There was nothing I could do, everyone's attention was elsewhere and I was able to slow down a bit and take stock of my career – from winning Olympic gold to breaking the world hour record to leading a professional team without much road-racing experience. I'd stepped off the plane in Barcelona in 1992 and someone had taken my life away.

Rules of the Mind

1. Control the Controllable

Through the British team, I have worked for a long time with the sport psychologist John Syer. He teaches visualization techniques, which I use for memorizing and tackling time-trial and prologue courses, but which otherwise didn't do a great deal for me. He helped me order my thoughts and structure the way I was doing things into a set pattern. He emphasized the principle of controlling the controllable and not worrying about what could not be controlled – for example, the weather or how anyone else performed. In the middle of an intense competition, there are so many distractions that it is critical to have a routine to follow, both in the physical and mental build-up to competition.

2. Try to Be as Good as You Can Be as Opposed to Being the Best

If you are as good as you can be, no-one can ask for more, which, on the starting line for an Olympics or evening track league, is a comforting thought. Again, it is a matter of good organization, which sounds very boring but is critical to mental and physical strength. Organization of my own thoughts and actions is one of the most important parts of mental training. All the details of a day's racing are taken care of. I turn up a certain amount of time before the race and have a meeting with all the people who are involved in the day – the team manager, my *soigneur*, my mechanic – and decide on exact timings for the day: what time to leave the hotel, what time to eat, when to warm up. Your mind has to be clear to focus on your performance and fitness; you can't afford time to worry about logistics.

At the Tour de France, the day's routine is well honed (see chapter 15); at the Olympic Games in Atlanta the management seemed to be struggling to cope with all the demands of such a big and complex event. I had a quick meeting with John Syer, and we decided that I would take charge of my own organization. I asked the relevant team managers to a meeting, and told them what I needed to get the job done. That wasn't as it should be, but it was important for my own peace of mind, and I had a big enough reputation to get away with it. The principles would be the same for a club competitor: be organized in your preparation. By taking control of all the variables you can increase your chances of dealing with pressure, and coming through difficult situations when you're under pressure also gives you a basis of confidence to build on for the next time.

3. Nobody Likes Pressure, But Some People Don't Show It

The best competitors turn pressure into a positive force, using it to intensify their commitment; others – maybe the majority – find it reduces theirs. That can just be a physical problem: taut nerves and constricted breathing. Almost every athlete will feel nervous and tense before a big event; the trick, if I can use such a non-scientific word, is to confront it and channel it. As a junior, I folded under pressure at times. A week before a race I would go out and keep trying to prove a point to myself by riding a 10-mile time trial, just to reassure myself that I could do it. On more than one occasion I left my form on the training road. It was caused by my psyche and, at that time, a certain sense of insecurity.

In Barcelona, on paper I was between three and four seconds faster than anyone else, which is quite a distance in pursuit. But on the startline, I sat there thinking, This can't be me; I'm just Chris Boardman from Hoylake, I'm not supposed to be an Olympic champion. My thoughts were negative: I can't win this; other people win Olympic gold. There were 102 countries watching on television, and I knew, deep down, that the next four and a half minutes could change my life. I would win or the Olympic machine would grind on and Chris Boardman would be just another British athlete who'd come second. Those are scary thoughts, but once the gun went off they all vanished and I was into territory I knew and understood. I was into an area I could control.

The pinnacle of pressure is the world hour record (see chapter 14) because there is no second place. In other events, if you lose, someone else wins; at the hour record, if you fail, everyone involved fails. Success or failure: those are the only options, and everyone is watching you. As I walked from the dressing room into the arena at the Manchester Velodrome, with 3,000 people there cheering me on, I remember turning to Peter Keen and asking him to remind me never to do this again. There is an added complication with the hour record. Under the rules of the record, a rider starts when he wants to, not at some prearranged hour, so the start of an hour's suffering is voluntary.

Preparing for the start begins weeks before and becomes more intense as the competition gets nearer. I try very hard, both on the startline and in the days leading up to the event, not to go through the 'what if' syndrome. It's easy to start throwing mental problems at yourself. What if I'm feeling bad? What if I have a puncture? What if a thousand things? I try to concentrate on things I can control because if my mind is working overtime, which it usually is, I want to make sure it's concentrating on something positive and not negative. When I race on the track or do a time trial or, most notably, the world hour record, I make sure whoever is working with me gives me as much information as possible. That gives me something to work with, which in turn helps to reduce the concentration on suffering. OK, I'll tell myself, I'm a second down, do I want to do something about it now or do I wait until the closing stages of the race, hoping my opponent will slow down? When the body is full of endorphins and adrenalin, if you have peaked at the right time, you don't feel pain as such. You can't go any faster, but you feel completely in control and you don't perceive the feeling as pain.

4. Motivation – Why Are You Doing This?

John Syer once told me that Keith Burkinshaw, the former Tottenham manager, recognized the self-motivated footballer by three things: he loved playing football; he had pride in himself, his team and his club; and last, and *least*, money. As I've already explained, I don't enjoy bike racing; it hurts and it's hard work. But I enjoy winning. Since I have enjoyed some success, my motivation has changed subtly from wanting success to fearing failure. Nowadays my main motivation is fear of failure.

Eddy Merckx won Milan–San Remo seven times. Each time he found a different reason for wanting to win it. One was the first time, the next was to repeat his success and show everyone it wasn't a fluke. Then he missed a year, so he wanted to win it a third time because he hadn't won it the previous year, and so on. Cycling is a predominantly working-class sport; it is also a boring, repetitive, mechanical exercise, which makes it harder to remain motivated. For someone like Miguel Indurain, as for many cyclists, the motivation comes from wanting a different way of life, from being given an opportunity and wanting to grasp it with both hands. They are not afraid of hard work. Indurain would have been working on the land if he hadn't made millions as a cyclist. The common shared factor for champions is their burning *need* to win. Merckx, or the Cannibal as he is known, is the prime example. He wanted to win every race he ever entered. Indurain was slightly different; he wanted to win the Tour de France every year.

I am slightly different. Failure makes me perform better because I hate it so much that I have to go out and discover how to do better next time. If I achieve my goal my motivation dies off a bit. In the winter of 1997–8 I had real problems with motivation because I had no strategy for the year; I didn't know why I was going out there and riding. I was doing the training, but I wasn't sure what it was for and I found that very frustrating.

This is the most important part of the book for me, and the principle that can be applied to every athlete, no matter what their sport. This is not about a type of bike or a type of training; it is the framework into which everything else fits. It is understanding why you're doing it.

Every day that I train, I need a reason to do so. It might be, as it was last winter, that I want to develop more explosive power, to give myself a better chance of winning one of the classics in the calendar. I want to win a classic because I don't think I can win a major stage race. And the reasons go on. That is my motivation, that is how I work. It sounds very clinical, and I have often been accused by the press of being dispassionate about my sport, which is untrue, but even if you've dreamed of winning Olympic gold or the Tour de France since childhood, you still need to know how to do it. One of the main reasons Peter Keen and I have developed such a good relationship is that he has always been able to answer my questions and, as a physiologist, he has been able to convince me that his plan is the best way of achieving the required result. The most important thing is that I believe in his methods, so every time I turn a pedal, I know the reason why.

Visualization Techniques

Visualization can be used in a number of ways to help confidence and instil positivity before an event. In the 1998 rugby league Challenge Cup at Wembley, John Kear, the Sheffield Eagles coach, used visualization techniques to prepare his players for their first appearance in a Wembley final. He got them to imagine walking out, meeting all the dignitaries and receiving the first kick of the match. When the time came, they already knew what to expect, even though they were novices compared to Wigan, their opponents. Kear said he knew the night before, after a team meeting, that it would be a special day. He sensed a common purpose in his players. He was right. The Eagles achieved the greatest upset in cup final history by beating Wigan 17–8.

In *Team Spirit: The Elusive Experience* John Syer recalls helping Glenn Hoddle overcome a particularly bad leg injury in November 1984. Hoddle knew his leg was fine, but was still reluctant to make a burst of speed during a game. Part of the treatment involved Hoddle recalling an incident in a match against Feyenoord before his injury when he'd felt totally confident. He did a mental rehearsal exercise twice a week, in the evenings, and then reinforced it with the written affirmation, 'I'm excited as I feel my opponent coming,' which, said Syer, later changed to, 'I'm in control of the situation.' Control, that word again.

We used visualization techniques during a ten-year period with the Olympic pursuit team. We imagined not just what we might be doing on the track, but the noise of the crowd and the environment. I use visualization for short, intense experiences, like prologues and time trials. For the prologue to the Tour de France, for example, I will ride round the course early in the year to make some initial decisions about equipment and bikes. I will ride the course a couple of days before the start, then again the following day and on the morning of the prologue, so that by the time the moment arrives I can close my eyes and go round the entire course in my mind, making decisions on how to approach each corner and climb and negotiate all the different obstacles. I know where all the manhole covers are and where the road surface changes.

I also visualize the effort needed for each section. If I'm not happy about a particular aspect of the course, my performance is never as good as it should be. My prologue in 1997, though good enough to win – just – was not as good as it should have been. I hadn't decided how to tackle a hill that came about thirty seconds after the start. Most people were battering up the hill because they were so fresh, forgetting there were still another six kms to go. I hadn't decided whether to thrash up it or take it steady, so the ride was a bit messy. The corners and technical aspects were right, but I hadn't quantified my measurement of effort effectively enough in my mind.

Concentration

There are two types of concentration: one is total focus on what I'm doing – descending, for example; the other is the type of concentration demanded by a time trial, where the skill is to balance on the anaerobic threshold, that fine physical line between maximum output and potential exhaustion.

A descent needs total concentration – on how much pressure to apply to the front or back brakes, on the type of road surface, on the trajectory through a given bend. There is no time to think of anything else. But perhaps because of my background in time-trialling, I now know exactly how fast I need to go round a time-trial course. When I'm in time-trial mode my mind can wander off somewhere else. I can be in the middle of a trial and be thinking about Ed's schooling, but still instinctively be able to monitor the situation as I go along. That is important if you're having to ride pretty well flat out for an hour and a half.

During a stage race, it is important to be able to switch your concentration on and off. In a quiet period, I will find someone to talk to for an hour or two. Neil Stephens, the Australian who used to ride for Once and Festina, but decided to retire in the aftermath of the Festina doping affair at the 1998 Tour, is a guy whose company I enjoyed. He always seemed to have the whole thing totally under control. He knew what he was good at and he knew his limitations. He had accepted that he wasn't quite good enough to win the big races, but was happy working his socks off for his team. He actually had the ideal mentality for a good *domestique*, someone who is very good, but not quite as good as the team leader, and accepts it. Neil was worth his weight in gold and had made a very good living from being an honest hard worker, and I was sad when he left the *peloton* at the end of the 1998 season. He said the only reward he needed was a little acknowledgement from his team leader that he had done a good job.

A lot of the Australians are like that. Henk Vogels, a member of both the Gan and Crédit Agricole teams, is the same. He doesn't analyse a race, or a day, too much. He reckons tomorrow is another day and that's it. It's a simple, robust philosophy that I envy. I will lie awake at night wondering where I've gone wrong and what I could have done better. It's not a healthy way to earn a living.

On the Tour de France, one minute you can be riding along gently, the next a break is on, the wind has changed and the race suddenly moves up a gear. It took me a few months to adapt my concentration to the different tempo of road racing, and to instinctively note where the wind is, where the best protection will be and where the dangers are. If the road becomes twistier and narrower, it is important to be near the front to cover breaks and avoid crashes. If the *peloton* is suddenly hit by a crosswind, you have to concentrate hard because it is the ideal time for a break. Yet, over twenty-one days and 4,000 kms of race riding, you have to find the time to relax. That is a key element in tackling the Tour, and one learned only from experience.

Tour of Romandie, Prologue, 1998

This was another occasion when my nerves won. I had done well in the Tour of Romandie the previous year, winning both time trials and finishing second overall. In 1998, my form was just beginning to return after a poor start to the season and I was desperate to get a good result under my belt, particularly in the wake of my disappointing 1997 season. When I'm nervous, I tend to sleep a lot. In the days leading up to the Tour of Romandie, I was asleep a great deal. The nervous tension just built up because I knew I could do well. The prologue was 4½ kms long – ideal for me – but included twelve bends, so it was all brake and sprint. I was so pumped up I went into the turns too fast, and had to compensate by braking halfway through and going wide on the exit. By the time I'd settled into a proper rhythm I'd lost too much time and finished seventh, behind Laurent Dufaux. The one bonus was that my form was nearly there. Physically, I felt good.

Emotional Control

The great riders are adept at controlling their emotions. The look on Miguel Indurain's face, for example, never seemed to change, whether he was pottering along on the flat on a gentle spring afternoon or climbing Alpe d'Huez in 40-degree heat. His face was a mask, and he often wore a cycling hat pulled down low over his face, with his eyes hidden by sunglasses. His rhythm never altered, either.

Often, with riders, you can tell from their style whether they're hurting or not; they start to roll or get out of the saddle more often. Laurent Jalabert and Jan Ullrich are the same; they never appear to suffer, which is highly unnerving for their rivals. I'm not sure whether you can control this by practice.

Stephane Heulot, who rode for the Gan team for a couple of years, just went red, so it was obvious when he was suffering. But Indurain, Jalabert and Eric Breukkink could be blown out or riding away from everyone and no-one could tell from their faces or styles. It would be a great asset to acquire because it makes it much more difficult for other riders to devise their tactics. The advantage is that once you have established the reputation for being inscrutable, you can use it to bluff your way through. On occasions, I am certain Indurain won Tours by bluffing his way through stages, frightening off potential attackers purely by appearing so strong. All the top riders store away bits of information each season and look for signs of weakness in their rivals. It becomes a long-term psychological chess game.

10

CLIMBING AND HOW TO SURVIVE IT

Sooner or later, if you want to compete with the best on the road, you have to find a way of surviving in the mountains. And for those of us not blessed with the lungs and physique of an Indurain or Pantani, it is simply a matter of survival, nothing more, nothing less. Even Indurain really did no more than survive on big mountain stages; he used his team to tire out the opposition and just sat there, covering all the breaks. Indurain was too big and heavy to be a natural climber, like the Colombians Pantani or Virenque, but he relied on his enormous strength to see him through. Jan Ullrich, the 1997 Tour de France winner, has similar qualities. Most of the *peloton* find a way of climbing that suits them, on good days at least. On bad days the riders just grovel, to use their lingo.

Climbing presents a whole host of new problems. There is no chance of slipstreaming, for a start, because of the low speeds, so there's nowhere to hide. On the flat, someone can be producing 800 watts at a certain speed and the guy on his wheel will only be producing 400 watts to keep up. That is how much difference slipstreaming can make. On a hill, the difference between the front man in a group and the guy at the back might only be 50 watts.

Often, particularly in the Alps and the Pyrenees in high summer, heat stress becomes a factor, not just because the weather is hot, but because the body generates enormous heat itself, and the lack of airflow at relatively low speeds makes for poor dissipation. Even under those extreme conditions the mind has to stay focused and sharp to anticipate attacks by rival teams, or simply to keep the body working. If you aren't a natural, climbing can hurt horrifically. I don't know the physiological reasons for this, but, for me, one of the most frustrating mental aspects is the lack of control. I am on the receiving end, at the mercy of some little Spaniard or Italian who skips off up the road as if it were flat. All you can do then is try not to get dropped, or at least not to drop off too far.

It's frightening how fast your feelings can change through a climbing stage. From being in a world of real pain, where you know you have another three quarters of an hour to ride and, as team leader, there is no respite, no help and no excuse, you can suddenly get to the top of the mountain, start the descent and completely forget how bad you felt five minutes before. Until, of course, the next mountain hoves into view and very soon the memories come flooding back. On the occasional good days you can feel like a true bike rider. Mostly, though, climbing is just damn hard work.

The secret, if there is one, is to try to ride rhythmically, and I think that holds whether you are tackling the Col du Tourmalet or the foothills of the Grampians. Pantani, for example, has a regular rhythm to his climbing style; he rides in the saddle more than Virenque, but can bounce up and down on the pedals for astonishingly long periods. Virenque has an upright style all his own. He sometimes climbs whole sections without sitting down in the saddle, which would seem a very uneconomical way to ride, but it works for him.

Often the best climbers do not have the purest climbing styles. I was interested to read recently that Julio Jimenez, six times King of the Mountains on the Tour, was described by one of his rivals as having an ugly riding style: 'He didn't sit right and he never looked comfortable,' he commented. There is a picture of the Spaniard perching on his saddle, his hair thinning, his seat position seemingly too far back. He looks as though he has never sat on a bike in his life, yet this man won on the Galibier (twice), Mont Ventoux, Aubisque (twice) and the Tourmalet (three times). So style isn't everything!

There are also exceptions to the general rule that climbers, more than any other cycling specialists, are born not made. I have mentioned Indurain and Ullrich, but Eddy Merckx was the prime example of a rider who was not a pure climber, but was able, through sheer force of personality and power, to impose himself on mountain stages. Legend has it that on his first Tour, going up the Tourmalet, the young Merckx was seen fiddling with his gears. His rivals thought he must have problems with them, but the Belgian was just engaging the big ring before heading off to win the stage by eight minutes. He was not a defensive rider; like Indurain, Merckx wanted to dominate not just for the day but for the year, and the mountains were as good a place as any to do that.

One of the criticisms of Indurain's domination of the Tour de France was that the balance of power had swung away from the pure climbers, towards the specialist time trialler. This is not a point of view I share. Pantani's victory on the 1998 Tour shattered the prevailing theory that climbers could no longer win the Tour. Marco had finally worked out that, if he could do an Indurain in reverse – namely, make time on the mountains and survive in the time trials – he could fulfil his ambition of winning the yellow jersey.

Climbing still remains the most romantic skill in cycling. The press, particularly in France, Italy and Spain, love a *grimpeur*, and they love their climbers to be individuals, frequently temperamental, always dashing. Often they are as slow going down the mountain as they are going up, fear of descending being a consistent failing of climbers. Jimenez's advice to other climbers sums up their attitude: 'Never conform, and race as spectacularly as you can.'

Climbing is about the ratio of power to weight, and weight is one aspect of climbing worth addressing because it is something you can control. Jimenez weighed 56 kgs, Pantani between 60 and 62 kgs. For any cyclist, at whatever level, it is possible to look in the mirror and see what weight can be lost and where. If you can lose only a kilo, it probably isn't worth the effort, but if you can lose three or four, which many amateurs could do, then it's worth it. Buying the lightest bike on the market is one way to help, but it's a bit daft when you're still carrying an extra 4 kgs.

Time trialling is less influenced by weight because you don't accelerate your mass the whole time, but the natural rhythms of road racing, the acceleration and deceleration, become far harder when you are carrying extra weight. The trick, as we have already discussed, is to lose weight without losing power, and this is one area the amateur can tackle as easily as a professional. It's just up to the individual. Most people don't need to come down much below 6–8 per cent body fat. Most survivors of the Tour, by the last day, might be down to 4 per cent, which is right on the limit of good health. In midwinter, I might have 11 per cent body fat when the average is 10–16. My lowest percentage is only 6 or 7. You have to lose weight over a long period, because, in my case, my weight can fluctuate by as much as 2 kgs a day when I'm doing large workloads.

As soon as the road starts going up, the graph of power to weight changes. On flat terrain, body mass assists forward momentum and slipstreaming can reduce your effort by as much as 40 per cent. On climbs, the extra weight not only has to be carried up, it also drags you back, so the heavier rider has to use extra power to compensate. Eventually, there comes a point when the power runs out, while the lighter rider has less power but is more effective because he has less to carry. Imagine putting a couple of bags of sugar in your saddlebags and riding up the twenty-one hairpin bends of Alpe d'Huez and you will get some idea of what it's like for heavier riders to climb. In *Cycle Sport* (October 1998), Lucien Van Impe, another great mountain rider, was once asked how he recognized a genuine climber. The Belgian replied, 'He is someone who regulates his pace while climbing without ever suffering from a lack of oxygen. Therefore, you've got to split your energy in the best way, to recover just in time, to change fluently into a bigger or smaller gear. You don't climb with the legs alone, but with the lungs, too. You've got to use special breathing techniques that are difficult to explain but can be taught.'

I'd like to know what those breathing techniques are. My own research led me to experiment with my riding position and emerge from some serious trials looking like a real bike rider climbing a real mountain, not just a converted time triallist flogging up the odd steep gradient. Over a winter spent on the treadmill at the Bebington Oval leisure centre on the Wirral, I negotiated a radical shift in my riding position. Peter Keen and I had looked at the whole problem of climbing and saw common traits in the riding positions of the best climbers and the cadence they would climb at – typically around 78 rpm. Their saddles were much further back, their trunks more stretched out and they would sit right back on their bikes. The technique is to use your legs as levers and your arms almost as anchor points, rather than hunching over the handlebars and pressing down on them. It seemed a logical area to explore, mostly for the long stage races with several big climbs, but it wasn't exactly a conventional move to be changing position so drastically in mid-career. I was pleased to learn that Eddy Merckx was a compulsive seat-shifter, always tinkering with his saddle and handlebar heights, even in mid-race. Most of the *peloton* have developed their own style and way of riding over many years and won't countenance any change at all.

We went into the performance laboratory at Eastbourne, where Peter was working, and adapted a special treadmill for use with a bike. By running a max test, ramping up the gradient by half a degree every fifteen seconds until I cracked, I found I could produce nearly 40 watts more power from a more elongated position. We filmed the work from side-on and then played about with different positions, tweaking the length here and there, adjusting the stem and the handlebars until we found a position that was really comfortable and productive. It was actually miles away from where we had started the session, but it was still quite a radical change for me. I was 9 cms behind the bottom bracket, 4 cms further than the position I'd been using for most of my career. I also used a slightly longer stem. Overall, I was stretched out by about 8 cms, if not more. The saddle height had to be lowered almost a centimetre to compensate for the additional length.

When I turned pro I had a 54-cm top tube and a 54-cm seat tube. Even now I still have a 54-cm seat tube, but the top tube is 59 cm, which surprises a lot of people. It looked OK, about right for a guy climbing a mountain in the Tour de France. I went out and used it, and stuck with it for a time. In the end the position was probably a little too extreme, particularly to be made in one leap. I have arrived at a compromise set of measurements now, between my old position and the extreme 'climbing' one.

Working on the treadmill also provided me with a good workout. On a treadmill I was able to control the gradient, speed and amount of time spent climbing. It was a novelty mentally, and it meant I could devote a lot of time to climbing without having to pound up some Welsh hills. I devised a couple of training programmes for the machine and went hunting for a similar long-wheelbase treadmill – PowerJog, the only one long enough to fit a bike – to use closer to home.

Peter Keen and I developed a series of different sessions: short, high-intensity climbing for the classics; longer, steadier climbs for the major tours. When the PowerJog at the local sports centre broke, I seriously considered buying another one for myself, but it would have cost £7,000. The great thing about the treadmill was that I could do an outing on the road, of equal length to a long Tour stage, finish it at the sports centre and simulate a Tour-type climb. I learned to climb in the saddle as opposed to climbing out of the saddle, which is very tiring. I became more efficient, pushing more power from the saddle than from jumping on the pedals. How useful it was in the long run is hard to assess, but it provided me with some good aerobic work and kept me interested, which, at that stage, was almost as vital. Robert Millar, a former King of the Mountains winner on the Tour, says that the only way to improve your climbing ability is to ride up hills. He is probably right, but that can be soul-destroying.

What marks climbers out from non-climbers in the end is the ability to recover, not just on a stage, but from day to day. A number of riders can hold their own in the mountains for a day, but they cannot recover mentally or physically in time to do the same again the next day or, on the Tour de France at least, the day after that. The abrasive effect is cumulative. If your body isn't performing to the limit, if you aren't in good shape, the mountains will expose your weaknesses ruthlessly. That has been the case for me over the past two Tours – 1997 and 1998 – when I have suffered from a loss of power. If I'm not on perfect form, I can't blag it through the mountains.

Climbing Tactics

I can hardly pretend to be a great expert on climbing matters. I have described earlier how agonizing a mountain stage can be, but I quickly learned to ride at my own pace and not be dictated to by others. Sometimes a break comes and you have to go with it, you have no choice. If you are in the leader's jersey and your team have worked their backsides off to get you into a decent position, sometimes honour requires that you give your all there and then. But in general, the shrewdest climbers are the ones who judge pace the best. Indurain was uncannily accurate in gauging the strength of the riders around him and in choosing the right moment to attack, often on the last climb of a long day.

One of the hardest disciplines for me to learn was when to let go. Usually, at the bottom of a long ascent, the climbers will leap off the front and attack up the first section, hoping to explode the leading group and do as much damage as possible over the length of the climb. The rest have to decide whether the early attacks are worth resisting. Often it is worth going over threshold to hang on because it might make life easier later on, but there is no hard and fast rule; it is a matter of feel. The mistake that even the most experienced riders make is to go over threshold for too long, too early, so that much of the remaining climb has to be spent recovering well below threshold. When that happens, it's just a case of finding your own pace and limiting your losses. In 1996 particularly, when I was climbing quite effectively, I would deliberately set my own pace and watch a whole bunch of climbers disappear into the distance, knowing that I would reel most of them in before the top.

Climbers are not, on the whole, the best descenders, so once over the top of the climb it is possible to make up some time on the descent before the next climb. It takes a lot of self-discipline for a competitive person to let others ride away from him; the instinct is always to follow. But five minutes over threshold and you can lose everything, so you almost have to block out the others and concentrate deeply on your own performance.

I remember speaking to Robert Millar and asking him how

important it was to reconnoitre a particular climb. He said he thought it helped to know where the flat bits were so that, if you were struggling, you at least knew there was a chance of a brief rest just around the corner. Whenever possible I have tried to follow his advice.

CB's Tips:

- Try to maintain a constant pace and rhythm when climbing. It is like running in that you can relax a little more if the breathing patterns and rhythm of cadence are good.
- Take the outside line round hairpins because, although longer, the incline is usually shallower.
- Ride mostly at your own pace unless the tactics of the race dictate otherwise.
- Try to start a long climb near the front of the bunch, particularly if you are not a pure climber, because then it will take longer for you to fall back through the field. Every little bit helps.
- The best way to improve your climbing is to ride up hills, as the man Millar said.

11

THE LOTUS POSITION, AERODYNAMICS AND OTHER EQUIPMENT

Equipment

This is a subject close to the heart of most young riders: looking at all the latest gear and seeing which new gadget might make you go faster. I used to love the creativity of putting together a new machine and trying to find ways of making it better. I still like nothing better than to disappear into my workshop and mess about with my bikes. The most important thing a bike must provide is an efficient, comfortable working position. So the priority when setting up your riding position is to work out what you are looking for and what it is you are trying to achieve.

Particularly with a bike used for time trialling, the compromise – and that is an important word – has to be between aerodynamics and mechanical efficiency. My own approach has always been to start with the most aerodynamic position the regulations allow, then work backwards to the point where I can actually sustain that stance for about an hour and feel as though I'm working efficiently. Since turning professional with road bikes, I have looked for a position that allows me to climb in the saddle for long periods without backache, to feel well balanced when cornering and efficient when I need to accelerate in the saddle in a small gear to exploit virtually non-existent gaps in the last 10 kms of a race. The different requirements of a road-bike position are easier to reconcile. My own road-bike position was sadly neglected until I turned professional, and people started to ask questions about it: Why do you have such a short reach? And why do you have your handlebars so low? I realized not only that I had no ready answer – unusual for me – but that my road position wasn't particularly comfortable.

I spent the winter of 1995 reviewing my position on a specially adapted treadmill, in conjunction with Peter Keen. The full account of the work we did is in the chapter 'Climbing and How to Survive It' because the changes were all designed to make me a better climber. But by the time we'd finished playing around with different positions and filming them from side on, I had lengthened my riding position and lowered my saddle.

The Mean Machine, Barcelona, 1992

I arrived in Barcelona for the 1992 Olympics with a sleak black Lotus bike that quickly captured the imagination of the press – almost more than its rider did. It was Jens Lehmann, the German I beat in the Olympic final, who had to remind the press that the man won the gold, not the bike. But somehow the combination of the cabinetmaker from Hoylake and Mike Burrows, the unknown British inventor from Norfolk who had designed the Lotus superbike, proved an irresistible story. There was a touch of the glorious amateur about the triumph for both of us.

I first came into contact with Mike in the winter before the Olympics. My fragile morale had been shattered by the World Championships in 1991 when Jens Lehmann suddenly went nine seconds quicker than anyone else in the pursuit. I had trained specifically for that event and was just beginning to believe that being a world champion was not out of my reach. In the qualifying round I did four minutes thirty-one seconds, a five-second improvement on the time I'd set in Japan the previous year. Then, out of nowhere, Lehmann produced a ride of four minutes twenty-two seconds. Nine seconds? I thought then, Well, that's it really, I'll never be able to match that. It was time to jump off the balcony. I'd clawed my way to where I'd thought the goalposts were only to find that someone had moved them into the next parish. At the time I questioned the legality of the ride, which I'd felt guilty about later, both when I got to know Jens, who is a very pleasant guy, and when I won the gold the following year.

At the time I felt like giving up, but instead I went back to basics. At the end of a year, if something has gone wrong or someone else has produced an outstanding performance, I'll pull my own year apart and see where and why I went wrong. The temptation is to sweep it aside and simply say, 'I'll do better next year', without knowing what went wrong the previous year and how to put it right. The German team had been using a one-piece moulded frame made out of carbon fibre for the previous couple of years. It was a really smart piece of kit and I had already admired it from afar. So when Mike Burrows rang up to ask if I would like to test his revolutionary new machine in the wind tunnel, he caught me just at the right time. The idea appealed to my sense of curiosity, too. I have always been ready to experiment in a way that many continental riders find strange and unnecessary. Many of them work on the time-honoured principle of if it ain't broke, don't fix it.

Lotus wanted to get their bike to the Olympics, and the only way they were going to do that was to get a rider on it. They claimed that it could make as much as a twenty- to thirty-second difference against another bike, which was ridiculous, but they wanted me to test the claim. I thought, Why not? Even if it made only a second or two's difference it would be worth the effort. A couple of seconds in a 4,000-metre pursuit is a comfortable lead. We went into the wind tunnel at the Motor Institute Research Association (MIRA) just outside Birmingham and, though it was the equivalent of measuring peas on a bathroom scale, I learned a lot about aerodynamics and how a different riding position can ease wind resistance and therefore increase speed.

The pursuit is short and intense, and any advantage that can be gained from machinery or aerodynamics is worth having; it's as precious as half a second in Grand Prix racing.

The tests involved me sitting on the bike in a stream of ice-cold air wearing nothing more substantial than a lycra racing suit. The initial results were disappointing until they discovered that if I folded up my body position and tucked in my elbows the drag would be considerably reduced. My rounded back, which is a bit strange in everyday life, was a real aerodynamic advantage when it came to riding a bike. What I liked about Lotus was that they came without any preconceived ideas. The problem was the air resistance stopping me from going forward, especially on a flat surface like the track. They were used to making cars and they saw **a** problem, not one specific to cycling. There were no constraints.

The Lotus bike was very radical and sexy; it was black, with yellow logos and a little Union Jack on the stem below the saddle. The wheels were only supported by a monoblade – a single-bladed fork on one side front and back – which made it look very disconcerting; the carbon frame was just one smooth piece. It would just about get through one four-and-a-half-minute pursuit round. Once, while training in France, the nut virtually came off the front wheel. Luckily it didn't feel quite right, so I stopped to have a look and spotted the loose wheel nut.

It was really pioneering stuff, and I knew it was the best bike available, which was important psychologically. When I reached the startline for the Olympic final, I knew I wasn't going to lose because of lack of preparation, and that was a very comforting thought. My bike was at least as good, if not better, than Jens's. We tried to keep it hidden as much as possible in Barcelona, but word soon got out that I was going quick on this strange machine. It must have been quite a shock, particularly to the Germans, who had dominated the event until then.

There were other carbon monocoque frames at the games, but, although excellent aerodynamically, they were more conventional looking and had a standard diamond-shaped frame. There are good energy transmission qualities in carbon, which means the material stores power as opposed to absorbing it. I could really notice the difference between the tubular steel bike I used for the team pursuit and the Lotus I used for the individual event. Imagine a bow and arrow made of copper and a bow and arrow made of really good ash. That was the difference between the two.

I became very attached to the Lotus, emotionally and psychologically, because my best rides were done on it. They produced a road-going version that was very aerodynamic but a little impractical. There was, for example, nowhere to put the water bottle. I set the fastest time ever for a Tour de France stage in the prologue at Lille in 1994 using a Lotus frame, but the problem was that by the end of the season we had broken about twelve frames. They were neither robust nor reliable. Lotus were having problems with their car manufacturing business and their interest was deflected from the development of a road-going Lotus bike. In my opinion, they should have made the superbike an advertisement for their engineering skills and produced a proper road-going bike. They estimated that the publicity from the Olympics was worth about £100 million and, in a sense, for all sorts of different reasons they wasted the chance to cash in. The basic principles of the Lotus bike have been carried through to my time-trial bike today.

Riding Positions and the Importance of Aerodynamics

My work at MIRA showed how important aerodynamics could be to a cyclist. Think how critical drag is to a Formula One car, then think how much it would mean to someone who is producing his own power. Riders even shave their legs to reduce wind resistance! Much of the development work I have done since, on bikes, racing jerseys, cycle shorts and all manner of equipment, has stemmed from the critical need to reduce drag. On a long stage event like the Tour de France, aerodynamic forces are relatively unimportant, though learning how to slipstream and protect yourself from a crosswind are subtle skills. In short time trials and on the indoor track for an event like the world hour record, every tenth of a second counts.

The rider himself constitutes about 80 per cent of the drag in the rider/bike aerodynamic package, and what I learned in the wind tunnel was how to reduce my frontal area. No-one has got a position as extreme as mine for a time trial bike. I have my handlebars about 4 or 5 cms lower than anybody else, which is something I developed with Lotus but which also seems to suit my own physiology. That reduced my frontal area, and the total drag, considerably. It is a matter of compromise – a word that will keep cropping up in this book – because in the quest for aerodynamic efficiency there will come a time when the cramped riding position will impair your mechanical efficiency beyond the aerodynamic payback.

From an aerodynamic point of view, Miguel Indurain had one of the worst riding positions in the world. He was a big guy anyway, but he rode quite upright, with his arms wide apart – a sure way to create maximum drag. He would have had to produce somewhere in the region of 20 per cent more power than me at around 50 kph to go the same speed. For his attempt on the world hour record, his team tried to get him to ride in a more aerodynamic position, but the conflict between his natural position and the new one cost him too much, so they simply accepted the fact that he couldn't conform and concentrated on his power and comfort. Indurain had such a big engine and such power that he was able to compensate for the lost time. I can't afford to be so free with the seconds, and nor can the average club cyclist. It helps that I can maintain a high level of efficiency in quite a tucked position. I have a curved back – which in this particular instance is very useful – long arms and short legs. The frontal area of your legs cannot change, but your torso can flatten out and even tilt down slightly.

Interestingly, in the winter of 1997, Ivan Gotti and Marco Pantani turned to the wind tunnel to improve their time-trialling technique. They are both good climbers because of their high power-to-weight ratio, but on the flat they are short of power. If they built up more power they might risk losing their natural climbing ability. In the tunnel, Gotti learned that the position of the handlebars was more important than his seat position. In an article in *Cycle Sport*, his bike designer, Chris Peck, said, 'Compared to last year, we've lowered the height of the handlebars and reduced the width of his arms a little. He's more tucked in now, like Chris Boardman . . . we tried to go as low as possible but found that at a certain point, the drag actually increased. We also discovered that a horizontal or slightly tilted-down position is much better than having the arms in front of the face, as LeMond did when he first started using tri-bars.' Gotti rode a time trial at the Giro in 1997 without a helmet and with his skinsuit open, but I doubt he will do that again after a couple of days in the wind tunnel. He also learned to ride with his head at a certain angle, making maximum use of the aerodynamic shape of his helmet, and rode with padding on his back to ease the flow of air across his head and back. Pantani realized that he could start winning the major tours if he could survive in the time trials. At the 1998 Tour de France, his ride on the final time trial, when he lost only three minutes to Ullrich in second place, clinched his first victory in the Tour.

CB's Tips:

- **Do not try to switch to an extreme tri-bar position too quickly. Do it gradually, because the position will seem cramped and unnatural at first. Changing too quickly could lead to injury and will not necessarily improve your performance if your muscles aren't given sufficient time to adapt to a new riding position.**
- **Comfort is the key. Find a riding position that is efficient, and slowly adapt it to become more aerodynamic.**
- **Ensure that your handlebars are neither too wide nor too narrow. The width between elbow pads on triathlon bars should be between 16 and 18 cms ideally. Too narrow and it will constrict your breathing, too wide and your bike handling will suffer.**

The Road Bike – the Workhorse

At any one time I will have four different types of bike on the road, either hanging in my workshop or out with the team. And that isn't including the spare bikes. There is my time-trial bike, my road bike, a prologue bike and at least one track bike.

The road bike is the workhorse of the team as it has to take a lot of abuse. Durability is as big a factor as speed with the road bike and nothing should be sacrificed for that little extra speed. There are, however, ways of saving weight, because even shedding a few ounces can have a significant effect during a race as long and arduous as the Tour de France, if you think how many times during the twenty-two days you will have to accelerate and decelerate. In essence, my bike is the same as the one you would buy and, though new materials have become available over the past decade, the shape is still pretty traditional.

The heart of any bike is the frame. It is the central component, mechanically and in terms of transforming your power into forward motion. The bike needs to be as light as possible, made of titanium, aluminium or carbon fibre, but above all it needs to be stiff and responsive. It should act a little like a bow, storing power as opposed to absorbing it. Carbon fibre is a relatively new material in the cycling world but it's ideal because it's incredibly stiff yet very light. A kilo and a half less weight at an average of 440 watts – the top rider's standard anaerobic threshold – could give a forty-five-second advantage up a long climb like the Tourmalet, and that's worth having. All my steel nuts, bolts and axles are replaced with either aluminium or titanium equivalents.

Strangely, perhaps, my time-trial bike is heavier than my road bike. But the shape, rather than the weight, is most important in a time-trial bike because, on the whole, there's not the same differentiation in speed. The road bike is always a product of compromise: it has to go up a mountain, but it also has to come down. New materials make that compromise easier. Carbon fibre is as strong as steel when used correctly, but it's much lighter, and titanium is almost twice as strong. For the club rider the main compromise will be with the bank. The downside of carbon fibre – and there usually is one with any material – is that it's difficult to repair safely. After a crash, you might need a new frame, which means more expense. If I had to buy a frame now, I would opt for the new breed of aluminium 'tig-welded' designs, combined with a pair of carbon forks. This option is stiff, light and cheaper than standard carbon-fibre frames.

Mountain Time Trial, St Etienne, 1997

Stage twelve was one I had targeted from the start of the 1997 Tour de France. It is a mountain time trial of 55 kms, smack in the middle of my range, with a sharp climb over the Col de la Croix de Chaubouret – 10 kms at a gradient of 6–10 per cent – midway. I had adapted my time-trial bike for the mountain stages, but had suffered a back injury on the first descent in the Pyrenees and couldn't get low enough in the saddle, so in the end I just used my ordinary road bike with some extras. However, I learned something new that day. A number of riders, including Richard Virenque, Jan Ullrich, Bjarne Riis and most of the top guys, switched bikes after the Col de la Croix, *but* they didn't change at the very top of the climb, they changed just before, which, if you think about it, is extremely smart. Instead of having to decelerate from, say, 45 kph and then accelerate back up to that speed, they only had to do so from about 15 kph. By lessening the time spent decelerating and accelerating they saved about fifteen seconds. I had estimated that the change of bike would cost me about thirty seconds and had therefore decided to stay on the same bike. Had I known the other riders' plan I probably would have switched bikes, too.

The Track/Pursuit Bike

This is the most extreme bike of the lot. The mass-start track bike is, fundamentally, a road bike without brakes and with only one gear. The pursuit bike is all about aerodynamics; the weight is of little consequence because you are only accelerating your own mass for the first fifteen seconds, then weight, to an extent, is working in your favour. It is a time-trial bike without gears, stripped down to the minimum. The riding position is lower and more stretched out because the event is only four and a half minutes long. My second world hour record was achieved on my pursuit bike, but we had slightly different tri-bars and I swivelled my arms round so that my elbows supported my weight instead of my shoulders.

The seasoned pro, all kitted out at a winter training camp with the Crédit Agricole team in Pau, 1998.
I am riding a mountain bike, which is a good way to develop endurance during the off season,
and adds a touch of variety to the training routine. © *Graham Watson*

We all have to start somewhere!
With my sister, Lisa, aged four. Note the stabilizers.

A boy scout, aged nine. 'Be Prepared' is a motto I have followed throughout my career, though I was never much good at tying knots or getting stones out of horses' hooves.

Aged fourteen, riding my first race: a Southport Schools 10-mile time trial in 1983. That day I began to discover the enormous pleasure of winning. Winning, and not just riding a bike, has always been my greatest source of enjoyment and motivation.

At the South Western Invitation 50-km trial in winter, 1990.

Riding for the Manchester Wheelers junior team on a frame inherited from Dave Lloyd, a former national champion. I had a compact crouched riding position even back then.

At the Motor Institute Research station in the Midlands, testing the aerodynamic efficiency of my bike and riding position before the 1992 Olympics. This was the forerunner of the 'Superman' position – arms outstretched, elbows tucked in – used to break the world hour record in Manchester in 1996.

The Olympic 4-km pursuit final in Barcelona in 1992. Four minutes and ten seconds that changed my life.
© Graham Watson

Olympic champion. The first British cycling gold medallist for seventy-two years.
© Graham Watson

The hour record – the ultimate time trial. It appealed to my logical nature and was ideal for my physiology. © Phil O'Connor

The 1993 attempt was successful, despite organizational problems and an unaerodynamic bike. It stimulated a lot of interest from the media, who were already in town for the Tour de France stage. Peter Woodworth, my manager, is standing behind me.
© Phil O'Connor

Manchester, 1996, was almost perfect in terms of preparation and execution. Riding in the later outlawed 'Superman' position, I raised the existing record by over 1km to 56.375. © Phil O'Connor

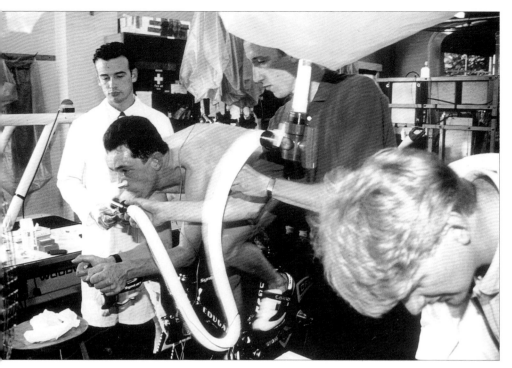

Doing a VO2 Max test to measure the efficiency of oxygen use, with my coach of fourteen years, Peter Keen, in the foreground. © Phil O'Connor

With Peter Keen just before the 1996 hour record attempt at the Manchester Velodrome. © Phil O'Connor

Teatime on the Tour: jam sticks and cake. The *musette,* or feedbag, is an important source of instant calories and mental succour. © Phil O'Connor

Wearing yellow at the end of my first day on
the Tour de France, Lille, 1994.
© Phil O'Connor

In Greg LeMond, the three-times Tour
champion, I found a fellow traveller, equally
inquisitive and unconventional. Here, we
reconnoitre the prologue stage in Lille before the
start of my first, and sadly his last, Tour.
© Phil O'Connor

Winning my second Tour prologue
in Rouen, 1997. © Phil O'Connor

Lying unconscious on the road between Cork
and Enniscorthy after crashing out of the race on
the second stage of the 1998 Tour. It was my
second big crash after St Brieuc in 1995.
I still don't know to this day what happened.
© Associated Press

Hard as I tried, I could never quite find the key to climbing consistently. I lost a lot of time on this stage to Les Arcs on the 1996 Tour. It was the same day that saw the end of the five-year domination of the great Spanish rider Miguel Indurain, pictured here, third from the right.

© Phil O'Connor

Indurain was psychologically impenetrable. Like most great cycling champions, you could never tell how much he was suffering. © Phil O'Connor

Two natural climbers, Richard Virenque (*left*) and Marco Pantani. Virenque has a very upright style of climbing, while Pantani, though here out of the saddle in an attempt to break Virenque, has a more classical climbing rhythm. © Graham Watson

Laurent Jalabert, the best French rider of his generation, has used his explosive power and determination to become the world number one. But his inability to climb consistently has cost him the Tour. Here he tests the resolve of the future Tour champion, Lance Armstrong, on the 1996 Paris–Nice spring classic. © Graham Watson

With two Spaniards, Abraham Olano, silver medallist (*left*), and the Olympic time-trial champion, Miguel Indurain (*centre*), after winning bronze at the 1996 Olympics. In Atlanta I suffered in the humidity, and having led for the first half of the race had to ease up in order not to pass out. I will be better prepared for Sydney 2000. © Phil O'Connor

Into the twilight. With my Crédit Agricole team at the start of another season.
© Phil O'Connor

I still had to take a rest from that position for a few minutes. My first world hour record was achieved on the least-aerodynamic bike ever made. Even though the tubes were teardrop shaped, they weren't the right dimensions. The length of a tube should be three and a half times the width to be aerodynamically efficient. If a tube is too round, instead of flowing round the tube, the air bounces off it and creates mini vortexes that actually increase the amount of drag. On the other hand, the bike was made of carbon and felt great to ride.

Gears

Like almost every other piece of equipment on a bike, gear mechanisms have improved considerably over the past decade. When I began racing I used the friction change. You just pulled on the levers on the down tube of the frame, waited until it changed onto the next sprocket and then centred it yourself, all of which was very time-consuming. Now gears are incorporated into the brake system and the pick-up for the chain is perfect, so you can be out of the saddle under full load and the change will be instant. Apart from the immediacy of the change, which helps maintain a cyclist's rhythm, the system allows you to brake and change gear at the same time, and to change gear when cornering. The sprockets are now manufactured in cassette form rather than individually. Most manufacturers of decent road bikes would have 53- and 39-tooth chainrings at the front and a 12–21 nine-speed cassette at the rear, though there is a move in the *peloton* towards ten-speed. Occasionally you might use an 11–23 sprocket on the major tours. Most of the year I ride 39–53 and 12–21 Shimano gears.

I use electronic gears only on my time-trial bike. They operate from two little switches on the handlebars, which are battery-operated and send a signal to the rear derailleur, which changes automatically. They have been around in the *peloton* for a few years now and Mavic, the manufacturers, keep saying they will revamp them. But many riders found the system too inconsistent and went back to the old mechanical one. Alex Zulle was once leading the Tour of Spain when his gears stuck. He changed bike and the same thing happened again. So the team just said, 'Right, that's enough, we won't use them.' I think that was the wrong decision. With the electronic system the most important thing is the set-up. The mechanics need to spend time making sure all the wires are properly soldered and that the mechanism is waterproof. Gan provided me with a set of electronic gears in the first race I rode for them in 1993.

With an electronic system, you can change gear a lot more often, perhaps 25 per cent more. With ordinary gears the temptation is to stay in too big a gear simply because changing would be disruptive. The electronic system is a little delicate for a road bike, but in four or five years of using them I've experienced only about three problems, which I think is acceptable.

CB's Tips:

- Maintain your transmission properly by cleaning the chain, sprockets or cassettes regularly. They will work better and last a lot longer.
- Resist the temptation to pedal in a big gear. The most efficient cadence on the flat is about 100 rpm and you should try for 80 rpm when climbing. You will have to train for this. Under pressure you will have the urge to use too big a gear. Resist it.

Wheels

The frame is the most important component of a bike, then the wheels and the tyres. After that comes the rest of the equipment. Wheels' general design has changed little over the last twenty years, but reliability and ease of maintenance have improved. In my opinion it is now possible to purchase one pair of wheels that are more than adequate for both road-racing and time-trialling. The wheels on my time-trial bike are standard size.

Before we did the second world hour record at Manchester we did a series of tests using power-measuring cranks. It's not a very attractive-looking piece of kit, but the strain gauge built into the cranks and a little box on the handlebars like a small computer give accurate readings of power and speed, among other information. The engineering involved is about ten years ahead of its time and measures power very precisely. We went to the Manchester Velodrome which, being indoors, is a controlled environment, and rode with different types of equipment at given speeds to monitor the power difference. At the time, Mavic disc and five-spoke track wheels turned out to be the best around. Theoretically the whole disc at the front should be better, but we found that the five-spoke was better than the disc because the surface area was smaller and it was aerodynamically more efficient.

The advantage of having a disc wheel at the back is purely an aerodynamic one, as there is less drag through the spokes. As the spokes come forward at the top of the wheel they are doing twice your forward speed, which can create an awful lot of drag. One spoke going through the air won't make much difference, but with thousands of them going round every minute the resistance increases just as the frame or the position of the rider does. A lenticular disc tries to re-form the air behind so the drag is minimized. The spokes on the hour-record bike, time-trial bike and track bike are elliptical section. The standard number of spokes for a road-race bike would be thirty-two on front and back, but I have twenty-eight in the rear and twenty-six in front.

Tyres

Tyre manufacturers make all sorts of claims. It's like ads for washing powders: each one is whiter and brighter than the last. In essence, there is a road tyre with some kind of tread pattern on it and a time-trial-type tyre which usually has a matt tread, but is thinner, lighter and generally narrower. The track tyre is made of such thin rubber that it looks as though it has been painted on.

The club racer will have two basic choices of tyre: high pressure or tubulars. Professional teams use both types. High-pressure tyres have a separate casing and inner tube and tubular ones have an integral casing and inner tube. Sizes vary: 19, 20, 23 and 25 mm are the basic choices. Thinner tyres are lighter and less flexible and are generally pumped up harder. A road-bike tyre will be pumped to a pressure of about 120–30 lbs per square inch, while, for a short time trial, it might be as high as 190 lbs per square inch. You will brake far less on a time-trial bike, so are less likely to lock up the wheels. There are, however, exceptions.

I use 'tubs' for racing, as they are more responsive than the normal tyre and tend to be more resistant to impact punctures. In a road tyre the qualities are low rolling resistance, lightness, good grip in the wet and reliability. In my amateur days, in an attempt to make the best of my performance, I often used tyres that were too light and ended up puncturing them. As a professional I have learned the lessons of poor tyre choice.

For the prologue at St Brieuc in 1995 I decided to change to heavier tyres as the rain set in. Unfortunately that was easier said than done. With nine riders all going off at different times it is impossible to have race and wet tyres, along with spares, for every-one, so some wheels are used twice. As a result, I went out with an ordinary road tyre on the front and a slick time-trial tyre on the back. I was also one of the few riders that night to use my time-trial bike. Most of the others – Indurain, for example – just used their road bikes, which proved a sensible decision. At a fast left-hand bend at the bottom of the Boulevard de la Mer, one of the fastest sections of the course, visibility wasn't great, so it was difficult to see which was clean road surface and which was not. This section is also smooth tarmac, baked under the sun. My front wheel gripped the surface, but my back wheel slid out and I careered into the barrier on the outside of the bend. Roger came within inches of running me over with the service car, so I can count myself lucky to have emerged with nothing worse than a badly shattered ankle and wrist. At the end of the day I was going too fast, but looking back on it, my tyres should have had matched tread. I now err on the side of caution where tyres are concerned. I often use road tyres that are thicker, heavier and have deeper tread, especially if there's a possibility of rain.

Helmets

Aerodynamic helmets provide little or no protection; they are purely to ease wind flow. In Barcelona, my spiky black helmet tended to trap air underneath it, so it had to fit perfectly. In Atlanta in 1996, in the time trial, I threw away my helmet after one lap because it was 80 degrees and I was about to faint in the humidity. A lot of professional road racers refuse to wear helmets because of the weight and increased heat. When they were forced to wear them one year by the UCI, the world governing body of cycling, the riders went on strike and the authorities were forced to back down, but whatever they say, vanity is the only reason not to wear a helmet. They weigh virtually nothing, the air flow is good because the vents are huge and they are about 90 per cent effective at protecting against impact injuries.

It has not been proved, but had Fabio Casartelli – the young Italian Motorola rider who died from head injuries in the Pyrenees on the 1995 Tour – been wearing a helmet, he might well have survived. Most of the sprinters now wear them, which makes sense; climbers, who are going more slowly, tend not to.

I wear a helmet virtually all the time now, and I would advise all club riders to do the same. Only in extreme cases – on mountain stages in 35-degree heat – have I ridden without one. Physiologists will say a helmet makes no difference to heat retention, but the perception of comfort is different on a grovel halfway up a mountain in a furnace. If the UCI made helmets compulsory I would have no objection.

Sunglasses

Strangely enough, I tend to wear sunglasses more in the rain because your eyes need protection from the spray and grit flying off the road. They are less gimmicky than you might think. On the track, riding in an extreme position, I wore specially adapted tilted glasses made by Oakley. My eyes were totally bloodshot after the first world hour record because of the concrete dust in the stadium. But, to be honest, I'm not a great fan of sunglasses. A lot of riders wear them for psychological reasons, I think, to help mask their facial expressions and make them look as if they're not suffering as much as they are. Indurain always looked deadpan anyway, but the effect was emphasized by his sunglasses.

Shoes

Shoes are more important than many riders think now that the clipless pedal, which is like a ski-boot binding, has been developed. At first the shoes weren't really strong enough to take the sort of force put on them. There was a lot of stretching on the top of the shoe, which was held down by a strap. With Kevlar straps, shoes are a really firm fit, but aren't too tight, so you won't lose any power through stretching. The soles are often made of injection-moulded carbon, which is extremely stiff, and they are moulded to the shape of your foot when riding rather than walking. They have to be light and aerated. They should click out easily with a turn of the foot and, in a crash, release the foot automatically. I use about six pairs of shoes every season. On the Tour de France, though, I have a spare pair in case the originals get wet or damaged in a crash. I've always stuck with Adidas, which makes life easier. They know what I want, my shoe size and the set-up of the plate. Changing brands can be risky and difficult because the plate will be in a different place. I also wear overshoes, which is purely to aid aerodynamics by covering up the rough edges.

Shorts

Along with shoes, shorts are the most important piece of non-bike gear, because saddle sores are a recurring problem for professional cyclists. Left untreated, they can end a career. Comfortable shorts, even if they cost a little extra, are worth the price. You need a pair that are well shaped when you are sitting in the saddle with your legs bent, not when you are standing in the shop. Most have an artificial chamois inside the shorts to ease rubbing and prevent creasing. I use tailor-made skin suits for time trials and the track because even the smallest crease can increase drag.

For early-season training and racing the motto is, 'Better too hot than too cold.' There is still a school of thought in pro cycling that says, I don't feel I can race without shorts on, even when it's three degrees and snowing. You should start with leg warmers, knee warmers and arm warmers, and discard them when the body starts warming up. For training rather than racing, there are now fleecy jackets, which are generally quite close-fitting, and sleeveless vests and breathable GORE-TEX capes. Clothing has developed a great deal for cyclists in the last decade, and not all of it is to make you look the part. It's worth investing in the right clothing to enable you to train in extreme conditions.

For an early-season race like Paris–Nice, which doesn't always live up to its billing as the 'Race to the Sun', my kit inventory would be something like this: shorts, overknee shorts, leg warmers, knee warmers, a few different types of undervest made of a light thermal material, fleece-lined arm warmers, two different road vests – one thick, the other ventilated – helmet or, if extremely hot, cloth cap, gloves, GORE-TEX cape, clear plastic cape for showers, neoprene gloves for rain, track mitts and loads of pairs of socks.

The First Bike

I would start a young child off on a BMX. Edward, my eldest son, had his first go on the track when he was eight, at a kids' session at the Manchester Velodrome. There were all different sizes of bike, and he had a miniature track bike, a tiny thing with 24-inch wheels, which he rode round a few laps at the bottom of the track. He thought it was great and now he wants one just like it, but he would never use it.

It's sad in one way, because he will probably never have the pleasure of building his own bike, finding bits from all over the place and learning how it's put together.

12

DIET AND INJURY

Diet is an integral part of any training programme. It's the fuel for the engine, if you like, and, like fuel, it can be supplied in different forms. Your stores of fat provide diesel – long-range endurance energy – and glycogen is the petrol – used more quickly but a much more efficient source of short-term energy. Endurance training is designed to make your body more efficient at using fat. Short-term explosive training – the race-winning stuff – comes from your reserves of glycogen.

It is only relatively recently that athletes have paid proper attention to what foods they should eat, when and why. The problem is that no-one has yet isolated exactly what effect diet and nutrition have on an athlete's overall performance. Research is still going on. Footballers have only recently begun to accept that pasta is a more digestible and efficient pre-match meal than red meat. Yet Bill Shankly's religious devotion to the nutritional powers of steak and chips before a game didn't seem to have an adverse effect on the performance of his Liverpool team. But then, very few other teams had the benefit of specialist nutritional advice.

Society has become more conscious of what we eat and why. There is no magic formula for athletes; a balanced diet is part of the whole training programme and has to be adapted according to the loading of that programme. The more exercise you take, the more calories you use up and the more you need to replace. It's both as simple and complex as that. The proportions of what you eat, the percentage of protein, fat and carbohydrate in your daily diet, will need to change depending on the intensity of your training schedule.

Matching workload and calorie intake over a twenty-four-hour period is impossible. It has to be done over a much longer time, say a week or a fortnight. If you have a rest day, for example, you might need 2,400 calories; on a full training day it might double. If you matched the intake to the output you would be bloated one day and starving the next, which isn't a particularly healthy way to live. As we saw in the section on weight loss, having a daily calorie deficit of more than 500 calories is not recommended. A deficit of 1,000 calories a day is the absolute maximum. A deficit of 500 calories a day will mean the loss of roughly a pound of body fat over a week, so the process is quite subtle, but shedding pounds every week is bad for the balance of the body.

When I am in a phase of controlled weight loss I am obsessive about the amount and content of what I eat. I can now usually tell without measuring it how many calories are in a particular portion. An average-sized apple, for example, is 60 calories. Most foods come in packages that give you the calorific, sugar and energy content and, after a while, you get pretty good at anticipating the calories.

Without getting too technical, the body needs energy in the form of glucose and fat, which are derived from food and stored in the body. Muscles store enough supplies of glycogen – polymerized glucose – for bouts of short, sharp exercise – about ninety minutes at race pace. Longer periods of exercise, like a day's stage racing, require the body to activate other supplies of glycogen and, sometimes, over long periods of intense exercise like the Tour, to dig into reserves of fat stored in the body. Low levels of muscle glycogen will cause fatigue. A healthy diet cannot stop exhaustion halfway up the Col du Tourmalet, but it can delay the onset of fatigue by providing extra reserves for an efficiently trained body to access. The most important elements in a diet are:

Carbohydrates: The main source of energy. They include wholemeal and white bread, breakfast cereals, oats, brown rice, potatoes, peas, beans and lentils, fresh fruit and vegetables, pasta, milk and yogurt. About 60 per cent of the energy used in a race comes from burning carbohydrate, the rest comes from burning fat.

Protein: The main building and repair kit for the body. Proteins are made up of amino acids and the most notable sources of protein are eggs, fish, milk, meat, cheese, bread, rice, potatoes, peas and beans. Many of these foods are also very fatty, so it's important to minimize the fat content by, for example, poaching rather than frying fish, cutting the rind off bacon and using only lean cuts of meat. Skimmed or semi-skimmed milk is also preferable to full-fat milk. Only two natural foods provide a perfect balance of amino acids: eggs and mother's milk. But a combination of foods can be well balanced: beans on toast, for example, or fish and chips. It has been estimated that an active 80-kg cyclist will need between 98 and 112 gs of protein a day, or roughly 1.2–1.4 gs of protein per kilogram of weight.

Fats: The energy conservationists of the body. Fat is the most con-centrated form of energy in food. It has twice as many calories per gram as carbohydrate or protein. Excess carbohydrate turns into fat, but the list of fat foods parallels the previous list for protein, and the two are often found together: eggs, meat, peanuts, fish, bread, butter, oils, cream, lard, margarine and ice cream.

Vitamins and minerals: If your diet is perfect you won't need these, but in the real world it does absolutely no harm to take out a little insurance by taking some multivitamin supplements. A good base is a high-quality time-release multivitamin, 1 g of vitamin C and 500–1,000 IU Vitamin E, an antioxidant, per day.

The rest is just common sense, really. Mostly I try to follow a normal healthy diet, controlling my intake by eating only when I'm hungry, not when I feel I have to. If I'm not hungry I don't eat, which sounds straightforward enough until you realize how often we eat out of habit rather than necessity. Every time I put a piece of food in my mouth I am aware of what it is and how many calories it contains. By simply taking notice of diet that can become a habit. This is not some-thing everyone reading this should follow religiously; the important thing is to develop a comfortable dietary regime, within reason, of course. I'll go out and have curry and chips if I feel like it, but only occasionally. It's important for morale sometimes to indulge yourself a bit. Try to live like a monk and you'll crack, no matter how strong your will-power.

A small example of that occurred in my first few months as a professional. I was using glucose polymer for feeding during a race, as it's absorbed very quickly from a physiological point of view and is an ideal way of ingesting fluid and food at the same time. At the feeding stations, others around me were tucking into normal food, bits of cake and biscuits, packed into the *musettes* (little bags) the *soigneurs* hand out during stage races. I thought it was most strange, but they performed no worse than me and, in the end, I discovered that it was a matter of morale as much as physique. After 150 kms on the road, you look forward to a piece of fruit cake or some such delicacy rather more than a slightly tasteless polymer drink. I revised my view a little and now eat what everyone else does.

The only time I force myself to eat is immediately after training because in the first hour after exercise the body is looking to replenish its stocks and can absorb a third more carbohydrate than usual. It is very important to eat in that time to aid recovery.

The timing of eating is almost as important as the content. Don't eat any closer than two hours before a significant training session or race. Your body needs to have that gap to digest and store the intake. If you have a lot of blood sugar flowing around because the body is trying to digest food while simultaneously providing energy for racing, apart from feeling bloated and a little sick, the body will automatically use the new influx of blood sugar as an energy source, and this can seriously impede the natural desire to burn fat later. The body will only burn immediate energy and won't learn to burn fat reserves. If I'm going out at 9 a.m., for example, I will have breakfast at 7 a.m.

Carbohydrate source is what you're looking for prior to racing. It is too late to digest fats, and there will be time to replenish fat reserves later in the day, after racing. The best pre-race food would be pasta – if you can stomach it for breakfast – or, more typically, toast, cereal and a pastry. On the Tour de France or a multi-day stage race, you will be eating for the following day, too, building up your reserves.

On a long stage a rider can go for six or seven hours without a proper meal, so I have begun to eat more solids while racing. I have my own prepared *musette* and, when possible, will eat congealed sticks of jam – about one every 15–20 minutes – as a top-up. Blocks of jelly are another good source of instant blood sugar, enabling the body to access extra fat stores. In the old days, riders would carry supplies of sugar lumps for the latter stages of races. It has to be something light and portable. Towards the end of the race there is time only to drink, so I will have a glucose polymer drink for the closing stages, when the glycogen reserves have largely been used up and the pulse rate drops, sometimes by as much as fifteen beats a minute.

On the final climb up to Les Arcs in the 1996 Tour de France, Miguel Indurain hit the '*bonk*' (wall) – or '*frangal*', as the French say – because he had forgotten to replenish his drinks bottle. The rules forbid riders from taking food or drink from their team cars in the closing kilometres of a race. Alex Zulle offered the Spaniard a drink from his own bottle, but Indurain refused to take it and he paid the penalty. There might have been other causes for Indurain's sudden decline, but this was a rare and costly mistake that highlighted the importance, for amateurs as well as professionals, of timing the intake and managing the content of food for racing.

Peter Keen strongly recommends eating a small meal, about 400 calories, immediately after the end of a race – the equivalent of a couple of power bars, some cereal or a sandwich – before having a bigger meal later. Alternatively, you can have a series of small snacks to help replenish the supplies.

CB's Tips:

■   **Don't be unrealistic. Be sensible with your diet and set realistic targets for weight loss and eating. Instead of lots of red meat, for example, try fish and chicken, maybe poached or grilled rather than fried. It's a matter of making little adjustments rather than** dramatically changing eating habits. If you snack on biscuits in the middle of the morning, try a muesli bar instead.

- Be aware. Watch closely what you eat and get a feel for how many calories there are in a particular portion of food. Try to get your family involved, too, so you eat the same as them; it helps with the shopping and the cooking. Try to learn about different foods and the way they might affect your performance. This is still a relatively new science and no-one knows the answers. What works for someone else might not work for you.

- Timing is as important as content. Never eat a big meal too close to racing or training; always try to eat some carbohydrate after heavy exercise.

- Eat in moderation, little and often. Don't go for more than four hours without eating something, even if it's just a snack bar. The body should be trained to absorb and make efficient use of small quantities of food, not be made to process very big meals, though there is no harm in the occasional blow-out.

- In competition, try to anticipate. Don't wait until you feel hungry before eating, and keep your fluid levels high before you start feeling thirsty.

The Physiology of a Cyclist

We have described the difference between aerobic and anaerobic capacity in the chapters on training and have outlined the various different physiological elements required for different types of cyclist, from the sprinter to the time-trial specialist to the dedicated climber, but it is still worth analysing the physiological characteristics of the cyclist before dealing with the problems of injury.

Cycling is a balance of elements: one morning sprinting hard for ten seconds, the next riding steadily for three hours. But some bodies are better suited to one sort of exercise than another. Most cycling on the road is endurance based, which means you must have the aerobic ability to absorb intense workloads for relatively sustained periods, from a one-day stage race to the twenty-two-day Tour de France. On top of that, an ability to produce anaerobic effort must be developed to cope with the increased lactic-acid levels caused by high-intensity exercise.

An elite cyclist will have a low body-fat percentage, good quadriceps muscle strength and above-average lung capacity (VO_2Max). VO_2Max is a measurement of the amount of oxygen the body can process, expressed as a percentage of oxygen extracted per litre of air inhaled. Typically, 75–80 per cent oxygen extraction means you're working very hard, and it would be quite impressive to reach that level for any length of time. Muscle strength can be developed, but studies have shown that maximum improvement for VO_2Max is liable to be no more than 10–15 per cent, as much of a person's natural aerobic capacity is inherited.

Equally, muscle-fibre type and the ability of the muscle to contract at speed are largely predetermined. Scientists have identified two basic types of muscle fibre, fast twitch and slow twitch. The fast twitch works at high speed and can contract rapidly without oxygen, though not for very long. The slow-twitch fibres contract more slowly, but for an almost infinite length of time. Humans are born with a certain ratio of muscle-fibre types. Only the muscle fibres you have can be made more aerobically or anaerobically efficient. Sprinters can improve their endurance, and endurance specialists can develop their sprinting abilities, but only to a certain limit.

Indurain, though the size of a sprinter, had the lung capacity and endurance to survive in the mountains. In reverse, Marco Pantani's ability to minimize his losses in the time trials, while establishing his lead in the mountains, was a significant factor in his victories in the Giro and the Tour de France in 1998. Race tactics can also play their part. If a rider can slipstream for long periods of a race, he can survive using only slow-twitch fibres and preserve his limited supply of fast-twitch fibres for the significant moments, such as a breakaway or a finishing sprint. If he has been forced into overworking his fast-twitch fibres, his sprinting ability will decrease in comparison to more endurance-based cyclists. The constraints of size, weight, power-to-weight ratio, oxygen capacity and proportion of muscle-fibre type will still mostly predetermine a cyclist's realm of excellence.

Injuries: Analysis and Cure

It is worth looking briefly at the main muscle groups that affect the pedal stroke, because these muscles are the most likely to suffer from strain or injury. Don't worry too much about the intricate muscular details of the three main areas of movement – the ankle, knee and hip – but it might help to know which are the main muscle groups, so that some form of early self-diagnosis can be made.

- **The quadriceps. The muscle on the front of the thigh, which is used to start the downward pedal stroke.**
- **Gluteus maximus. The biggest muscle in the buttocks, critical to the extension of the knee from the hip joint in the downward stroke and in the reverse process in the upward stroke.**
- **The hamstring. Cyclists have quite inflexible hamstrings because the pedal stroke doesn't stretch that muscle. The hamstrings, the long muscle on the back of the thighs, combine with the quadriceps, calf muscles and gluteus maximus to propel the knees through the pedal stroke.**
- **Calf muscles. These help to push the front part of the foot down at the bottom of the pedal stroke, and to bend the knee, assisted by the hamstrings.**
- **Tibialis anterior. The muscle used to pull the front of the foot upwards on the upstroke.**

Cycling is a relatively injury-free sport. The motion of cycling is repetitive, so the muscles can be properly trained to do their job and, except under the severe pressure of a steep climb or sudden sprint, the muscles are not forced into overload. As in swimming, the body weight is supported. Being a non-contact sport – unless you count the roads of St Brieuc or the stone walls of Ireland – cycling injuries occur mainly from the breaks, cuts and bruises of high-speed crashes, or from some fault or change in riding technique.

During his riding career, Neil Stephens built up a medical file the size of a dictionary. His list of injuries reads: a cracked femur, seven broken collarbones, torn tendons in both shoulders, operations on his collarbones and knees (two apiece), an operation on his Achilles tendon, three stomach operations for hernias and a broken nose, the latter inflicted by Raul Alcala during an altercation on Mont Ventoux in the 1994 Tour de France. Further tendon problems, combined with his disillusion over the Festina drugs affair on the 1998 Tour, finished his distinguished career at the end of the 1998 season. But Stevo always rode hard and his body paid the price. Most amateurs will not have to cope with those extremes.

The areas that are most at risk in crashes are the ankles, the wrists – both of which were damaged in my fall in St Brieuc – and, as Stevo's casualty list above confirms, the collarbone. Sean Kelly was forced out of the Tour de France in 1989 by this injury, and broke the same bone again in 1991. Rest is about the only cure, though when my wrist was fractured at St Brieuc I did manage to get gingerly back onto an exercise bike once my ankles had recovered. Such an enforced period of rest can even prove beneficial. Certainly, a period soaking up the sun in my garden in that summer of 1995 gave me time to recharge a few empty batteries. At the time it's frustrating, and the temptation is to get back on a bike too soon.

The physical damage is often the easiest thing to cope with, as you have no choice but to let it heal, but the mental scars from a crash can prove more difficult to quantify and harder to heal. Footballers who have been seriously injured in a tackle often have problems committing themselves fully in the early stages of their comebacks. Their minds recall what happened last time. Confidence will only be rebuilt as the negative images of the injury are replaced by more positive thoughts, and that takes time. My crash in the wet at St Brieuc will always be in the back of my mind when I'm descending and the road is wet. The first time you're a bit cautious, the next is better and so on, until confidence in similar situations has been almost completely restored. The danger for any cyclist is to feel that this is in some way abnormal, that you should just be able to get back on a bike and steam off again at the same speed.

The knee and the back are the two most common areas of muscle pain in a cyclist. On long stages you will see a lot of riders lift out of the saddle and press their stomachs forward to stretch the muscles in their backs. The cycling position is ergonomically very awkward, and the lower a rider gets to decrease the aerodynamic drag, the greater the risk of stretching those back muscles, particularly for riders like Eros Poli who are very tall. Doubled up at an angle of 45 degrees is not a healthy posture in which to spend half your life, but it is an occupational hazard for a cyclist. By the end of the Tour de France, I doubt you would find one rider who wasn't suffering from knee or back pain.

Prevention: Stress and Saddle Height

Though it isn't possible to rule out every ache and pain, there are some preventative measures.

The first is perfectly straightforward, particularly for the amateur. When returning to serious training, don't try to ride in a gear that might put extra strain on your muscles, and don't try to ride too far too soon. The body needs to be broken in gently.

The second thing is to make sure that your saddle height is right and comfortable. Sean Kelly rode too low and bunched up for classical tastes, but it seemed to work for him. When Greg LeMond arrived in Europe with the Renault team in 1980, his coach Cyrille Guimard persuaded him to raise his saddle height by an inch and a half. LeMond did and, once he'd got used to the new position, found it looser and much more efficient. If you sit too low on the saddle, your legs will be bunched up and you won't be able to utilize their full muscular force. Your legs will also quickly become tired because they are having to work harder to achieve the same speed as a rider in the correct position. A too-low position will also put added strain on your ligaments, cartilage and tendons.

Riding too high, on the other hand, means you will stretch the body out too much and this will prevent you achieving full power on the downstroke of the pedal. There is also a danger you will overstretch your muscles.

These are the key dimensions in my own riding position:

- **738 mms from the centre of the cranks to the middle top of the saddle.**
- **The point of the saddle is 70 mms behind the bottom bracket.**
- **610 mms from the point of the saddle to the centre of the handlebars.**
- **100-mm height difference between the top of the saddle and the top of the handlebars.**

No cyclist would know these measurements precisely, many still ride on feel, but they reflect my predetermined physical body position – a long trunk and short legs. I did stretch my position during my experiments with climbing, as we have discussed, but the essential dimensions have remained the same.

What all riders must beware of is a sudden, radical change of riding position, as this can seriously affect the way certain muscles are used. If you are going to change your saddle height, pedals, length of crank-shaft or riding position, do it gradually so that the body gets used to it, and do it during the winter months, not the racing season. I suffered in the early part of the 1999 season from a misaligned shoe plate. It was only a fraction out, but on 10,000 repetitions in the course of a day's racing, the very smallest change can aggravate the muscles in the knee and ankle.

The most common problem with knees is pain behind the kneecap, often known as anterior knee pain. Cyclists, on the whole, have to cope with some pain in the knee for much of the time, but some simple measures can be taken to minimize or alleviate the problem:

- **If in doubt, cycle at a higher cadence in a lower gear; don't force extra pressure on the kneecap by riding in too high a gear.**
- **After some time away from the bike, don't try to compensate by doing too much too soon. It's not so bad coming back during the off-season because there's no pressure, but when returning from injury in mid-season the temptation is to rush straight back to a high workload, and this can aggravate the old injury, or even trigger another one. It's amazing how often injuries come in twos or threes, and I'm sure it has something to do with overcompensation.**
- **Don't make too many radical changes to saddle height or crank length; make them gradually.**

Riding only on the flat, and at a high cadence with low pressure, can help to ease knee pain. Try anything to lessen the instant pressure on the knee. The same principles apply to the back, which is subject to enormous and constant pressure on the road. With the back, it is important to be relaxed while riding and, when not riding, to keep it as flexible as possible by using stretching exercises. Developing greater strength in the abdominal muscles is another way to ease the pressure on the back. I'm not sure that it is possible to eliminate back pain, but you can ease it. If the muscles in the back are well developed and flexible, and the muscle balance is correct, there is a greater chance of keeping the back in good shape.

It is always difficult to know when to ignore pain as an occupational hazard and when to go to the doctor and risk being sidelined for a few weeks. If in doubt with any injury, it is best to get specialist advice from a doctor or a sports clinic, but getting to know your own body can help enormously in distinguishing the different aches and pains and prompting an accurate diagnosis.

Above all, be very careful when changing your pedals or shoe plates, as misalignment is the most common cause of knee problems. If you change models of either, or both, so that a direct imitation of your old shoe-plate set-up isn't possible, use the position of the ball of your foot in relation to the pedal axle as a reference point, i.e., how much higher and how much behind or in front is it? If possible, stay with the same combination of shoe, pedal and plate brand.

Forward/aft of axle; this should remain constant, regardless of pedal type

Height above axle varies between pedal types and will change your saddle height

Pedal axle

13

WHO NEEDS A COACH?

When I was young and open-minded and didn't have as firm opinions as I do now, I came across a guy called Eddie Soens, who had an incredible track record as a coach not just in cycling, but in a whole array of sports. He trained John Conteh the boxer and Geoff Smith the marathon runner, as well as a host of international athletes, but cycling was his first love. He was a hard, no-nonsense man, a former sergeant-major, with a brusque manner, who believed in self-discipline and a certain code of conduct, and expected athletes to follow it. He died relatively young, and it was almost as if he knew it was going to happen because he had no time to suffer fools. I can see now that his tough exterior masked a very gentle man, but to me he was just big and brusque, and I was totally in awe of him.

Norman Sheel, who was a pretty good road man, rang Eddie up once and said, 'I'd like to have a little go at pursuiting.' Eddie replied, 'Don't do "little goes",' and put the phone down. Norman phoned right back and corrected himself. 'Eddie, I would really like to give pursuiting a real go,' and Eddie said, 'OK,' and the guy became a multi world champion pursuit rider.

That was Eddie to a T. People either loved him or hated him. He either got right up your nose or his particular brand of abrasiveness spurred you on. But his best talent was motivating people and giving them self-confidence, and he had a huge influence on my early career and the way I prepared myself and thought about my sport, through my development as an amateur club cyclist into a performance professional. He was the only person to whom I gave complete control of my career, probably because I was still in my teens. If he said do something, I did it. I never questioned whether it was the right thing to do.

When Eddie died, he had coached me for only two years, but his death left an enormous hole in my cycling life. I was seventeen at the time, and I just drifted that year. I had only really started getting into cycling seriously and had always done what Eddie had told me. In a sense, he had transformed my career. In my early teens I'd raced but never trained, and he made me see that cycling was what I wanted to do. I transferred to a sponsored club – the only junior rider they had ever taken on – and started to contend for the National Championships. Two days before he died, I was a member of the Manchester Wheelers senior team that won the National Team Pursuit Championships.

Finding the right coach is a problem for all young athletes. Parents aren't necessarily the best people to give advice or to coach because they are too close to you personally. It is hard for them to step back and be objective. My own father, though an Olympic-class rider himself, recognized that fact. He would help me do as much as I wanted, but one of the best things my parents did was give me space. They were incredibly supportive, ferried me all over the country, but they never crowded me. If anything, in my early days I was actively discouraged from competitive cycling; I was encouraged to enjoy the social side of cycling first and foremost.

I discovered fairly early in my teenage years that cycling was a great sport for a young person because, though it is essentially an individual sport and cyclists tend to be individualists, there is a great camaraderie between cyclists that crosses age, gender and generations. One of the beauties of the sport is that you can engage in conversation while you ride. Not many sports have that luxury. The club runs down to a café on the Wirral still hold a special place in my memory all these miles later, and I'm still riding the same roads!

Being a more obsessive character than most, I began to find that the competition was more enjoyable than the riding itself. Perhaps that was Eddie's influence. I have always said I'm not a natural bike rider; I'm a natural competitor. When I retire I hope to pursue cycling for what it is, a mode of transport and a good way to enjoy the countryside, and I intend to follow my father's philosophy with my own children, which is to encourage but never push.

A year after Eddie's death in 1986, I was sent down to a laboratory near Chichester with the national squad. There I met Peter Keen, who was conducting the tests, and I liked his approach straight away. Firstly, the tests he had devised were quite interesting and secondly, he explained the results in a very imaginative and positive way. Whatever question I asked, he would suggest a course of action and then explain the bulk of the evidence that had led him to that conclusion. He had the vocabulary and creative ability to explain in great detail why he thought a certain type of training was a good idea. At the time he was still a very active cyclist, very lean and gaunt. He looked like an athlete, which helped give me confidence that he might know what he was talking about, and that he had practised virtually everything he was preaching. He seemed to know what it felt like, which was a bonus. Some coaches can calculate to the letter the physical strains of a training schedule, but they forget about the mental toll.

In the mid-Eighties Peter Keen began to get more involved with the national squad, so I spent a lot of time with him, pestering him with all sorts of questions. Slowly we began to form a good working relationship, and I contacted him directly, so that he could help me set up some training programmes. In 1990 I had just recovered from a major stomach operation and went on to finish sixth in the World Championships, and it was at that moment that both of us realized the possibility of winning the world title. Before that, the very idea had been completely out of reach for a skinny boy from the streets of Hoylake. From then on our relationship developed into a more formal coaching arrangement, though it was a long time before I could afford to pay Peter for his services. The rest, as they say, is history.

What Should You Require from a Coach?

I am suspicious of coaches and coaching methods. I need to trust someone before I will listen to what they have to say. I try very hard to be open-minded about coaches, but too often they're more interested in trying to discredit someone else's theories than constructing or creating any of their own. At coaching conferences, people ask Peter questions just to try to catch him out, not because they're really interested in learning from what he says. In that sense, it's a very unhealthy profession. I see too many coaches more interested in themselves than their athletes.

A good coach should be inspirational and helpful in making you enjoy your sport. A coach has to provide perspective and must have an independent eye without taking away from the ultimate significance of personal pride and passion. Sometimes, in the middle of a race, there is no logic. Though every fibre of your body might be saying the opposite, it becomes a case of, I am not going to let them drop me. It all comes down to passion, determination and aggression.

The first point about coaches is that they must be honest and open with you, and you with them. They must be willing to tell you the bad news as well as the good, so that a trust can be built up between you. The athlete must have faith in the training programmes he is having to endure, and the coach, particularly if he doesn't see the athlete every day, must trust the athlete to follow his programme. Second, they have to be dispassionate and not get drawn into the athlete's success. A coach must be objective about a performance and be able to absorb all the implications of a victory or defeat before moving on.

Personally, I need a coach to explain *why* I'm doing something. If I know what the benefits *could* be, I will do the sessions with a lot more purpose. Not all cyclists and athletes are like that. Some are quite happy to do what they are told and get on with it, as I did during my early days with Eddie. Peter Keen rarely said 'will' when he was explaining a particular programme, as in 'will make you go faster'. He would more normally say, 'There is evidence to suggest . . .' which appealed to me. He wasn't trying to pretend he knew more than he did and he always put a positive spin on bad news and was there to pick me up again after knocking me down.

Coaching is a deeply creative job; it requires real dedication and a sixth sense in anticipating and understanding how an athlete might feel at any given moment. Peter and I developed a relationship where he can set workloads for a training programme – on an ergometer, for example – and they will be uncannily on the limit of what I can handle on that day. That intuition comes from developing a really close relationship over a number of years.

Much of his coaching has been done by phone and fax machine. I would phone him at the end of every day's racing or training and fax through my race reports so he could tell without seeing me what I needed to work on. I have come across too many people who have great ideas for training but don't tailor them to the needs of the athlete at that particular moment. They don't ask whether, mentally, the athlete can handle that volume of work or whether they should think of something more creative. For example, there's a big psychological difference between riding 120 miles and riding from my home to Derby. 120 miles is a slog. Sixty out, turn round, sixty back – mind-blowing stuff. Peter Keen discovered fairly early on that I'm not like that. Riding to Derby for a dinner is a lot easier on my mind; it then becomes an expedition. Peter is first and foremost a creative person, and he is an excellent judge of mood.

A coach *must* listen. It's a very two-way relationship, and a coach must be able to impose his own methods without being in awe of the athlete. There was one coach in the England set-up who was an excellent physiologist, but he didn't have the confidence to speak his mind to me. That was partly my fault. Whenever I argued a point with him he would back down, when in fact he may have been right; all he needed to do was persuade me of the significance and benefits of his way. To me, coaching is a very personal thing. The coach has to get inside your skin, understand your moods and know what you're like at various points in the season. This obviously takes time and a commitment by both parties, but if you find the right person, someone you really feel comfortable with, it will be worth it in the long run.

There has to be respect on either side. I don't think you necessarily have to like your coach, though if you actively disliked them that would be hard, nor, in my case anyway, do they have to be great motivators in the conventional sense. I am motivated by fact, and if I know what I'm doing, why I'm doing it and why it might work, then I will have complete commitment to a training programme. Peter Keen gave, and continues to give, me self-belief. The drive to succeed comes from within, and I'm not sure a coach can instil it if it's not there already.

One notable example of Peter's ability to think beyond the ordinary came in 1990. I was still an amateur then and the world hour record had been held for a long time by the great Italian cyclist Francesco Moser. Peter was sitting down and number crunching one evening and he worked out that what I was doing would develop enough power to translate into a speed that, in the not too distant future, would put the world hour record within range. It was a ludicrous thought then, but he hadn't looked at tradition or convention; he had just looked at the figures and reality.

The coach of a pro-cycling team is always in a difficult position. He sets the riders' training programmes and gets close to them, yet when the boss will ask how a particular rider is doing, he will have to be honest, so he's regarded as the boss's man, too. The riders are therefore prepared to tell him all their good news and be a touch absent-minded about the bad news. Honesty is an essential ingredient in coaching. Sometimes coaches forget how hard it is to do the programmes they set. They tend to work week by week, rather than stepping back and looking at the bigger picture. They have a vested interest in us riding well, and some coaches will transfer a lot of pressure to their riders. In our team, if we're not doing well, our coach sometimes pushes harder, which can have the opposite to the desired effect on a rider's form.

In my opinion, a good cycling coach cannot deal effectively with more than half a dozen riders. He wouldn't have the time or the commitment to take on more than that. The trouble is that, in Britain, coaching has never been a professional occupation. No-one really expects to pay for coaching; so coaches have generally been willing amateurs, but the more that attitude has taken root the more difficult it has been to adopt the same professional approach as, say, the Italians or the French. Amateurism is a hard and vicious cycle to break.

Most clubs will have a coach, but, for a club cyclist who wants to improve, there is no point in taking on a coach just for the sake of it. You have to find the right person for the job, someone to bounce ideas off, who will appraise your performance dispassionately and not get too carried away by their own enthusiasm. To me, qualifications are the least-important factor. I would much rather have a coach who learned as we were going along than someone who had lots of letters after his name.

One of the difficult factors in my relationship with a coach is pay, as it is hard to calculate accurately how much a coach should receive. If Linford Christie wins Olympic gold, how much of that is down to his coach? I hold the world hour record, but how much of that record really belongs to Peter Keen? Coaching isn't quantifiable, yet the best coaches consider their job as a way of life. They don't work nine to five; their job is a passion and a vocation. I might even become a coach myself when I retire, if I can find the right athlete. But if I did coach someone, I would be sure to demand money, and quite a lot of it, not for the money itself, but as a means of getting the athlete's attention.

Coaches are too often taken for granted because they aren't paid. If an athlete has to part with his hard-earned winnings, he will listen and make sure he gets the most out of his investment. If you had spent good money on buying a really smart car, you wouldn't treat it like an old banger, would you? The principle is exactly the same. I worked with Peter in the traditional amateur way when he was a student. Then he became a lecturer, then a senior lecturer and, until the end of 1993, he was basically unpaid. When I turned professional and started to earn a good salary, it seemed reasonable that I should pay him for his time. His career had advanced like mine, we had both given each other credibility in different ways, so we drew up a letter of intent, which we both signed. That was it.

In my career I have been lucky enough to run into the right people at the right time. What wasn't luck was recognizing them and hanging on to them. Nor should my wife Sally's role in all this be forgotten. Not only has she been an emotional support as my partner, she has also given me strong and good opinions on all aspects of my career. I've sometimes been tempted to ignore them, but often she has been right. The people I rely on for advice make a good combination. Peter Woodworth is great at looking ahead and anticipating the consequences of a particular course of action. Sally is able to look at how a particular plan might affect my general health, not just the cycling. As the coach, Peter Keen is able to analyse the physiological and psychological aspects of my schedules. And I act as chairman of the committee, assessing all the opinions and coming up with a plan that suits me. Together we make a formidable team.

Towards the end of the 1999 Tour de France, I was beginning to despair of ever finding my form again. I had survived the Tour, no more, without putting any real passion into my riding. It was time to make a decision. Should I quit the sport and take the honourable way out? Or should I try to refind my focus and drive myself hard for the last year of my career, with all the sacrifices that would mean for me and my family? But what I found I needed, answering the question posed in the title of the chapter, was the strong influence of a coach.

After a timely phone call towards the end of the Tour, Peter and I began to explore the possibility of working together again. We had never been totally out of touch, but daily contact had stopped. Peter had taken up a post with the British Cycling Federation, and I'd thought I had enough experience not to need the sort of day-to-day guidance that Peter had been providing. I could always tell with Peter, as soon as he picked up the phone, whether he had just started thinking about a problem I'd given him or whether he had already spent time crunching numbers and giving it serious thought. Over the past two years his mind had clearly been on other things. What I hadn't been able to do was control my training and objectively evaluate the work I'd been doing. Peter had always been able to do that instinctively, and when we met up I told him, 'I have fourteen months of my career left and I need you to make it happen.' With the Olympics a year away and a shortage of medal prospects for his elite programme, it turned out that he needed me, too.

The first question we had to ask was whether we wanted to work together. The second was whether it was feasible, given that we both had other jobs; his at the BCF, mine with Crédit Agricole. For me, there was only one answer to both questions, and I was quite prepared to make it as convenient as possible for Peter. I would make the phone calls and instigate the training programmes; what I needed from him was that element of control. We've gone back to basics, looked at my riding position and standardized it between my road bike and my time-trial bike. We've also reviewed the objectives for the rest of my career. In Sydney, my main objective is the time trial, with the team pursuit and individual pursuit as further possibilities. We are working on the same framework as before, with main and interim objectives, but, unlike in the two years since 1997, I now have a coach I believe in and who gives me that edge of self-belief I've been lacking.

The whole process has helped to clarify the importance of the coach's role for me, and made me realize how much I need one. I regarded most coaches as training advisers, whereas a true coach is someone who gets inside the athlete's head, finds out how they tick and is able to marry their psychology with their physiology. A trainer tells you to do this on Monday and this on Tuesday, but without providing any mental support. It is critical for both coach and athlete to have belief in each other. I've learned the hard way how difficult it is not to have that support.

The Qualities of a Good Coach:

- Good base of physiological knowledge.
- An ability to listen. Ignore people who just agree when you're talking, because they just want to talk themselves. Those people don't learn, so their advice is probably faulty.
- A willingness to ask questions and be open-minded.
- An ability to communicate ideas simply.
- A passion for sport and coaching.
- An ability to inspire and motivate and to help you enjoy what you are doing. It's a challenge not a problem.

14

THE HOUR RECORD

A Brief History of the Hour Record to 1993

On 11 May 1893, Henri Desgrange covered 35.325 kms in an hour riding round the Buffalo Stadium in Paris on a big steel-framed bicycle. Unwittingly, the Frenchman set a record that would capture the imagination of the cycling world as passionately and intensely as the Tour de France, his later creation. In the century that followed Desgrange's epic ride, only nineteen men successfully challenged one of the toughest records in sport. The list included three of the sport's great champions: Fausto Coppi, Jacques Anquetil and Eddy Merckx. By the time Francesco Moser of Italy had broken the record for the second time, in Mexico in 1984, the distance had risen to 51.151 kms – far enough to discourage any further serious attempts.

To understand the significance of Moser's record it is important to understand the nature of the hour record and the fascination it holds for cycling *aficionados*. The hour record is a deceptively simple concept: ride as far as you can in an hour. But mentally and physically it is cycling's Mount Everest, a monument to cycling's hard men and a definition of cycling generations. All great champions have attempted the hour record as a matter of honour. For a number of reasons, Moser's record seemed definitive. Achieved at altitude, using disc wheels and a one-piece skin suit, the Italian not only broke the mystical 50-km mark, the equivalent of the four-minute mile, but, during his two successful rides, he broke Merckx's record by almost 2 kms, a rise unprecedented since the turn of the century.

Psychologically, Moser put the record out of reach for another decade or more, just as Merckx himself had done in 1972. Merckx's record, set at the end of a season of extraordinary domination, was equally long-lasting, mainly because the Belgian was regarded by all the other potential riders and record holders as invincible. That has been the way with the hour record: short bursts of activity, punctuated by long dormant periods while a new generation emerged to challenge the old masters. Coppi's record, set in 1942, lasted for fourteen years, Merckx's 1972 record lasted for twelve and Moser's for ten.

The history of the event, like most in cycling, has not been without its moments of controversy. In 1913, Richard Weise covered 42.276 kms on a track in Berlin, only to have his record nullified by the previous holder, Oscar Egg, who claimed that the track in Paris where he'd achieved his record had been wrongly measured. The track turned out to be 1.7 m longer than first thought, raising Egg's record to 42.36 kms. In 1966, Jacques Anquetil claimed the record, only to be disqualified by the UCI for refusing the obligatory dope test. There were strong protests, ignored by the UCI, about Moser's oversized rear disc wheels and his low-profile-design bike when he broke the record in 1984. But the record was allowed to stand, and Moser, three times winner of the legendary Paris–Roubaix, gained a special place in the distinguished history of Italian cycling.

On the continent, only the champions of the Tour de France have higher status than world hour record holders. Yet, in Britain, the record has not attracted its share of attention or acknowledgement over the years.

The Quest for the Hour Record

Though I don't remember it, Eddie Soens apparently used to enthuse about Moser's record to me when I was growing up. It would have been Ed's sort of record – uncomplicated and tough. Whether any of his influence rubbed off on me subconsciously is hard to say, but slowly and surely, the hour record has come to be my sort of record, too. Peter Keen had an eye on it much earlier than I did. He was quoted once as saying that if he couldn't beat the record himself, he would like to be involved in preparing a rider for it. He was nineteen at the time, but it required a person of his analytical and often detached manner even to consider tackling a record that had stood for more than a decade.

I have already written about how Peter Keen sat down in 1990 and, as an academic exercise, computed a performance graph that translated my speed over a certain distance into a quantifiable and plausible attempt on Moser's record. As the history of the hour record shows, sometimes it takes a new generation, who don't appreciate how tough the record was, to break down the barriers. Neither of us looked at Moser and said, 'He's a great champion; this can't be done.' We had the enthusiasm and the arrogance of youth. Above all, we looked at the figures, and though I took a lot of persuading, the figures said it could be done. At the time the thought was put to the back of our minds. I was still an amateur, two years away from winning gold in Barcelona, and it was hard enough trying to make ends meet without having to worry about a record set by one of Italy's great champions. It still seemed like a dream, but Peter didn't forget it.

What both of us liked about the hour record was the neatness of it. It was a calculable equation: × amount of power for × surface area = × distance. The one variable was my human weakness. Yet it suited my particular abilities. Focusing on the data and turning a great record into a set of figures also helped to block out the difficulty of achieving it. I knew what the record was and what it meant. Moser was a cycling megastar and the prospect of a cabinetmaker from Hoylake challenging his terrain was difficult to come to terms with. The record had a touch of magic to it and the press had talked it up so loudly for so long that no-one had considered trying to break it.

The shift in my confidence began back at the World Championships in 1990 when, for the first time, I'd realized that becoming a world champion was possible. Winning gold at the

Barcelona Olympics transformed my life almost overnight. From scrounging about for a living, people were ringing up every day asking me to open this and that and make television appearances. The press suggested that I could earn £1 million simply by signing a piece of paper that would turn me into a professional, but the idea of riding for a foreign team for 110 days a year on the roads still didn't appeal to me greatly. But a few months of hammering around television studios and cutting the tape on supermarkets quickly ordered my thoughts on what direction my career should take.

I knew what I didn't want to do. Though I'd been offered a chance, and a lucrative one, to turn professional with a British team, the idea of pedalling around Britain for the rest of my life didn't appeal very much, but nor did becoming a *domestique* in a continental team. You have to remember that winning Olympic gold doesn't hold the same kudos in France as it does in Britain, particularly in cycling, where champions are measured in terms of the classics and the major tours. Staying amateur was an option, though not an appealing one now that we had two children, Edward and Harriet, to feed, and I was aware that the celebrity status I'd gained from winning gold would quickly fade. I might be big in Hoylake, but opening church fêtes wasn't quite what I had in mind, however robust and touching the support of my own community was. So in the year after Barcelona, the idea of breaking the world hour record grew from simple paper calculations to a full-blown attempt.

I travelled down to Brighton one day to have a meeting with Peter, and I can remember sitting in a lecture room with him while he covered the blackboard with figures that supposedly explained why I could break Moser's record. I still wasn't fully convinced, because on recent tests monitored by Peter I hadn't been able to hold 400 watts for ten minutes, let alone the 430 watts for an hour required to break the record. But Peter went through the whole thing, analysing Moser's physique and ability, looking at the real advantage his hi-tech bike had given him and comparing it with the up-to-date technology, and I began to believe in what he was saying. The idea started to appeal to me.

There was another factor that came to influence both the timing and the venue for the record attempt. On 23 July 1993, the Tour de France was due to finish a stage in Bordeaux. We – myself, an old friend Harry Middleton, Peter Keen and a cycling colleague Paul Jennings – had trekked over to the indoor track in Bordeaux to do some testing, both on different bikes, pulse rates and power watts. We hadn't intended to use that track for the hour record until Harry pointed out that the Tour de France was passing through. One thing led to another, and in about five minutes the whole thing had mushroomed into a full-blown attempt on Moser's record in front of the world's cycling press on the morning of the Tour stage finish.

For six months my training was geared specifically to the hour record. All my other races were tailored to that goal. I spent about six weeks doing really specific training, working just over threshold and doing a lot of track work. Only in the final two weeks before the attempt did I taper down my preparations and work on keeping myself fresh. But the period leading up to the first record attempt in 1993 was the most stressful time of my life.

I have already outlined my methods of dealing with pressure. As long as I arrive on the startline knowing that everything that could have been done to get me there in the best possible physical and mental shape has been done, then I can cope with the rest. In Bordeaux we were all learning as we went along, and yet there was a massive focus on what we were doing. At the Olympics I knew I had the most modern bike in the competition, which gave me confidence, and I also knew that, though the four minutes or so of the final would change my life, there was still a silver medal to be won if I didn't win gold. That, believe it or not, was a comforting thought. With the hour record, a second or so either way means the difference between success and failure. There is no consolation prize.

In contrast to my second attempt, in Manchester in 1996, which was near perfect, the lead-up to 1993 was fraught with problems. First, my Corima bike, which we chose from four different makes of bike on the basis of some very crude testing by today's standards, was state-of-the-art but very stiff. The material was right, but it proved to be the least aerodynamic shape imaginable. Second, we had no control over the humidity inside the arena and minimal control over the temperature. Only on the morning of the attempt would we know how high the humidity levels would be inside the arena. To add to the problems, the owners refused to turn off the arc lights, which were needed for the television crews. To combat the effects of the heat, Peter Keen had to spray me with ethyl alcohol, which evaporates twice as fast as water, taking the heat with it.

The tone was set by the first problems we experienced in finding a van to transport our equipment. In the end I had to ask an old friend, Alan Dunn, who managed the Rolling Stones. He spoke to Mick Jagger, a cycling fan, who agreed to let us borrow one of their tour trucks, and then we were stopped at Customs because we didn't have the proper documentation. The whole expedition was fraught with difficulties that could have been sorted out with a bit more planning and a lot more experience, and it taught me an important lesson for the future.

My motivation had also been hit earlier in the week by the news that Graeme Obree had got to Moser's record before me.

Graeme had arrived on the cycling scene burdened with an 'eccentric' tag, which he has never managed to shake off. His bike, built in the shed at his home near Turnberry, incorporated parts of a washing machine. Of course, the press loved that story and they loved it even more when he broke Moser's record. So typically British. I was pretty upset about it. He had every right to go for the record, and to do it when he wished, but he had even tried to get on the track at Bordeaux before me. He went to Norway and failed on his first attempt. We heard about that as we prepared in Bordeaux and thought that was it. But Graeme being Graeme, got up the following morning, had another go and did it. It was a tremendous feat, but for a time it took the wind out of my sails. One moment there was Francesco Moser's glittering record, unbeaten for nearly ten years, the next I had to beat the record of some Scottish guy who'd built his own bicycle! It took away a lot of the impact, though, to be fair, it also heightened the interest surrounding Bordeaux. All those factors impinged on my preparations.

For a time, in the month or so before the occasion, I was close to having a nervous breakdown. At least that's what it felt like. When I went home, I felt like I was a spectator in my own house, as if I wasn't really there at all, I was just watching everyone else, but wasn't part of it. I didn't realize how close I came to something quite serious. I was in a right state.

On the day, Peter kept trying to calm me down and put the attempt into perspective so it didn't seem like do or die, but to me it did. I was at the hub of this great big wheel and it was all my fault. The worst moment was just before the start. The crowd were going wild, waiting for the start, and yet there's no official start time. It is entirely up to the cyclist. You go when you feel ready. So you sit there and count to three, like a child jumping into a cold swimming pool. At that moment, like the start ramp in the Tour de France prologue, when expectations are so high, you wish you were anywhere else in the world. In Bordeaux I can remember the silence, broken only by the sound of a Chilean radio commentator jabbering into his microphone. Everyone told him to keep quiet, but I was thinking, No, keep going, mate, you're doing a great job.

The Hour Record: Mind Over Matter

Our training had been geared to riding as efficiently and rhythmically as possible over the whole hour rather than blasting away for the first few minutes, as Merckx had done, and then dropping away. That happened to be Eddy's style. But the graph of his record in 1972 shows a steady drop from an initial speed of over 51 kph down to just over 49 kph after 35 kms, before picking up again to finish with 49.431 kms. My own race profile shows a steady increase in pace up to 5 kms and 52 kph, then a slow but steady increase through to a peak of over 52 kph after 40 kms, before a slight drop-off to the finish.

Mentally, the hour record is as tough as it gets. It wouldn't seem like it from the outside, just going round in circles for an hour, but there is so much to think about. For a start you're trying to minimize the distance covered on each lap, because the lap is measured round the black line on the bottom of the track and you waste time and energy when you deviate from it. After a while the black line becomes almost hypnotic, and following it becomes tiring in itself. You are also trying to minimize aerodynamic resistance by keeping as low as possible on the bike to sustain your effort just on or below threshold.

On top of the technical issues you worry about keeping to schedule. We had a system adapted from my pursuit riding whereby Peter Keen would walk away from a set mark if I was ahead of schedule and the other way if I was behind it. It is absolutely critical to keep to schedule and not ignore it, even if you are feeling good at a particular moment. It is very easy to stray over threshold and pay the penalty by having to slow down for ten minutes. That's what Merckx did.

In Bordeaux the heat prevented me from matching the schedule we'd set. On the day we bottled it a bit and went for a pretty conservative 53-km schedule, which was still over the record, but not as far as I thought I could go. After ten minutes it became clear that, with the heat, 53 kms was going to be unrealistic. I started to fall off our initial schedule, so Peter Keen began to give me information on the record, not my schedule, because dropping away isn't good for morale.

Only later did we discover that there are little tricks to keep a steady power output on the track – an essential part of an efficient, successful attempt. If you ride up the track slightly through the bend, maybe a foot or a foot and a half above the black line, then drop off the bend back onto the line on the straight, it smooths the power profile. Though you travel further, you sustain a more even pace and power output. There can be a 300-watt difference in power output from the straight to the bend in some SRM computer printouts taken from pursuit riders. That's a massive difference, and not very efficient or rhythmic over a long period of time like the hour. For the second hour record I did three years later, in 1996, we had the benefit of the power profile from the first record, and we found that my cadence had to increase as I went round the bend to minimize the speed difference between the straight and the banking.

From a mental point of view, the hardest part is between fifteen and forty minutes. After a quarter of an hour the fatigue is already starting to build up, but there are still another forty-five minutes to go. It's just a question of keeping the mind busy, but those thirty minutes or so are interminable. After forty minutes the bulk of the work has been done and the end is in sight. The last ten minutes is a terrible mixture of fear and rising elation; fear that a puncture might deprive you of the record, elation at knowing that the record is within your grasp. The very best bit comes in the few seconds when you've beaten the record and there is still some time to run.

In Bordeaux, the overwhelming feeling at the end wasn't triumph or glory, but relief, sheer ecstatic relief that I hadn't let anyone down. Strangely, though I had broken Obree's record by 674 ms, ridden more than a kilometre further than Moser and become only the twentieth rider to hold the hour record, I wasn't entirely happy with my performance; that's what the hour record does to nominally sane minds.

The finish was bedlam. I had intended to do a few extra laps to warm down, but had missed the final bell because of the noise and only knew it was all over because the two Peters were dancing a jig down the main straight. Once the press and photographers had swarmed onto the track there was little chance of a warm-down. I was absolutely drained, but I also knew that I could do better, which was an important motivating factor for my second attempt in the summer of 1996. That evening I shared a podium with Miguel Indurain, the leader of the Tour de France, my first taste of life as a professional cyclist.

The Hour Record: 1993–6

Graeme Obree, an amateur rider from Turnberry in Scotland, broke Moser's hour record in Norway a week before my attempt in Bordeaux in the summer of 1993. Obree failed at his first attempt but, with typical panache, tried again a day later and established a new record of 51.596 kms. In Bordeaux I succeeded in raising that limit to 52.270 kms, but the fact that two amateurs had shattered a record regarded as impregnable for the past decade brought renewed interest from the world's best riders. Only a few had the courage to go ahead with their challenge. So incensed was Moser that his record had been beaten by a couple of amateurs from Britain that he returned to the track in Mexico in 1994, at the age of forty-two, and tried to regain his record, only failing narrowly in his attempt.

The first of the big boys to attempt the record was Miguel Indurain, who, like Eddy Merckx twenty-two years before, simply got on his bike and rode for an hour round the track in Bordeaux to take the record beyond 53 kms for the first time. The Spaniard had done the minimum preparation for his attempt; he rightly believed that, as he was a class bike rider, he should be able to beat the record. He did it on pure ability, but I'm convinced he didn't get anywhere near his capacity, which was probably just as well for the rest of us. Had he prepared properly, made his quite upright riding position more aerodynamic and learned how to pace himself, Indurain had the capability to take the record out of sight for another decade.

As it was, Tony Rominger, one of Indurain's great rivals in the early Nineties, and the world number one, took advantage of Indurain's lack of serious preparation by extending the record to 55.291 kms, a figure most regarded as unreachable. Rominger won the Giro and the Vuelta and finished on the podium in the Tour de France, but he was unlucky to be at his peak during the years when Indurain dominated the Tour. Within the *peloton*, the Swiss rider was a star, but he never quite got the recognition he deserved from the general public because he never won the Tour. He was a superb time triallist, with a methodical, analytical nature, and he was the first person of that stature in the early Nineties to dedicate himself totally to breaking the hour record. He was coming to the end of his career and saw the record as his great swansong. His first attempt, in October 1994 at the indoor track in Bordeaux, took the record to 53.832 kms, but that was no more than a preface to his second attempt, again in Bordeaux, the following month, in which he annihilated his own record.

Within the space of just over a year, the distance for the hour record had risen by more than 4 kms. Most of the cycling world, myself included, thought that Rominger had shut down the record for another decade, at least. But Peter Keen didn't take much notice of instinct. He looked at the statistics from Rominger's ride, at my potential power output and aerodynamic forces, and calculated that the record was still within reach.

Superman and the Second Hour Record

Rominger's distance of 55.291 kms, like those of Moser and Merckx before him, seemed to define the potential of a generation of riders. That was the best we could do. But, undaunted, we put some numbers on the sort of power that would be required to break the record and, to my surprise, so good was my form during some equipment testing in Manchester after the Atlanta Olympics, I started to get quite close to the power that was needed. I was aiming at a speed of 55.5 kph. In tests, I was quite capable of riding close to that pace and staying under control. The time was right: camera crews were over for the World Pursuit Championships in Manchester and they would stay on if we announced the record attempt. All that was needed was a little motivating factor for me to make the effort once again and ensure that the odds were a little more weighted in my favour. There was no point in going just for the sake of it, without a realistic chance of success. That would have been a waste of everyone's time and an embarrassment for me. We then tested the last piece of equipment – the new 'Superman' bars, with my arms stretched right out in front of me. It looked stupid and it wasn't bike riding as I knew it, but I'd learned long ago how foolish it is to write something off just because it looks wrong, and my early tests in the wind tunnel at MIRA had shown how important the science of aerodynamics is to riding a bike faster. We devised a handlebar set-up that was fully adjustable in both height and reach, and a pair of triathlon bars that were telescopic, so they could be altered in length and width. To start with we copied the position Graeme Obree had used, trying to find out if it made any difference to power output. We were suitably impressed and tested a load of equipment before refocusing on the Superman position again, seeing how extreme we could go before compromising on a more comfortable stance.

From there we had some special handlebars made. When I tested them, on the first ride round, I thought, Oh my God. I knew it would give me that margin for error that I wanted to take into another attempt on the record. With the new riding position, I had a small comfort zone, enough to make an attempt worthwhile. The next move was to call Roger Legeay and explain the position to him. We told him that if I rode in this strange, elongated position, I could cover this number of kilometres in an hour and, being a passionate fan of bike racing and loving the hour record, he was seduced by the idea. He wanted to see it, and, for me, there wasn't quite so much pressure as the first time. If I failed, it wasn't a catastrophe.

The disadvantages of the Superman position became apparent during an invaluable thirty-minute track trial before the record attempt. The day after I'd won the world pursuit title with a world-record speed of 53.5 kph, I rode for thirty minutes in the position and found that, after half an hour, I began to get real muscle problems in my arms. It was as if someone had flicked a switch in my body. The muscles were taking all the weight, but every time I went round the banking, the centrifugal force was pushing my head down so that I couldn't sustain the position comfortably. I had to come out of position twice to ease the pressure on my arms and neck. Peter Cook, an engineering friend at Liverpool University, worked on the problem and produced another set of extension bars that allowed me to rotate my arms inwards so the bones, not the muscles, were supporting the weight. We planned a couple of breaks from the Superman position into the schedule, but by the end of a week's training we'd reduced that to just one spell of rest. In almost every other way, the preparations were as perfect in Manchester as they had been fraught in Bordeaux.

For a start, logistically, the arrangements were simple: I was an hour from home, so able to train on the track pretty much when I wanted. All the officials were already in place because of the World Championships, so we didn't have to worry about finding and accommodating them. Last, and not least, everyone spoke English. My own training, though hardly ideal for a world-record run, had left me at pretty much exactly the right level of fitness and confidence. Having completed the Tour de France for the first time, I had the basic levels of endurance and, having trained hard and specifically to cope with the explosive pace of the pursuit, I had enhanced my lactic-acid threshold. Above all, at the end of a gruelling Tour, I had the glycogen stores to fuel the engine and the confidence to ride hard for an hour. During the seven weeks that included the Pursuit World Championships and the hour record, I was in the form of my life. I won seven races in seven weeks, set two world pursuit records and broke the hour record. It felt great.

In spite of my form, I still thought the attempt would be really close. Even a couple of days before, my training had been good but not great. I was still a little under par. Even on the morning of the record, when I went for a gentle ride with Peter Keen, there was no sensation of feeling fantastic, which proves the point we made in the chapter on finding form: there is no way of predicting when it will come.

As soon as I kicked off in front of a full house at the Manchester Velodrome, however, I began to feel great, and I was soon seconds up on the board. Tennis players use the term 'in the zone' to describe the feeling of being almost omnipotent. Your confidence is so high that you feel as if any shot you try will succeed. On a bike, this translates into the feeling that you can't go any faster but you aren't suffering. The one regret I have about that ride is that I didn't take my pulse, because I would be fascinated to know what it was, for future reference.

After it was all over, I said to Roger Legeay that I was never going to do the hour record again, which was a Steve Redgrave-type statement. Steve said, after his fourth Olympic gold, that anyone who saw him go near a rowing boat again had his permission to shoot him. I knew exactly how he felt. Unlike him, I intend to keep my word. The tension and expectation is just too draining, despite the fact that, in comparison to Bordeaux at least, everything went like clockwork. All the preparations were absolutely spot on.

I warmed up on the rollers in a room underneath the track and, remembering the humidity in Bordeaux, I wore the absolute minimum. I'm not particularly superstitious, but I always use locker number fifty-six when training at the track – 56 kms was the mark I was aiming for. I did a couple of laps on the track and then got on with it. Peter Keen was at trackside to tell me, in increments of a second, whether I was up or down. He used a small flip board: red on white for down, white on black for up. After a few laps I was one second up on my schedule, then two. Pete gestured to me at one point to ask what was going on; he was frightened I was showboating, going too fast too soon. I had to tell him not to worry. In truth, I couldn't believe it, either. I did one minute flat for the last kilometre, which is about a second off the world record for a standing kilometre. That is how good I felt.

Because I'd known from the start that I was going to do it, I was able to enjoy the whole experience much more than in Bordeaux. It was as if the whole event had been choreographed. Eddie Soens's wife was there and it felt as if I was repaying some of my debts to her and Eddie. To be able to do that, and to see the reaction on the faces of the crowd, made the pain endured during the hour worthwhile. It was an honour. I might be wrong, technology will progress, but I believe I've taken away the insurance for anyone – except maybe Jan Ullrich, Abraham Olano and Lance Armstrong – who wants to break the record. It's a big leap from 55.1 kms to 56.3. If someone attempts it, they can only hope to break it by metres not kilometres, so that person has to be prepared to fail, and that is quite a disincentive. I was actually quite cross that subsequently the UCI banned the Superman position, because it seems to imply that the record was won solely by that factor. I hope that if anyone attempts it in years to come they will use the same position, as Rominger said he would.

15

THE TOUR

A Voyage of Discovery

The Tour de France is one of the great annual events in sport. It is much more than a race: it's a national obsession, a reassertion of national identity played out across nearly 4,000 kms of France for three weeks each summer. The image of the Tour suffered terribly from the drugs scandal in 1998, but the people still flooded onto the streets of their towns and villages to see the 1999 Tour pass by as if nothing had happened. That is the hold the Tour has on the nation that began it all the way back in 1903.

Most newcomers to the Tour find the scale of it breathtaking. I was no exception. No matter how much you watch it on television, the reality is three times as big. The Tour is part circus, part bike race, part national holiday, part mobile advertising hoarding, part travel show. If you are French and ride a bicycle, there is only one dream: to ride the Tour de France. But when you are inside its vast inflatable bubble you experience a whole range of different emotions. For the rider, it is quite simply the make or break part of the season.

Unlike so many others, I never dreamed of riding the Tour. But once I'd made the decision to become a professional bike rider there was no choice. The Tour came close to destroying me because it slowly drained my spirit. It forced me to question the way I had always looked at my sport. The Tour is the limit. It is the Olympics, Wimbledon and the World Cup all rolled into one. It is the highest level of the sport. Perhaps it would be different if I had the all-round capacity of Jan Ullrich or Miguel Indurain or Lance Armstrong; I don't know what that would feel like. But, for me, the Tour has been a source of joy and frustration in equal measure.

I've had some great days on the Tour. I've won three prologues – Lille, 1994; Rouen, 1997; Dublin, 1998 – became the first rider to wear the coveted yellow jersey on his first day on the Tour (Lille, 1994) and broke the record for the fastest stage win, also in Lille. But I realized in 1997, after I had focused my whole preparation on the Tour, that I was not going to be able to compete for overall victory. A lot of people reckoned they could have told me that long before. But, as a born competitor, I thought differently. In my naivety I thought anything was possible.

Once that ultimate goal had been denied me, my motivation changed subtly. I could win the prologue, maybe the odd road stage, but not the overall yellow jersey. It became a matter of trying to do the same thing again, which is a very negative ambition; striving to achieve new goals is much more positive. But suddenly there were no new goals in front of me, and for a couple of years I drifted, partly as a result of overtraining through the winter of 1997, partly because of mental fatigue. For years I knew exactly why I was doing a particular type of training: I was always looking to progress and improve. But suddenly I couldn't muster the same passion for training just to repeat what I had already achieved. The Tour can do that to you. In 1999 it became a personal challenge. I wasn't going to beat it, but I wasn't going to be beaten by it, either, and that thought kept me going when Stuart O'Grady and I were ploughing away at the back on some of the long, hot, perpetually rolling stages through the Massif Central that year. You think to yourself, Oh, come on, just let it happen, let's get off and go home. But you know you couldn't live with yourself if you did. The Tour takes on a character, that's why people identify with it and that's why it is called *the* Tour.

There are lessons to be learned here for any racing cyclist. There will come a point in everyone's career when they feel they've reached the limit. It might come in a 10-mile club time trial, on the track or on the road. For those who simply enjoy going out and competing, win or lose, the shock is probably not as great. The problem for me was that my motivation throughout my cycling career had always been winning and when the winning dried up, I began to question the reason for competing. Constant defeat destroyed the whole philosophy that I have set out in these pages. I lost the passion.

From the outside it's hard to comprehend how much the Tour dominates the life of a professional bike rider. There are many chances to succeed or fail outside the Tour. We have seen the ten-month professional calendar and how many prestigious races are featured on it. But in the three weeks of the Tour, success and failure are magnified tenfold. A team can win sixty races a season, but if they don't perform in the Tour, then their year is deemed a failure, and vice versa. I've always said that the bigger the risk, the bigger the reward, and the Tour is the most eloquent expression of that.

Most riders have a love/hate relationship with the Tour de France. They love the tradition of the race, the excitement, the crowds, the camaraderie and the intensity of those three weeks. Anyone who rides bikes for a living wants to compete in the Tour because it is the absolute apex of their professional career, and to have even one completed Tour on your CV is the sign of a serious professional. To win a stage, to wear the coveted yellow jersey, just for a day, is to stamp your name on the sport. Sean Yates completed thirteen Tours, yet he will be remembered for the one day he wore the yellow jersey of the race leader.

Yet the Tour's domination of the calendar and, for a few years at least, my life was also a source of frustration. The week before the start of the Tour is one of the most unpleasant in the calendar. You step off the plane into a little capsule of pressure that increases every day until the start of the prologue, which is often the make-or-break moment of my season. There is a particular routine you have to follow: the signing-in ceremonies, the medical examination, the end-less interviews and, all the time, that feeling in the pit of your stomach that the next three weeks are going to hurt and the overwhelming desire to get on with it. Patience is a good virtue to have on the Tour, both in not expending too much energy or pumping too much adrenalin in the week before the race, and in pacing yourself through the first week. Whether the Tour's domination of the season is healthy is a matter for debate. The Tour eclipses every other event in the calendar. A poor Tour usually means a poor season, and though the top riders can maybe afford to have one or two bad days on the Tour, the average *domestique* has to keep performing day after day.

It is that unrealistic pressure to perform that lies at the heart of the drugs issue in the sport, which is not an excuse for it, just an explanation of why it might happen. For someone who likes to be in control, the monolithic structures of the Tour can be daunting. You can find yourself being pushed this way and that and doing a thousand things that have nothing to do with being better prepared for the primary objective of the season. In some ways I used to resent the extent to which the Tour dominated my life. For a couple of seasons, when I still wanted to do well in the overall classification, all my training schedules and my entire racing calendar were geared to performing at maximum potential on the Tour. There was no safety net.

The race itself can be divided into distinct phases. During the first week the racing is extremely nervous and aggressive. Every *directeur sportif* wants every one of his riders in the top twenty positions, covering breakaways, shepherding the team leader and keeping out of trouble, which invariably occurs in the middle of the *peloton*. Mostly the races are ridden on the flat and, after a series of attacks, they come together for the final few kilometres to the finish, where the sprint teams jostle for position to get their man to the front. The rest of us quietly retreat and watch the show, making sure that no unexpected gap opens up in the *peloton* before the finish.

The first time trial, which is usually after about ten days, begins to establish the pattern of the race, as it did with Lance Armstrong at Metz in 1999. Lance won from Alex Zulle by almost a minute and took the yellow jersey, which he held to the end. Depending on who is leading, the team of the yellow jersey will always try to control the race, covering breaks and making sure that no-one can gain time on their leader.

The complexion of the race changes once it reaches the mountains, where the specialist climbers hope to do some damage and the balance of power can change dramatically in a matter of minutes. Here the race becomes quite tactical, but more individual. The leaders usually ride near the front, often unable to rely on a team-mate for support, covering each other and trying to explore the physical and mental strength of their rivals. The mountains provide the most compelling spectacle if you happen to be riding on a motorbike or watching from your armchair. For those of us who are not, and never will be, natural climbers, the mountains are hell, nothing more glamorous than a matter of survival. Avoiding the personal humiliation of finishing outside the time limit and being carried away by the broomwagon are the only two sources of motivation.

I used to watch the Tour on television while I was growing up and thought it looked long, hard and definitely not for specialist time triallists like myself. Only when I'd won the Olympic gold and decided to become a professional road-racer did the thought of riding the Tour occur to me. At the start, I didn't realize what the Tour meant, which was an advantage in one way. In my first year, when I won the prologue on my first day, I barely had a clue how hard the race was. I didn't even intend to be in it for too long, just long enough to get some experience under my belt for the following years. It has been a voyage of discovery for me, sometimes euphoric, often agonizing, but the Tour tells you the truth about how good you can be and where your limits lie. I have learned the hard way, and the lessons are as relevant to an amateur cyclist as they are to a professional. If you fail to reach an objective, what is the next step? How do you pick yourself up? How do you react in training? How does it affect your motivation and morale? These are all questions that riders at any level will face. I just happened to face them at the very highest level in the sport.

The Prologue

From the start the prologue was always going to be my main objective in the Tour. It was my specialist event, but at roughly eight minutes and 6 or 7 kms long, the prologue is an insignificant factor in the overall race. It is a way of deciding who wears the yellow jersey on the opening road stage and a way, too, of introducing the Tour to new venues and selling the race to sponsors. Yet, with every stage so competitive and every column inch of newspaper report or second of television exposure being worth money to the sponsors, the prologue is a valuable prize for teams, and even Robert Millar said it was one of the most stressful days of the Tour. It is the only day on the Tour when the winner of the stage is certain to wear yellow.

There are other benefits to winning the prologue in terms of heightened early motivation and confidence in the team that has the yellow jersey. The team is in credit with the bank even before the race has started. It is also an early measure of form. Bobby Julich, who finished third in 1998, said that he gained a lot of confidence from his performance in the prologue. To his credit, Roger Legeay, my team boss, was shrewd enough to realize the growing importance of the prologue and he used me to exploit that.

The Ecstasy: Lille, 1994

I'd already seen the course on paper earlier in the year. I knew it was flat and I knew it was a U-shape out and back. Luckily the road was closed on the day before the race, so I went out and rode the circuit twice. There were some very big sweeping bends, which were no problem to corner but were going to be interesting at speed. So, just to make absolutely sure that nothing shocked me, we took the team car up to racing speed, roughly 60 kph, and took the corners at race pace. It proved a very effective preparation method, and one I used on subsequent courses. A case again of leaving nothing to chance. Riding round a course at 30 kph as opposed to 60 kph can be very different. I gained a lot of confidence from knowing that I could take those corners comfortably at race pace.

One thing I've learned is that I prefer riding round a course on my own. Other riders tend to do it in groups. It's not wrong, I just prefer to ride on my own. They might be able to visualize what it's like taking a corner at 60 kph, but I'm not a natural, so I have to practise it. I went away having ridden most of the corners twice. A prologue can be decided by less than a second, but this is the few minutes of the year I earn my keep. I also tried to visualize the course while lying in bed that night, remembering every particular corner and picturing the whole circuit so I knew instinctively how I was going to tackle each phase.

Once I was happy with the course, I rode back to the hotel, having checked where the start ramp was and where I would have to sign on. I worked out where I was going to warm up and how far that was from the start and, with Greg LeMond, I rode down from the hotel to see how long it would take. The evening before the race I planned all the pre-race timings, working backwards from my start times: stop warming up ten minutes before the start time, twenty minutes' warm-up – five minutes to kill some time, five minutes in the 130s, five in the 140s, five in the 150s, going slowly through the band, and in the last five minutes adding in two ten-second sprints to simulate the start. Otherwise it can be quite a shock.

On the day of the race, I arrived at the camping car about an hour and a half before my start time. Everything was laid out and ready, and I signed on as early as possible to get that out of the way. In the camping car I tried to read, but mainly rehearsed the race in my head before going out for the warm-up.

I started the course in a 53×16 gear and switched quickly to a 53×12, where I stayed for the rest of the prologue. From the start ramp, there was a sharp corner after about 200 ms. I had to brake for that, but from there on the whole course was on a road about 10 ms wide. A kilometre-long straight led into a sweeping 90-degree left-hand bend that could be taken almost flat out; I just stopped pedalling slightly. This is a reasonable place to explain my method of cornering at speed. I'd picked up something from Stephen Roche once. He'd said that a rider should never enter the apex of a bend until he can see the exit. Riders often turn into a corner too soon. If you get parallel to the bend before entering it, it makes the entrance fractionally slower, but the exit much quicker, because you can start getting back on the power faster. The other tip is: always look where you're going, not at the bend.

From the left-hand bend, it was straight down round a traffic island, which could be taken flat out, and back up to the same corner, which

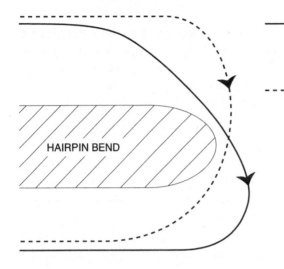

Chris Boardman's line.
Late entry, lower speed,
but earlier acceleration
out of the corner.

Orthodox line.
This is a common
mistake. An early turn
into an apex that
results in corrective
breaking and loss of
speed on exit.

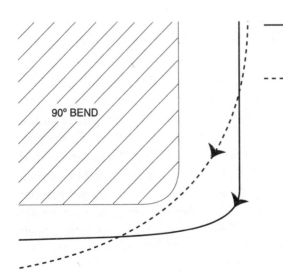

Chris Boardman's line.
Slower in, but quicker
and safer out.

Orthodox line.
Faster, but runs the risk
of crashing out if speed
on entry is too high.

was now a right-hander. It was the only corner where most people would brake. I actually covered the brakes but didn't use them and ran wide, almost touching the barriers on the exit. That was a key corner for me. From there it was a straight road ahead to the finish, and I caught Luc Leblanc just as I was coming up to the line. I'd managed 120+ cadence for an average of 56 kph, seven minutes and twenty seconds. I wasn't hurting, but I knew I couldn't go any faster. I beat Indurain by thirteen seconds that day, and for a few days after that I enjoyed some of the best form of my life. I was floating.

Rouen, 1997

I was under a lot of pressure in 1997 to win the prologue again, yet it can never be quite the same because people start taking your success for granted. I won the prologue that year; I got away with it by one second from Jan Ullrich, the eventual winner of the Tour. I overgeared because I was under so much pressure, and the course included quite a nasty climb some 600 ms after the start, which caught me out. I wasn't comfortable with the course and hadn't really worked out how to tackle it. When it came to the climb, which was about a minute long and a big gear climb, I completely fluffed it. I didn't attack nearly hard enough because of my indecision. The start was on one side of the bridge, which we crossed into a slight dip and then started the climb, out of the saddle all the way. It was important not to expend too much energy on the climb because you would then spend the flat part of the course at the top of the hill recovering rather than re-accelerating. The flat section lasted for about 800 ms, then curved to the right with a descent back down to the town, a right curve almost onto a motorway, a long straight and one final right-hander to the finish. I used 54×11 gear, but it wasn't a good ride.

There is a lesson to be learned here. In Rouen I knew I was capable of winning, and I knew I should win, so if I didn't I knew it would be my fault, which triggered the what-if syndrome. What if I lose, what if my wheels fall off, what if . . . ? I became tied up through nerves. In Dublin the following year, I came to the Tour in very poor form and with low expectations. I had reconciled myself to doing my best. I thought, If I lose, they can't hang me, they can't shoot me, they can't put me in prison, and that cleared my mind before the start. Be as good as you can be – that was the phrase we'd decided to hang on to that weekend, and it helped me to relax and concentrate on the ride.

Dublin, 1998

I've no idea where this one came from. My preparation was poor and I had no right to win it. What I hadn't counted on was the depth of work that had been put in place over previous years. I had been training hard in the build-up, doing some intense work, but at no point did I feel on anything like decent form. On the day I had resigned myself to losing, so winning was a real shock. It was a physical course, which required riding in a good position at high speeds. The start was in Castle Street into a sweeping left-hand curve, then a 1-km straight into a 90-degree turn along the park. I actually started slower than I wanted because I was having difficulty finding explosive speed at that time. In this particular course that helped, because many of the guys started too fast and then blew up. It takes a lot of confidence not to start like a greyhound, particularly when it's an event you want to win so badly. There were three corners I had to brake for, but the one coming back over the bridge was the sharpest. I was slightly over-geared for the final straight, which is also a temptation. If you overgear it takes a few precious seconds to get going.

When you're riding, it's an exercise in pure concentration. I don't hear the crowd at all, which is extraordinary when you consider how close they are. It's the moments before the start that I hate. On the ramp, all you feel is fear and the total desire to be somewhere else. But a few minutes later it feels great because it's all over.

Riding the Tour: Tactics and Technique

There are plenty of things to learn about stage racing in the *peloton*. One is to how to deal with crosswinds by forming an echelon across

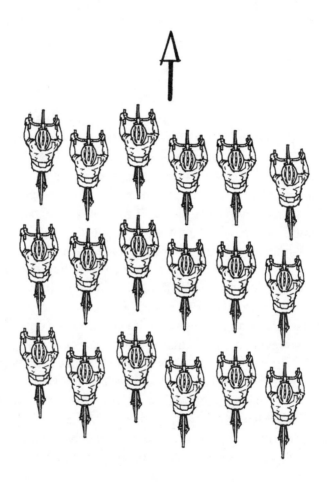

The *peloton* cruising.

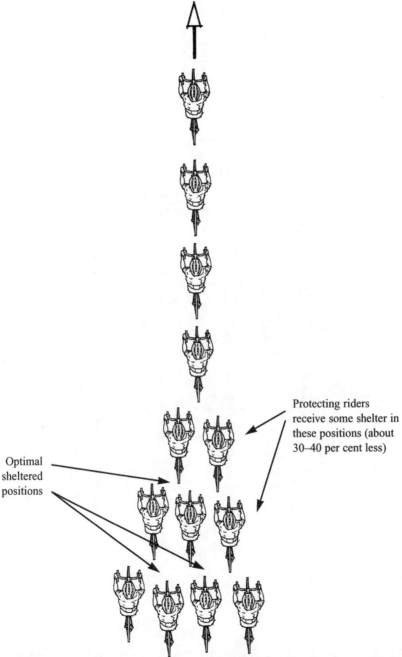

Protecting riders
receive some shelter in
these positions (about
30–40 per cent less)

Optimal
sheltered
positions

The formation of the *peloton* when teams are working to keep up the pace, usually to chase down a breakaway, or in the last 20 kms of a stage that will be contested by sprinters.

WIND DIRECTION

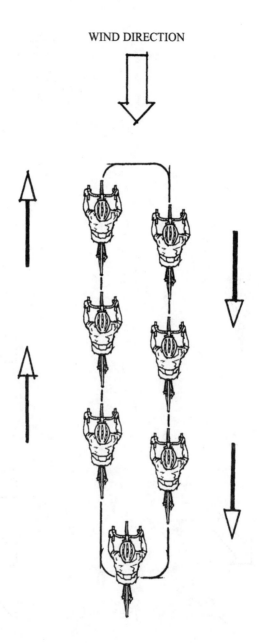

The principle of 'through and off' used to drive the *peloton* or a breakaway group. Riders take their turn at the front before dropping away to the back in a constant circular motion.

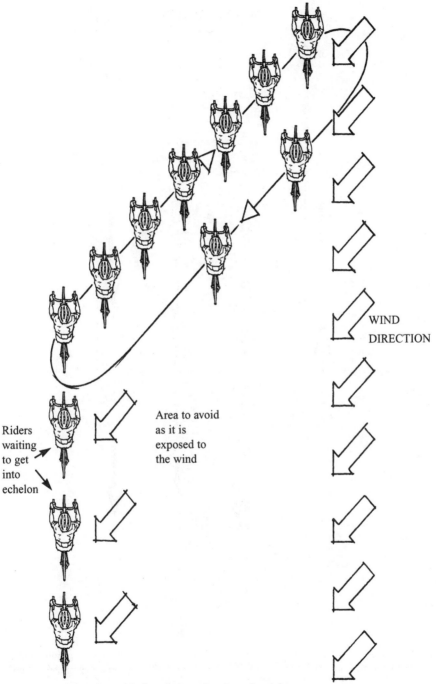

Riders
waiting
to get
into
echelon

Area to avoid
as it is
exposed to
the wind

WIND
DIRECTION

The echelon formation, with the wind coming from the right.

Rider B   Rider A

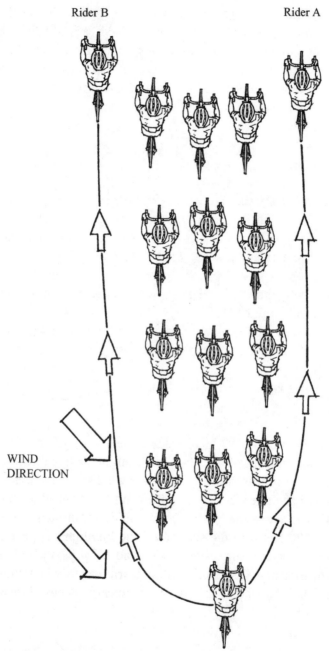

WIND
DIRECTION

Attacking into the wind. Rider B has attacked on the windward side of the bunch, which will be much harder than the protected side taken by Rider A.

the road. If the wind is coming from the right, the front of the echelon is in the right-hand gutter of the road and the back is in the left. On paper, the echelon looks straightforward enough. It's a moving ellipse with riders constantly falling off the front and moving down the order to join the back rank again in the left gutter. The temptation if you can't find shelter is to jump out into the wind and try to queue jump, as it were. The power demand to ride fully in the wind is so great that, generally, you have about ten seconds to get into the echelon before you start to fall back. Once riders see you falling back, they will nip in front of you, not wanting to be caught behind a potential split. If the wind is coming from the right, the best place is on the left, but to find a gap it's important to ride in a very low gear and at a high cadence, ready for the moment a gap opens up. Crosswinds are dangerous for stage riders because gaps can open up between the separate echelons very easily. Echelons are fluid, with riders coming past and around you and everyone trying to find the best place. Fred Moncassin told me: high cadence, low gear.

Greg LeMond also passed on a tip about making ground through a corner. If there are a hundred plus riders gutter to gutter and you need to be nearer the front of the *peloton*, when you go round a left-hand bend, a gap will appear on the right-hand side of the road. What people watching on television seeing those lovely aerial shots of the *peloton* fail to understand is the rider's eye view of the bunch. When you're in the middle of them it's like driving behind a big truck: you can't see anything in front of you. The truck might change direction, stop or come back towards you. You can't see what shape the road in front is, or whether there's a left- or right-hand bend ahead, or how sharp it is. All you see is the guy in front. You don't, in many cases, have any idea who has won the stage until the highlights appear on television later in the evening or when you read *L'Equipe* to find out the result in the morning. It's quite a skill to learn how to ride in those circumstances, and it's scary, particularly in the early stages of races, which tend to be very nervy. If the road bends to the left, everyone's instinct is to corner close to the left, so gaps appear on the right-hand side of the road. If you don't learn these tricks of the road you end up having to expend a lot of unnecessary energy making up ground and, over a long and gruelling race like the Tour, preserving energy is one of the keys to success.

On the Tour, as in other stage races, the tactics are dictated by circumstances. Often, the first day or two of stage races are mayhem because everyone comes with fresh legs and attacks occur all over the place. Once the pattern develops and the main contenders are sorted out, the race starts to settle down. That only happens after a week or so. If you happen to be leading, the critical thing is not to waste energy chasing shadows.

I rode a four-day stage race with a time trial to finish at the end of the 1999 season. On paper, if I could keep the race together I had a reasonable chance of winning overall. But I made a big mistake on the first day. There were some crosswinds, and attacks were going on everywhere, bodies all over the place, and I couldn't follow them all. I should have cut my losses, looked to see who was the best time triallist in the race – in this case, Christophe Moreau – and stuck close to him. In alliance, our teams might have had a chance of holding the race together. But I tried to chase too many things and suddenly a group formed from twos and threes up the road and disappeared into the distance. All my potential allies were in that group and that was that.

In the 1999 Tour, Armstrong's US Postal team did a good job of protecting the yellow jersey, but they couldn't defend every move. Often, they had to rely on joining forces with the second- and third-placed teams, who also wanted to protect their positions by ensuring that no rival was allowed to make a decisive break.

You have to be careful not to use up energy in the wrong places. Indurain was a past master at using other teams to further his own cause. Often, towards the end of the Tour, other teams would have accepted that the Spaniard was going to win and would be solely concerned with getting their teams on the podium in Paris. It's a matter of psychology and finding out who wants what and how everyone can fulfil their ambitions.

Most *directeurs sportifs* want you at the front the whole time, but it's easier said than done because everyone wants to be there. A lot of time in the *peloton* is spent in conversation about bank managers, families or schools, but there is an underlying level of competence and concentration that comes from riding an inch from someone else's wheel all your life. I hate having to join in something like an echelon because I've had some bad accidents and the scars are beginning to show. When you are aware of the consequences of crashing, you start to avoid putting yourself in dangerous positions. The rest of the *peloton* soon pick up on that and start nipping round you, which makes you feel like the most timid of learner drivers. Then you end up at the back, which hits your self-esteem further, until being in fiftieth place feels like being at the front. And so it becomes a vicious circle. When the stakes become high enough and I know I'm on the verge of some good form then I force myself to mix it, but I really have to force myself. In the Tour, the safest place is either right at the front to miss the trouble or right at the back so that you can spot the trouble and avoid it, as I did when so many fell on the causeway on an early stage of the 1999 Tour. The worst place to be in those situations is in the middle.

Descending is another acquired skill. When a group is in a straight line on a descent, the best place to be is first or between tenth and fifteenth. You should watch the guy at the very front, not the guy directly in front. If you see him start to pedal round the bend, he has seen round the corner and knows it's clear, which means you can start pedalling that little bit earlier. It's also important to get behind someone who is a good descender and a good bike-handler, someone who brakes smoothly and follows a good line round the corners. Most riders brought up on road-racing are naturally good bike-handlers, they think nothing of rubbing their front wheel against the rear wheel of the guy in front and can ride all day surrounded by a hundred other cyclists. For those of us more used to riding alone on a track or road against the clock, the *peloton* can become almost claustrophobic. Certainly, riding in the bunch was not a skill I acquired overnight, yet when I asked Greg LeMond to explain the tricks of doing it, he couldn't really tell me. He wasn't being unhelpful; it's like asking a footballer how he kicks a ball. Mostly, he just does it.

LeMond was a great poker player on a bike. I would have liked to see him together with Indurain at the peak of their powers. When I joined the Gan team in 1994, Greg was on the last stages of his extra-ordinary career. One of his greatest attributes was his ability to think clearly and tactically under enormous pressure. He was a great bluffer, able to cover up the fact that he was suffering by asking his rivals questions, pushing them into riding too hard and making mis-takes, much as he did with Bernard Hinault, his team-mate and rival, on the famous 1986 Tour.

Indurain had the same inscrutable face and ability to pressurize others by the relentless rhythm of his riding. You could never tell what he was thinking or how much he was suffering. Like boxers looking into each other's eyes before the first bell, it was unnerving to find that your opponent didn't blink. Indurain was like a boxer on a bicycle.

An example of LeMond's tactical brilliance, which he relates him-self, came in the 1983 World Championships. This is a perfect example of how flexible top riders have to be, tactically and mentally. LeMond had an American team with him, but they were of no real consequence when it came to the final, while the Italians and the Dutch had strong professional teams quite capable of supporting their leaders. With about 60 miles to go, the Australian Phil Anderson broke clear and established a lead of a minute. LeMond let him go because he knew the course was difficult and the other teams would combine to reel him in eventually. LeMond joined the chasing group of Dutchmen and Italians, who caught Anderson with about 25 miles to go. Robert Millar attacked, but when the chasing group caught Millar, at which point there is always a brief let-down psycho-logically, LeMond attacked and broke off the front with two other riders. Once away, LeMond had to play cat and mouse with his two rivals, Moreno Argentin of Italy and Faustino Ruperez of Spain. He accelerated a little to gauge how strong the others were, and found that the Italian dropped off. Then LeMond pretended he was tired and asked Ruperez to share the work at the front. Not wanting to be caught, the Spaniard agreed. Stuck to his back wheel, LeMond could tell how strong Ruperez was and, using that information, he was able to monitor his own strength, use it to his best advantage and break away just before the finish to win the world title.

Tactics in the Tour are dictated by the pattern of the race. The yellow jersey team will defend their man. The trick for anyone who wants to win a stage after the first ten days or so is to make sure they are no threat to the overall leader. If they are a threat, they stand a good chance of being ridden down by the top teams. Some riders who have no chance of winning overall from the start will even purposefully lose some time early in the race to make sure that, when they attack later, none of the leading teams will bother to waste their energy trying to catch up because they pose no threat to the general classification. The problem in the first week is that the sprinting teams have an interst in keeping the race together at the finish.

The Tour can also expose weaknesses in the spirit of a team. The pressures can blow you apart or pull you together. It depends on the individuals in the team and how they deal with that pressure. You often find that a team needs a mutual enemy, and if you're not careful that enemy can come from within. I've been there, on the pursuit team at the 1992 Barcelona Olympics, which I mentioned earlier in the book. Because I was riding the individual pursuit, the others were suspicious of my commitment to the team. They found it irritating that I was doing something else as well. A good psychologist defused that situation, but as a pro you're riding to preserve your living, too, which adds to the complications. If you're on the last year of a contract and you give your all in a race to help someone else win, that's better for the team, but at the end of the year you have less to sell. Unless the team boss recognizes your work and pays you accordingly, it would surely have been better to have got third place for yourself as opposed to nowhere for yourself and first for the team. There are plenty of individuals who think like that.

A Day on the Tour

This is really very straightforward and, after a time, thoroughly tedious. It's a matter of getting to the next hotel, having a massage, eating, going to bed, waking up and doing the same again. The timings are dictated by the start time in the morning, which, in turn, depends on the length of the stage. All stages tend to end at about

4–5 p.m. continental time for television, so the start might be 11 a.m. Teams begin to arrive at the start area about half an hour before the off, time enough to have a chat with journalists, if necessary, sign on and have a coffee in the *village de depart*. A lot of race gossip flows through the village in the mornings: who's saying what about whom and little psychological games played out through the pages of *L'Equipe* or *Le Monde*.

If the start is at eleven, the riders will have been woken at about 7 a.m. in time to have some breakfast and pack their bags ready for the *soigneur* to take to the next hotel. There will be a short team meeting to work out the tactics for the day and to see who might be strong enough to join a break. It's a question of trying to anticipate the tactics of the other teams, while gauging the individual potential within your own team. If you're struggling with your form, as I was in the 1999 Tour, you hope that one member of the team gets in an early breakaway and takes the pressure off the rest. In the mountains, without a specialist climber, it's simply a matter of hanging on.

At the end of the race, you go straight to your *soigneur*, into the camping car, back to another hotel, onto the massage table, have dinner and go to bed. That's the routine, but you get surprisingly used to it after three weeks and it's quite a culture shock when it all comes to an end.

The Bad Days: The 1999 Tour

I have had plenty of bad days on the Tour. The first at St Brieuc in 1995, when I crashed and broke my ankle; the second on the Col de Soulor in 1997, but 1999 was probably the most disappointing of my six Tours to date. I came into it short of form and confidence, knowing that I was going to suffer without any hope of success. If you suffer and win, then there's a point to it all, but if things aren't going well and you're dropped in the mountains and are struggling simply to stay inside the time limit, it's soul-destroying.

My mood was apparent at the final time trial. I had ridden the whole Tour defensively, trying not to put myself into any difficult situations, riding purely to survive, which isn't my style. The time trial, though, at Futuroscope, the day before the finish in Paris, should have been good for me. The course was 57 kms and not too hilly. Ordinarily, I would have been up for it, but after three weeks of being pummelled day after day, I'd become scared of suffering. It was a result of constant overtraining; I never felt on top of it. You not only go slower, you hurt more, and over a period of time – about eighteen months – that was all I was achieving. In the end, like a boxer, you just don't want to get hit any more. On that last time trial I didn't feel it was worth suffering for fifth place. You can see it from my pulse, which rose quite a bit over the last few kilometres, so I was obviously capable of more than I was giving. I was prepared to suffer for ten minutes, but not for an hour.

Strangely, on the 1999 Tour I got through the Alps as well as I've ever done. I just aimed for the easiest group and rode tempo. But I had some bad days in the Massif Central, during the transition between the Alps and the Pyrenees, and on the first day in the Pyrenees, on the stage from St Gaudens to Piau-Engaly, a day of pure torture with four mountains stacked one after the other, I was at the back and punctured at the bottom of the first climb.

Stuart and I had actually calculated beforehand where we could afford to be dropped if we were going to arrive inside the time limit for the stage, but we were dropped way before that spot, which meant we had to get back to the bunch or it was all over. We survived and I finished my second Tour, but only after climbing off in Paris did I realize the extent of my disappointment. It wasn't enough just to say I'd finished. I was a shell. For the first time in my career I hadn't performed to the best of my ability.

Learning the Lessons and Looking Forward to Sydney

Every rider will go through bad patches, be they in club races or at a professional level. It's just not possible to perform well all the time. The trick is to plan and identify when the best opportunities are and prepare yourself to dig deep for those moments. Don't ask yourself to do it week in, week out. The words of the Pirelli ad sum it up: 'Power is nothing without control'. Through 1998–9 I had all the knowledge and physical ability, but I had no control. I wasn't properly focused. But the 1999 Tour will, hopefully, prove a crossroads in the latter stages of my career.

The final week or so of the Tour is the usual place for negotiating deals for the following season. It's a place where agreements are made rather than contracts signed, but it's a good time to talk. Roger came to see me and we talked about what I had in mind for the future. I was signed up for another year, but I knew he was concerned about my form and motivation, and he had every right to know what was going on. I wasn't going to renegotiate my contract, but the discussion made me feel very uncomfortable, because I knew I had let him down and I wanted to redress that. It would be easy to say I don't owe him anything – I've generated good publicity for his team, given off a good image and, until the last year, done the best I could – but Roger has been very supportive to me throughout my career and I wanted to give him more of what he was paying for. But how? That was the question.

Within an hour of that discussion, Peter Keen phoned, which was a coincidence because I had wanted to speak to him. He'd been occupied with the elite performance programme for the British Cycling Federation, but had missed doing his high-performance coaching, and I was desperately in need of some guidance to get my career back on track for the run-up to Sydney and retirement. So, in a sense, we both came back together at the right time. That was the one positive thing to come out of the 1999 Tour.

The 2000 season will be my last. I have always thought that thirty-two was about the right age to retire, and I would like to retain some element of control in the decision and not be forced out because I couldn't find a contract. I have mixed feelings about the season. Much of my childhood and all my adult life have been devoted to cycling. I've given it all my time, put my heart and soul into it and I earn the majority of my income from it, so it will be quite a shock to stop and I'm not sure how I will cope. It feels like doing the very last interval in training; it doesn't matter if you trash yourself because there are no more. I want to do well and go out with some good memories, but, being a perfectionist, I'm a little apprehensive that it won't finish quite as neatly or conveniently as I would like.

My programme for the early part of the season will stay the same until the Tour. My winter training was geared towards adding more explosive power to my riding and improving my ability to jump and attack on short climbs. It was good to be back working with Peter Keen almost full time again. After the Tour, my time will be given over predominantly to national team training, with a view to riding the Olympic time trial and, potentially, the team pursuit. There is still an outside chance I will try to regain my individual pursuit title, but I think it will be just the two events. Depending on what happens in Sydney, I will contest the World Track Championships which, as luck would have it, are right on my doorstep in Manchester. That would be my ideal swansong, but I won't ride if I don't feel I'm up to the job, because not being able to give my best would be an awful way to go out.

The fairy tale would be to win a second Olympic gold in Sydney and complete the circle that began in Barcelona in 1992. I will be up against riders who are extremely motivated, who eat, drink and sleep cycling, and the reason I'm stopping is because I don't feel that way any more. In reality, winning gold would only add to the pressure to continue, but throughout my professional career I've always looked forward to the second half of the season, and the opportunity to finish on a high note will give me all the motivation and passion I need one last time.

16

DRUGS

A Personal View

There are two ways of looking at the 1998 Tour de France and the persistent revelations about drug abuse in the *peloton*. The first was to lament the fact that my sport was being brought to its knees by the rumour, speculation and accusation. The other, more positive response was to say that at least that Tour brought the whole problem out into the open. Faced with such disturbing evidence, the authorities could not just sit back and do nothing. The use of drugs had clearly spread deeper and wider than I or anyone else had suspected.

I was lucky in 1998. I fell off on the third stage in Ireland and was sitting back at home when the chain of events, begun by a raid on Willi Voets's Festina car on the French–Belgian border on the eve of the Tour, escalated into a full-scale investigation by the French police. The Festina team, including Richard Virenque, was expelled from the race in dramatic circumstances, the Spanish teams went home in disgust and the Dutch-based TVM team abandoned the race after their team hotel was raided and some of their riders had been forced to spend the night in a police cell. At one point, as the riders refused to race, the Tour de France was on the verge of collapse, and only some very persuasive talking by Jean Marie Leblanc, the head of the Société de Tour, kept the race going till Paris.

What lessons have been learned from that Tour? I said at the time I was happy to be out of such an unpleasant atmosphere, but, though the 1999 Tour, which began as the Tour of Revival and ended as the Tour of Transition, was run without a hitch, it was far from clear that the drug problem had been eradicated from professional cycling. A constant undercurrent of innuendo and rumour accompanied the race, and there were strong suspicions voiced by a minority of riders, one publicly, the others privately, that there was a 'two-speed' Tour, one for the French riders, who were subject to regular and rigorous blood tests throughout the season, and one for the other teams, who didn't have such strict dope controls. The fact that the home riders did not manage to win a stage in the Tour for the first time in twenty-six years only added to the speculation. The problem, both for individual riders and for the wider credibility of the sport, is that now no performance is above suspicion.

Lance Armstrong's recovery from testicular cancer to win the Tour is one of the most remarkable stories in its long history. Yet the extent of his domination was regarded with great cynicism by the French press in particular. How, people asked, could Armstrong break the record for the fastest ever climb to Sestrière after a 200-km stage when the original record, held by Bjarne Riis, was set when the stage had been shortened to a mere 40 kms? Why, they asked, did the *gruppetto* contain seventy riders, nearly half the *peloton*, when usually it consisted of between only thirty and forty? How could a man with only a 50–50 chance of life two years before come back so quickly to win one of the most gruelling sporting events in the world? To them, nothing added up.

It was all circumstantial evidence, but the problem with such an atmosphere is that now no performance can be viewed objectively. No-one can say, 'Wow! That was great.' Anything that is remarkable is regarded as suspect, and Lance's victory came firmly under the banner of 'remarkable'.

I would be lying if I said I hadn't harboured my own suspicions about other riders. I know my form and I know what times I am capable of, so I find it strange when a rider who I can usually beat by five minutes mysteriously beats me by five minutes in the Tour.

When I turned professional in 1994 I wasn't completely naive. I knew drugs were an issue and I joined Roger Legeay's Gan team because I knew he would be totally and utterly straight on that. We discussed the issue and I told Roger what my personal standpoint was. Roger said he wouldn't be able to live with himself if he felt he had helped to shorten the lifespan of one of his riders or put their lives at risk simply to win a bike race. He said that if I did my job, worked hard and applied myself, I would win races anyway, maybe not as many or as major, but I would win.

I've never speculated about what I might have been able to achieve by taking drugs because it has never been an option. My way of dealing with the drugs issue is to draw a line in the sand and say, 'I'm not prepared to do that.' I've set out to be as good as I can and to see where that gets me. In my narrow field, it's got me quite far. I have habitually low testosterone levels; in forcing my body to endure my regime day after day I've lost bone density at such a fast rate that I'm on the verge of suffering from osteoporosis. I had the engine to compete and I was lucky in that I found things I could do within professional cycling. I could win prologues if I arrived completely fresh and I could pull off the odd time trial within a stage race. I could even climb pretty well on good days. But I couldn't recover quickly enough to repeat the performance consistently, day after day.

I have been accused of not taking a strong enough stance against the drug-takers. Nicolas Aubier, a member of the Gan team in my first season, claimed that ninety-nine out of a hundred riders had taken drugs. I was the hundredth. He couldn't believe my suitcase contained only clothes, books, a few vitamin C and E tablets and my toothbrush. But though I am an acknowledged 'clean' rider, I'm not going to cast stones at others. For one thing, I don't *know*. It's not a subject widely discussed over coffee and a croissant in the morning. One of the things that annoyed me about those who were found guilty in the 1998 Tour was their presumption that every other team was taking drugs, too. I don't know who's taking drugs, so how can they? Yet despite that fact we were all tarred with the same brush.

Cycling is a tough, and predominantly working-class, sport. The choices facing a lot of riders are quite stark. You can go and work in the local factory, the garage or on the family farm, or you can ride your bike, which is what you enjoy doing, and, by the way, if you take a little of this, you'll be able to earn a good living. That's a pretty horrible choice to have to make, particularly when you suspect, or are led to believe, that everyone else is taking drugs, too. If boxing is a way off the streets, cycling is a way out of the fields. Neil Stephens, one of the Festina team who admitted to taking drugs and who retired after the 1998 Tour, was a good friend of mine. I don't regard him as a bad person because he took drugs. Anyone who says he hasn't considered it is a liar. It's just not the choice I've made in my career.

One way of tackling the problem is to go straight to the source, which is the incentive for taking drugs in the first place. By making the risk greater than the reward, you remove the rider's incentive to take drugs, which means that sponsors have to be more responsible in their attitudes to the sport.

Alex Zulle, who was suspended for six months for drug-taking, claimed that the pressure of producing results for sponsors had pushed him into it. If sponsors instigated a rule that stated that one positive test within a team meant they would forfeit their whole sponsorship, the risk of detection would become greater and the gap between reward and risk would narrow.

Sponsors have brought more money into cycling, but in doing so they have demanded more from the cyclists, who are already stretched to the limit by their relentless race schedules. The calendar has speeded up and races that were used to warm up for the season are now more aggressive and competitive. Everyone wants to win something somewhere because the rewards are so much greater. By their very nature, cyclists are obsessive; they don't just want to do well, they're desperate to succeed. So when they get put under intolerable pressure, taking drugs is one way out.

Advances in physiology and medicine mean that we are now able to supplement what the body does artificially, right down to controlling our hormonal levels. On the second rest day of the 1999 Tour, every rider left in the race was breathalysed for a drug called Perfluorocarbon (PFC), which expands the body's haemoglobin and enables the recipient to carry more oxygen in the blood. It is used in hospitals as an emergency product for casualties who have lost a lot of blood and can't undergo transfusions. It's a sophisticated form of EPO (Erythropoietin) because it doesn't increase the haematocrit level above the 50 per cent laid down in the UCI's health checks. It does the same job but doesn't show up. The authorities think they have found a way of detecting PFC because the product deposits a gas within the body for up to seven days after it is used. The depressing news is that anyone might be willing to take it, but the good news is that, if there are health checks for haematocrit levels and an effective test for PFC, the sport might begin to tighten up its act.

The authorities have a very tough job to do. It is easy to say they should do more, but what and how? By introducing regular blood tests, cycling has done more than almost any other sport to detect drug-takers. But if people are prepared to mess about with their hormones in order to ride faster or for longer, then the whole business is becoming a nightmare. One way of tackling it in the long term is to have regular and compulsory blood and urine testing of riders throughout their careers, so that any abnormality in the body can be quickly identified and checked. They are starting to bring that sort of scrutiny into athletics and it could be tried in cycling.

The authorities also need to be tougher on those who are caught. A six-month winter ban is not exactly a great hardship for a cyclist. Sentences have to hurt; the risk has to be made bigger.

The drugs issue hasn't made me want to quit cycling, but it has helped to confirm my original decision to retire at the end of the 2000 season. It is just one more thing which has been eating away at my enthusiasm. The way I've countered it is to repeat one of my favourite phrases over and over: 'Be as good as you can be.' I need to do that for my own sense of honour, so that I can look my boss in the eye at the end of it all and say, 'I'm sorry I couldn't do that, that and that, but I gave it everything I had.' That's important to me and it should be important to *every* cyclist at *every* level.

APPENDIX A

Chris Boardman
Race Schedule Early/Mid Season 1997

Date	Event	
21 Jan 97–30 Jan 97	Team Training Camp	FRA
22 Feb 97	Tour de Haut Var	FRA
25 Feb 97–1 Mar 97	Tour de Valence	SPA
5 Mar 97–9 Mar 97	Tour de Mercie	SPA
16 Mar 97	Porthole GP	GBR
29 Mar 97–30 Mar 97	Critérium International	FRA
1 Apr 97	Paris–Camembert	FRA
7 Apr 97–11 Apr 97	Tour du Pays Basque	SPA
16 Apr 97	Flèche Wallonne	BEL
20 Apr 97	Liège–Bastogne–Liège	BEL
4 May 97	Grand Prix Grimpeur	FRA
6 May 97–11 May 97	Tour de Romandie	SWIT
27 May 97–1 June 97	GP Midi Libre	FRA
8 Jun 97–15 Jun 97	Critérium du Dauphine Libéré	FRA
19 Jun 97–26 Jun 97	Tour de Catalonia	SPA
5 Jul 97–27 Jul 97	**Tour de France**	**FRA**
9 Aug 97	San Sebastián	SPA
17 Aug 97	Leeds Classic	GBR

24 Aug 97	GP de Suisse	SWIT
31 Aug 97	GP Eddy Merckx	BEL
6 Sept 97–28 Sept 97	Tour d'Espagne	SPA
9 Oct 97	World Time Trial	SPA

Training Camps

21 Jan 97–30 Jan 97	Pau basic conditioning/weight loss
9 Mar 97–29 Mar 97	Target venue undecided
20 Apr 97–4 May 97	Weight loss programme (venue undecided)
11 May 97–21 May 97	Mountain Reconnoitre Alps or Pyrenees

Chris Boardman
Race Schedule 1998 Season (Provisional)

Date	Event	
20 Jan 98–29 Jan 98	Training camp	FRA
4 Feb 98–8 Feb 98	Bessèges	FRA
21 Feb 98	Haut Var	FRA
24 Feb 98–28 Feb 98	Tour de Valence	SPA
8 Mar 98–15 Mar 98	Paris–Nice	FRA
22 Mar 98	Cholet Pays de Loire	FRA
23 Mar 98–29 Mar 98	Critérium International	FRA
6 Apr 98–10 Apr 98	Tour de Pays Basque	SPA
19 Apr 98	Liège–Bastogne–Liège	BEL
5 May 98–10 May 98	Tour de Romandie	SWIT
16 May 98–17 May 98	Tour de l'Oise	FRA
23 May 98–31 May 98	Prutour of Britain	GBR
7 Jun 98–14 Jun 98	Dauphine Libéré	FRA
18 Jun 98–25 Jun 98	Tour de Catalonia	SPA
11 Jul 98–2 Aug 98	**Tour de France**	**FRA**
26 Aug 98–27 Aug 98	World Pursuit Championship	FRA
30 Aug 98	GP Eddy Merckx	BEL
13 Sep 98	Formies	FRA

16 Sep 98	GP des Nations	FRA
20 Sep 98	GP Isbergues	FRA
27 Sep 98	Polymultiplee	FRA
1 Oct 98	Paris–Bourges	FRA
8 Oct 98	World Time Trial Championships	HOL
18 Oct 98	Chrono des Herbiers	FRA

Chris Boardman
Race Schedule 1999 Season

Date		Event	
FEB	3–7	Bessèges	FRA
	15	Team Camp – Seillans	FRA
	16	Lagueglia	FRA
	20	Haut Var	FRA
	24–28	Training Camp – Nevers	FRA
MAR	7–14	Paris–Nice	FRA
	21	Cholet	FRA
	27–28	Critérium International	FRA
APR	6	Camembert	FRA
	7–10	Circuit de la Sarthe	FRA
	14	Flèche Wallonne	BEL
	18	Liège–Bastogne–Liège	BEL
MAY	4–9	Four Days of Dunkerque	FRA
	14–16	Tour de l'Oise	FRA
	23–29	Prutour	GBR
JUNE	6–13	Dauphine Libéré	FRA
	19–22	Route de Sud	FRA
JULY	**3–25**	**Tour de France**	**FRA**
	31	Bretling GP Time Trial	GER
AUG	17–20	Tour de Limousin	FRA
	24–27	Poitou Charente	FRA
	29	GP Eddy Merckx	BEL

SEP	6–12	Tour de Pologne	POL
	18	GP Nations	FRA
	19	GP Isbergues	FRA
	22–26	GP Guillaume	FRA
OCT	6	World Time Trial Championships	ITA
	17	Chrono des Herbiers	FRA
	20	**Track Worlds**	**GER**

APPENDIX B

**Chris Boardman
Proposed Training Plan 1999
Overview First Draft**

Phase 1 Commencing: December 1998

4 weeks: Base conditioning, general maintenance and final recovery.
Increase of bike-specific training from 8 to 16 hours per week; as yet no target heart rate, but generally averaging above 145 bpm and maxing approx. 179 bpm.

Phase 2 Commencing: 1 January 1999

5 weeks, 3 days: Pre-race preparatory conditioning.
Increasing on the bike volume from 16 to an average of 18 hours per week. Phasing in of pulse-specific training with the emphasis on **self-control!** Endurance rides increasing from 4 hours max to an occasional 6 hours. This phase will also include the team's 8-day training camp (18–25) which is generally overload in both volume and intensity.

Apart from the camp, this period is mainly aimed at creating a strong endurance base and conditioning my body to be able to absorb and profit from the more intensive training to follow. Target weight by end of phase 2 – 70.5 kgs.

Weight loss

2 January also heralds the start of a **controlled** weight-loss programme from an estimated 73 kgs to a stable 68.5 kgs by 14 March.
Approximately 11 weeks, averaging a loss of 450 gs per week. This
would seem to be a reasonable objective but **should not be allowed
to become my primary objective!**

Note

At this point I am mindful of the length of this season, a potential 10
months if it is to include the World Track Champs, and the need to
exercise self-control early in the year if I am to be physically and
mentally ready for the bigger objectives later on.

Phase 3 Commencing: 7 February 1999

**5 weeks: Intensive road preparation culminating in objective no.
1, Paris–Nice on 14 March.**

This is a very mixed phase to include climbing L2–4, threshold work
L3 on track and road, intervals from 10 seconds to 2 minutes. I anticipate the majority of endurance work will come from the racing and
that the total weekly volume should be 17–25 hours. I would like to
go to the races in this period with a clear idea of what I am trying
to achieve; this will help motivation in a period where I am likely to
be getting a good hiding!

Phase 4 Commencing: 15 March

5 weeks: 'Peak' maintenance programme.

This is the first mentally intense period in the season, containing 3
objectives. The volume should be about the same or even less to
facilitate recovery from the races and the emphasis should be more on
maintenance of what has hopefully already been created; if not, then this
period can also be used to concentrate a little more on areas of concern.

Again, endurance should not be a problem now racing is well under
way, and I hope my objectives during each race should be clear and
very obvious.

End of spring campaign!

Phase 5 Commencing: 19 April 1999

2 weeks: Active recovery period.
This period is shorter than I would have liked but is governed by the races appropriate to me.

I think it would be difficult to lose much form in such a short period, but it would be possible to carry over fatigue into the main part of the year if I don't exercise sufficient self-control. This would be potentially disastrous to the rest of the year as there are no other obvious opportunities to stop and recover before the end of the season. Consequently, I think this break period should be viewed as of key importance to the year and a light-maintenance phase of about 10 hours per week mixed L2 should be the aim. This also provides a mental incentive after the spring campaign.

Phase 6 Commencing: 4 May 1999

4 weeks, 5 days: Specialized climbing and T.T. work.
16 hours to 25 hours per week. This phase contains a high volume of racing (16 days), but these are mostly secondary objectives for me and so I anticipate riding them hard even if my form is only at about 85 per cent. This, then, should take care of my endurance needs and hopefully some of the L4 work. With the time that is left, I intend to concentrate on specialized L3 and L4 work, also some long climb simulations utilizing the treadmill.

Again, if I assume correctly and the Tour is the year's most important objective, I think caution is important in this period, carefully starting to reach peak condition no sooner than the Dauphine on 6 June.

Any minor weight adjustments can also be addressed in this phase with an average stable weight of **no less** than 68 kgs.

Phase 7 Commencing: 14 June 1999

5 days: Recovery.
10 hours. Hardly a phase, but I anticipate needing something positive to look forward to mentally here. This could also serve as a pressure

valve physically after what is likely to have been a very tough 5 weeks.

3 of these days will hopefully include some very short L4 prologue work.

Phase 8 Commencing: 23 June 1999

10 days: Recovery, final prologue preparations and taper.
This section is well known to me and I intend the preparation to be much the same as previous years.

Conclusion
I have based this programme on previous experience – mistakes and successes. I have also tried to take into account the potential length of this year (10 months). In my opinion this format gives me the best chance of some early-season results for both my own morale and that of the sponsors, whilst remaining capable, both mentally and physically, of performing when it really matters in mid-season.

APPENDIX C

Chris Boardman's Performance Test Reports

I do one test a month for the first few months of training. The first in a new season marks the start of serious training. I find them useful not only as a measurement of my current state of fitness, but as a means of comparing my fitness with that of previous years. It also helps to redefine the parameters of my training programme, whether we're on the right lines or not. The examples began in 1989, when I was twenty, and include a couple of reports before the 1992 Olympic Games. On the bottom of each of them Peter Keen has put his own comments.

Physiological Performance Test Report

NAME: CHRIS BOARDMAN
SPECIALIST EVENTS: PURSUIT/TT
DATE OF TEST: 25.7.89
WEIGHT: 68.8 kgs

DATE OF BIRTH: 26.8.68
AGE: 20
TIME OF TEST: 1 p.m.

Exercise Data
MAXIMUM HEART RATE: 189 bpm

MAXIMUM POWER OUTPUT:	470 watts
MAXIMUM POWER-TO-WEIGHT RATIO:	6.83 watts/kg
PEAK LACTATE LEVEL:	9.2 mmol.1^{-1}
THRESHOLD POWER OUTPUT (4mmol.1^{-1}):	375 watts
THRESHOLD POWER-TO-WEIGHT RATIO:	5.45 watts/kg

Target Heart Rates For Training

LEVEL 1	up to 145
(recovery rides etc.)	
LEVEL 2	150–160
(steady state riding, 1–2 hours)	
LEVEL 3	175–180
(high-intensity paced work, TTs)	
LEVEL 4	180+
(intervals, hill work etc.)	

Physiological Performance Test Report

NAME: CHRIS BOARDMAN	DATE OF BIRTH: 26.8.68
SPECIALIST EVENTS: PURSUIT	AGE: 21
DATE OF TEST: 13.8.90	TIME OF TEST: 1 p.m.
WEIGHT: 71.0 kgs	

Exercise Data

MAXIMUM HEART RATE:	196 bpm
MAXIMUM POWER OUTPUT:	504 watts
MAXIMUM POWER-TO-WEIGHT RATIO:	7.1 watts/kg
PEAK LACTATE LEVEL:	13.2 mmol.1^{-1}
THRESHOLD POWER OUTPUT (4mmol.1^{-1}):	360 watts
THRESHOLD POWER-TO-WEIGHT RATIO:	5.1 watts/kg

Target Heart Rates For Training

LEVEL 1	up to 155
(recovery rides etc.)	
LEVEL 2	155–170
(steady state riding, 1–2 hours)	
LEVEL 3	175–180
(high-intensity paced work, TTs)	
LEVEL 4	185+
(intervals, hill work etc.)	

Comments

VO_2MAX = 5.6 L.min, 79.0 ml/Kg^{-1}/min $^{-1}$.
Just lacking basic volume work, but the power is there.

W.S.I.H.E. Human Performance Laboratory – Test Report

NAME: CHRIS BOARDMAN	DATE OF BIRTH: 26.8.68
LAB TEMPERATURE: 18°C	AGE: 22
DATE AND TIME OF TEST: 11 a.m. 19.4.91	
WEIGHT: 72.4 kgs	

Exercise Data

MAXIMUM HEART RATE:	196 bpm
MAXIMUM POWER OUTPUT:	515 watts
MAXIMUM POWER-TO-WEIGHT RATIO:	7.1 watts/kg^{-1}
VO_2max (ABSOLUTE):	5.86 L.min^{-1}
VO_2max (BODYWEIGHT RELATED):	80.9 ml/Kg^{-1}/min^{-1}
PEAK LACTATE LEVEL:	11.3 mmol.1^{-1}
THRESHOLD POWER OUTPUT:	395 watts
THRESHOLD POWER-TO-WEIGHT RATIO:	5.46 watts/kg^{-1}

Target Heart Rates For Training

LEVEL 1	up to 147
(recovery rides and low-intensity training rides of many hours' duration)	

LEVEL 2   147–157
(general regular training rides – brisk steady state
rides up to 2 hours long)
LEVEL 3   167–177
(maximal steady state quality work – short-distance
time trials, paced work, extended intervals of 3 mins+)
LEVEL 4   OVER 177
(maximal and near-maximal efforts, interval work,
hill sprints etc.)

Comments

This is an excellent test result, Chris. You are clearly fitter for this
stage in the season than in any previous year.

W.S.I.H.E. Human Performance Laboratory – Test Report

NAME: CHRIS BOARDMAN   DATE OF BIRTH: 26.8.68
LAB TEMPERATURE: 22°C   AGE: 23
DATE AND TIME OF TEST: 10 a.m. 16.4.92
WEIGHT: 72.3 kgs

Exercise Data

MAXIMUM HEART RATE:	191 bpm
MAXIMUM POWER OUTPUT:	494 watts
MAXIMUM POWER-TO-WEIGHT RATIO:	6.8 watts/kg^{-1}
PREDICTED VO$_2$max (ABSOLUTE):	5.51 L.min^{-1}
VO$_2$max (BODYWEIGHT RELATED):	76.2 ml/Kg^{-1}/min^{-1}
PEAK LACTATE LEVEL:	9.3 mmol.1^{-1}
THRESHOLD POWER OUTPUT:	410 watts
THRESHOLD POWER-TO-WEIGHT RATIO:	5.67 watts/kg^{-1}

Target Heart Rate For Training

LEVEL 1   up to 145
(recovery rides and low-intensity training rides of
many hours' duration)
LEVEL 2   145–155
(general regular training rides – brisk steady state
rides up to 2 hours long)
LEVEL 3   165–175
(maximal steady state quality work – short-distance
time trials, paced work, extended intervals of 3 mins+)
LEVEL 4   over 175
(maximal and near-maximal efforts, interval work,
hill sprints etc.)

Comments
There don't seem to be any major problems here, Chris. Indeed, your
threshold power is very high, only your max power is a little lower
than expected. There seems little reason to worry about the training at
the moment, at least until after Circuit des Mines.

W.S.I.H.E. Human Performance Laboratory – Test Report

NAME: CHRIS BOARDMAN   DATE OF BIRTH: 26.8.68
LAB TEMPERATURE: 22°C   AGE: 23
DATE AND TIME OF TEST: 11 a.m. 13.5.92
WEIGHT: 70.1 kgs

Exercise Data
MAXIMUM HEART RATE: 196 bpm
MAXIMUM POWER OUTPUT: 504 watts
MAXIMUM POWER-TO-WEIGHT RATIO: 7.2 watts/kg^{-1}
PREDICTED VO$_2$max (ABSOLUTE):   5.60 L.min^{-1}

VO$_2$max (BODYWEIGHT RELATED):	80.0 ml/Kg^{-1}/min^{-1}
PEAK LACTATE LEVEL:	11.8 mmol.1^{-1}
THRESHOLD POWER OUTPUT:	412 watts
THRESHOLD POWER-TO-WEIGHT RATIO:	5.87 watts/kg^{-1}

Target Heart Rates For Training

LEVEL 1   up to 150
(recovery rides and low-intensity training rides of
many hours' duration)
LEVEL 2   150–165
(general regular training rides – brisk steady state
rides up to 2 hours long)
LEVEL 3   170–179
(maximal steady state quality work – short-distance
time trials, paced work, extended intervals of 3 mins+)
LEVEL 4   over 180
(maximal and near-maximal efforts, interval work,
hill sprints etc.)

Comments

This is starting to look promising, Chris. The endurance base, i.e.,
threshold, is all there, all we need is to put in the higher-quality work
to bring up the max power. However, with 10 weeks to go there's no
rush to do this.

W.S.I.H.E. Human Performance Laboratory – Test Report

NAME: CHRIS BOARDMAN   DATE OF BIRTH: 26.8.68
LAB TEMPERATURE: 22°C   AGE: 24
DATE AND TIME OF TEST: 10 a.m. 16.2.93
WEIGHT: 71.8 kgs

Exercise Data

MAXIMUM HEART RATE:	192 bpm
MAXIMUM POWER OUTPUT:	512 watts
MAXIMUM POWER-TO-WEIGHT RATIO:	7.2 watts/kg^{-1}
PREDICTED VO$_2$max (ABSOLUTE):	5.72 L.min^{-1}
VO$_2$max (BODYWEIGHT RELATED):	80.0 ml/Kg^{-1}/min^{-1}
PEAK LACTATE LEVEL:	9.5 mmol.l^{-1}
THRESHOLD POWER OUTPUT:	n/a
THRESHOLD POWER-TO-WEIGHT RATIO:	n/a

Target Heart Rates For Training

LEVEL 1 — up to 150
(recovery rides and low-intensity training rides of
many hours' duration)
LEVEL 2 — 150–165
(general regular training rides – brisk steady state
rides up to 2 hours long)
LEVEL 3 — 170–179
(maximal steady state quality work – short-distance
time trials, paced work, extended intervals of 3 mins+)
LEVEL 4 — over 180
(maximal and near-maximal efforts, interval work,
hill sprints etc.)

Comments

Things are looking fine. Your max HR was a little lower than I would expect if you were very rested and recovered, so it is possible that you were a little tired from the weekend, or that it was a bit early in the day for a max test. The message is clear, though: All is well – let's keep on top of it!

Physiological Test Report
Performance Evaluation Centre
National Cycling Centre, Manchester

Athlete Details
NAME: **Christopher Boardman**
DOB: 26.6.68
AGE (yr): 29
WEIGHT (kgs): 70.2

Lab Details   Date: 13.3.98
TEMP (C): 22°
HUM (%):
BP:
EVENT: ROAD/TRACK

Ergo Maximal Ramp Test

	This test	Last test
START POWER/(w):	200	200
RAMP RATE (w/min^{-1}):	20	20
MMP (w/min^{-1}):	**481**	**450**
(highest average power in any minute):		
P/W (w/kg-1):	**6.85**	**6.33**
(power to weight):		
PEAK HEART RATE (bpm^{-1}):	186	?

Sum of Skinfolds
bicep, 3.1; tricep, 5.2; scapula, 8.2; supraspinale, 5.7.
Total = 22.2mm

Levels of Training Estimated From Peak Heart Rate
L1 up to 140 (recovery rides and long endurance rides 3–4 hrs+)
L2 140–150 (endurance rides between 2 and 4 hrs)
UL2 150–160 (shorter endurance rides 1–2 hrs)
L3 160–170 (high-intensity endurance rides, intervals or sustained efforts)
L4 170+ (maximal efforts, repeated intervals, 10–20 secs or exhaustive efforts 30–90 seconds)

Comments
Your last ramp test was over 30 watts lower than the present test, which suggests that, even though you are ill, your basic engine is still there, and has improved considerably over the winter. The problems

you are facing with your form at the moment are probably through a combination of both training load and health issues. At this stage in the season it may be effective – obviously once you are back to full health – to focus on maintaining your endurance with lower-intensity rides (L1) and fine tune your form when your programme allows, with structured L3 L4, rather than progressing your training load and allowing the races to give you the form you require. Finally, your total skinfold measurements are OK. In conclusion, a very good test, considering your current health status.

APPENDIX D

1984
National Schoolboy
Championship, 10 miles.

1985
Gold medal National Team Pursuit
Championship.
(At 16, the youngest person ever to
be selected to represent Great
Britain at senior level at World
Championships in Italy.)
Represented GB at Junior World
Championships in West Germany.

1986
Gold medal National Junior 25-
mile Championship.
National Junior Best All-rounder.
Gold medal National Team Pursuit
Championships.
Represented GB at World
Championships in Colorado, USA,
in individual and team pursuits.

Bronze-medal winner Team
Pursuit, Commonwealth Games,
Edinburgh.

1987
Represented GB at World
Championships in Austria in the
team pursuit.
Gold medal National Team Pursuit
Championships (record time).
Silver medal National Hill Climb
Championship.
Gold medal National Hill Climb
Championship (winning team).

1988
Gold medal Road Time Trial
Association 100-km team time
trial.
Gold medal National Team Pursuit
Championships.
Silver medal BCF 100-km Team
Time Trial.

Silver medal National Individual Pursuit.

Gold medal National Hill Climb Championship (winning team).

1st Grand Prix of France International Time Trial.

Track cycling team captain for GB in Seoul Olympic Games.

1989

Senior National 25-mile Champion.

Gold medal National 25-mile Championship Team.

Gold medal Road Time Trials Association 100-km team time trial.

Gold medal BCF 100-km team time trial (fastest time recorded by a British team anywhere).

Gold Medal National Individual Pursuit.

Gold medal National Team Pursuit.

Gold medal National Hill Climb Championship (winning team).

1990

Bronze medal winner Team Pursuit, Commonwealth Games, New Zealand.

Bronze medal winner Team Time Trial, Commonwealth Games, New Zealand.

Gold medal National 25-mile Time Trial (winning team).

Silver medal National Individual Pursuit.

Best British Rider (qualified 7th fastest Individual Pursuit, finished 9th Individual Points Race) World Track Championships, Japan.

1st in all three October Classic Mountain Time Trials.

Fastest 50-mile time trial of the year.

Broke 12-year-old 50-mile team record.

Other notable records 1984–1990

Junior national record holder at 25 miles – 52 minutes, 9 seconds (aged 15).

Winner Isle of Man International Mountain Time Trial on TT Course 1987, 1989.

Winner Circuit of the Dales Classic 50-mile time trial, 1987 and 1989.

Four-times winner Merseyside Wheelers Circuit of Delamere Pro/Am Classic.

Winner Porthole Grand Prix. Pro/Am Classic Time Trial.

Represented GB at senior level since 15 years of age.

Stage winner Tour of Lancashire. Pro/Am (3rd overall best amateur).

1st Douglas International Critérium.

Stage winner Tour of Texas 1990.

1991

24 wins.

1st National 25-mile Time Trial Championship (record time).

1st National 50-mile Time Trial Championship.

1st 100-km Team Time Trial Championship BCF (record time).

1st 100-km Team Time Trial Championship RTTC.

1st Individual Pursuit Championship (record time).
1st Team Pursuit Championship.
2nd Pre-Olympic meeting Team Pursuit, Barcelona.
5th Qualifier World Championship Pursuit, Stuttgart.
1st National Hill Climb Championship.
World Amateur 5-km record – 5 minutes, 47.70 seconds.
1st Hope Valley Classic Star Trophy.
1st Pro/Am Tour of Lancashire.
(numerous Classic wins.)

1992 (short season)
1st (10 times).
2nd (3 times).
3rd (twice).
Olympic gold medal and Olympic record.
World record.
World 5-km record attempt.

Recent Career Highlights

1999
1st Breitling GP '2 Up' Time Trial with Jens Voigt
2nd Grand Prix des Nations
Bronze Medal World Time Trial championship
119th Tour de France (second completion)

1998
1st Prologue Tour de France, Ireland
1st Prologue Prutour
1st Stage 1 Prutour
1st Prologue Tour de Catalonia
1st Time Trial Tour de Catalonia
1st Tour de l'Ain
1st Dauphine Libéré Prologue
1st Dauphine Libéré Time Trial
2nd Overall Prutour

1997
Bronze Medal World Time Trial Championship, Spain
1st Prologue Tour de France
1st Prologue Tour de Catalonia, Spain
1st Stage 4 Tour de Catalonia, Spain
2nd Grand Prix Eddy Merckx, Belgium
2nd Stage 3 Critérium International, France
3rd Stage 5 Tour de Catalonia, Spain

1996
World 1-hour record 56.375 kms, Manchester
World Champion 4000-metre Pursuit, Manchester
Silver Medal World Time Trial Championship, Switzerland
Olympic Bronze Medal Time Trial
1st Overall Critérium International, France
1st Grand Prix des Nations, France
1st Grand Prix Eddy Merckx, Belgium

1st Time Trial Paris–Nice, France
1st Telecom '2 UP' Time Trial,
Germany
1st Duo–Normande with Paul
Manning, France
1st Stage 3 Time Trial Four Days
of Dunkirk, France
1st Prologue Dauphine Libéré,
France
1st Stage 2 Route du Sud, France
1st Chrono des Herbiers, France
2nd Prologue Tour de France
2nd Stage 6 Paris–Nice, France
2nd Stage 3 Critérium
International, France
3rd Overall Paris–Nice, France
3rd Overall Tour de l'Oise, France
3rd Stage 6 Dauphine Libéré,
France
3rd Stage 2 Critérium
International, France
4th Overall Midi Libre, France
5th Overall Dauphine Libéré,
France
7th Overall Tour Mediterranean,
France
89th Overall Tour de France

1995
1st Stage 4 Time Trial Four Days
of Dunkirk, France
1st Stage 4 Tour de l'Oise, France
1st Time Trial Midi Libre
1st Prologue Dauphine Libéré,
France
2nd Overall Dauphine Libéré,
France
2nd Stage 3 Dauphine Libéré,
France

2nd Stage 7 Dauphine Libéré,
France
2nd Stage 2 Route du Sud, France

1994
**World Champion Individual
Time Trial, Italy**
**World Champion 4000-metre
Pursuit, Italy**
**Held Tour de France Yellow
Jersey for 3 days**
1st Prologue Tour de France
1st Prologue Dauphine Libéré,
France
1st Stage 3 Dauphine Libéré,
France
1st Stage 7 Dauphine Libéré,
France
1st Stage 6 Tour of Switzerland
1st Prologue Tour of Murcia, Spain
1st Stage 6 Tour of Murcia, Spain
4th Stage 4 Tour de France
4th Tour de l'Oise, France
5th Time Trial Tour de France

1993
22 – 1sts
8 – 2nds
1 – 4th
World 1-hour record 52.270 kms
3rd World Individual Pursuit
Championships
1st 25-mile Time Trial
Championship, team and
championship record
1st National Team Time Trial
Championship and championship
record
1st Isle of Man Time Trial and
course record

1st Tour of Lancashire Pro/Am
25-mile Time Trial record: 45 mins
57 secs

Professional Début
1st Grand Prix Eddy Merckx,
Belgium
1st Duo–Normande with Laurent
Bezault, France

1st Chrono des Herbiers, France
1st Milimetro del Corsa, Venice,
Italy
2nd Baden-Baden Telecom '2 Up'
Time Trial with Claudio
Chiappucci
2nd Firenze–Pistoia, Italy
4th Grand Prix des Nations, France

APPENDIX E

Useful Addresses

Audax UK
History: AUK was formed in 1976 to register and validate qualifying *randonnées* with Audax Club Parisien so that British cyclists could ride the 1200-km Paris–Brest–Paris.

Objectives: AUK aims to promote non-competitive long-distance cycling. The club represents the International Randoneurs in the UK and annually runs over 300 events, including 200-, 300-, 400- and 600-km *randonnées* and shorter introductory rides, for which nationally and internationally recognized awards may be claimed.

Contact: AUK calendar available from Ray Smith, 43 Marriot Grove, Sandal, Wakefield WF2 6RP.

Bicycle Association
Objectives: the Bicycle Association is the national trade body for UK-based manufacturers and importers of bicycles, components and accessories. Its members supply over 80 per cent of all the cycling products available on the UK market. It works by providing a forum for the industry, lobbying government, developing technical standards, assisting exporters and monitoring the worldwide market.

Contact: Brian Furness, 14 Deneside Road, Darlington, Co Durham DL3 9HZ. Tel/Fax: 01325 482052.

British Cycling Federation (BCF)

History: formed in 1959 following the amalgamation of the National Cyclists' Union and British League of Racing Cyclists.

Objectives: the BCF aims to be *the* organization of choice for competitive cyclists. The federation is committed to competition cycling at all levels, from the structured development of grass-roots cycling, through the provision of effective cycle coaching, to the implementation of the Cycling World Class Performance Programme.

Contact: membership services. Tel: 0161 230 2301. Fax: 0161 231 0591. Email: Info@bcf.uk.com. Website: www.bcf.uk.com.

British Cyclo-Cross Association (BCCA)

History: founded in 1954, controls cyclo-cross in England and Wales under an agreement established in 1960 with then newly formed BCF. Manages international cyclo-cross activities on behalf of the BCF.

Objectives: to promote, develop and encourage the sport of cyclo-cross at all levels, from foundation to excellence, with particular emphasis on ease of access to competition and the participation of young people. Main season – September to February. Any type of bike is welcome in domestic races. 1999–2000 handbook available in July, priced £4.

Contact: Brian Furness, 14 Deneside Road, Darlington, Co Durham DL3 9HZ. Tel/Fax: 01325 482052.

British Cycle Speedway Council (BCSC)

History: cycle speedway has existed since 1946. The BCSC was founded in 1971. British competitions are run annually and World Championships bi-annually. There are approximately forty clubs in Britain; there are also clubs in Australia, Poland, Holland, Sweden, Bulgaria and Ukraine.

Objectives: to maintain and develop the sport by encouraging participation, particularly in the youth and junior categories, by the promotion of equal competition, from grass-roots level through to national and international competition.

Contact: Central Office, 57 Rectory Lane, Poringland, Norwich NR14 7SW

British Schools Cycling Association (BSCA)

History: formed in 1967 as the English Schools Cycling Association to encourage and promote the participation of school children in cycling, either as a sport or leisure activity. Renamed the British Schools Cycling Association in December 1997.

Objectives: BSCA seeks to encourage the participation of school children in leisure and competitive cycling activities across all disciplines of cycling. BSCA also provides leader courses across several disciplines for adults interested in safe cycling with children.

Contact: Mrs Susan Knight, 21 Bedhampton Road, North End, Portsmouth PO2 7JX. Tel: 01705 642226. Fax: 01705 660187.

CTC (Cyclists' Touring Club)

History: founded in 1878 as the Bicycle Touring Club, the CTC has promoted recreational and utility cycling and protected cyclists' rights for over a century.

Objectives: the CTC is Britain's largest cycling organization, providing its members with a bi-monthly magazine, travel and technical advice, legal aid and insurance and access to local groups. The CTC is also an independent and powerful voice at local and national level, campaigning to improve facilities and opportunities for all cyclists.

Contact: CTC, Cotterell House, 69 Meadrow, Godalming, Surrey GU7 3HS. Tel: 01483 417217. Fax: 01483 426994. Email: cycling@ctc.org.uk. Website: www.ctc.org.uk.

Road Time Trials Council (RTTC)

History: in 1922 a group of cycling clubs formed the Road Racing Council to ensure uniformity in the conduct of time trials. The name was changed in 1937.

Objectives: the RTTC today still aims to provide a national uniformity in the conduct of time trials. The RTTC will take any steps necessary to ensure the continuance and well-being of the sport for everyone aged twelve years and over who wishes to compete in the 'Race of Truth'.

Contact: Phil Heaton (national secretary), 77 Arlington Drive, Pennington, Leigh WN7 3QP. Tel: 01942 603976. Fax: 01942 262326.

Scottish Cyclists' Union (SCU)

History: the Scottish Cyclists' Union (SCU) was founded in 1889 and reconstituted in 1952, giving the SCU over 100 years' experience in the sport of cycling.

Objectives: the SCU is an integral part of the BCF, encouraging and governing all aspects of cycle sport in Scotland, whether mountain biking, road-racing, time-trialling, cyclo-cross or track-racing. With over 100 clubs and 320 events per annum, there is something in the SCU for you.

The SCU runs the Scottish cycling teams and structured coaching activities, allowing cyclists the opportunity to follow in the footsteps of famous Scots such as Tour de France King of the Mountains Robert Millar and former World Champion Graeme Obree.

Contact: Jim Riach, Scottish Cyclists' Union, The Velodrome, London Road, Edinburgh EH7 6AD. Tel: 0131 652 0187. Fax: 0131 661 0474. Email: Scottish.Cycling@btinternet.com.

Sustrans

History: formed to build the Bristol–Bath cycle path in 1978. Registered as a charity in 1984. Built 300 miles of traffic-free paths before starting on the National Cycle Network.

Objectives: to promote sustainable transport, primarily through the implementation of the 8,000-mile National Cycle Network, to be completed by 2005. A £400-million project of safe, high-quality signed routes which will run within 2 miles of 20 million people in the UK. Aim: to develop and promote safe routes to schools.

Contact: Lindsey Smith, Information Officer, 53 King Street, Bristol BS1 4DZ.

UCI (Union Cycliste Internationale)

The UCI are the world governing body of cycle sport.

Objectives: the mission of the UCI is to develop and promote all aspects of cycling, without discrimination of any kind, in close co-operation with national federations and major associates.

Contact: UCI, 37 Route de Chavannes, Case Postale 1000, Lausanne 23, Suisse. Tel: +41 21 622 0580. Email: admin@uci.ch. Website: www.uci.ch.

Welsh Cycling Union

History: the union was formed on 1 September 1973 on the amalgamation of the former BCF, North and South Wales divisions.

Objectives: the union exists to promote, develop and control the sport and pastime of cycling in all its forms, among all sections of the community in Wales. It is actively seeking to establish new facilities, expand the opportunities for membership of the union and bring the sport's various disciplines closer together.

Contact: Rae Hughes (Hon Sec), 15 Palmeria Gardens, Prestatyn, Denbighshire LL19 9NS. Tel: 01745 888754.

Women's Cycle Racing Association

History: the WCRA was formed in 1949 to further the cause of women in cycling. Women did not have World Championships or Olympics at that time, but, due to the work of the WCRA, they finally had a World Championships in 1956 and were allowed into the Olympics in 1984.

Objectives: to continue raising the profile of women in the sport, introduce more riders to international racing and encourage a balanced race programme in domestic racing. The WCRA has its own newsletter, which covers all the news not found in other magazines. Women-only track, road and critérium championships and handicap racing. Caters for all abilities.

Contact: Membership Secretary, Tina Codling, 38 Bedford Street, St Neots, Cambs. Tel: 01480 392957.

BRITISH CYCLING FEDERATION IM*PRU*VE CLUBS

Region	Im*pru*ve Clubs	Contact Details
North West	Manchester Community CC	Gina Upex: 0161 773 8009
	Mossley CRT (Manchester)	Vince Mercer: 0161 445 4870
	Ribble Valley C&RC (Preston)	Ivor Armstrong: 01772 745647
	Border City Wheelers (Carlisle)	Steven Angus: 01228 596 575
	Red Rose Olympic (Preston)	Philip Woodhouse: 01772 722 633
	VC Cumbria (Whitehaven)	Gerard McCarter: 01946 64576
North East	Holme Valley Wheelers	Peter Root: 01484 607830
West Midlands	Bromsgrove Olympique CC	Ian Billington: 01527 833847
	Royal Sutton CC (Birmingham)	John Birch: 0121 748 3707
	Wolverhampton Wheelers	Paul Wedge: 01902 751 769
East Midlands	Matlock CC	Harry Gould: 01629 822259
	Ashfield RC/Frederic Gent (Nottingham)	Ian Drake: 01773 783826
East	West Suffolk Wheelers (Bury St Edmunds)	Justine Wallace: 01359 232151
	Welwyn Wheelers	Simon Layfield: 0171 637 8471
	Colchester Rovers and affiliated Clubs	Anthony Asplin: 01206 522 680
South East	VC Jubilee (Shoreham-by-Sea)	Shelly: 01273 462928
	Team Darenth	
Greater London	Hillingdon Slipstreamers	Keith Wilmot: 020 8813 5498
	Willesden CC	Mike Ellison: 01895 672398
	Sutton CC	Peter Fordham: 020 8641 2859
South	Palmer Park Velo (Reading)	Shane Benson: 01344 750617
	Farnborough and Camberley CC	Ron Dowling: 01252 5443596
	VC Venta (Winchester)	Stuart Gough: 01962 714091
South West	Decoy Bicross BMX Club (Newton Abbot)	Dave Drew: 01626 335799
	Bournemouth Arrow CC	Lynda Humphreys: 01202 510863
	Exeter Eagles BMX Club	Mandy Jenks: 01884 258052

Region	Im*pru*ve Clubs	Contact Details
	Newport Phoenix CC	Mike Davies: 01633 420856
Wales	Maindy Flyers (Cardiff)	Debbie Wharton: 029 2061 9713
Scotland	Edinburgh CC	Neil Muir: 0131 447 0224

INDEX